CORPORATE VENTURE CAPITAL

Since the start of the 1980s there has been a significant rise in the number and forms of collaborative inter-firm relationships, driven largely by increasing competitive pressures in the global marketplace. One form of collaboration is Corporate Venture Capital Investment, or Corporate Venturing. This involves large, non-financial companies taking minority equity stakes in small unquoted firms, and can be beneficial for both parties. The levels of corporate venturing are, however, reportedly low in the UK, particularly when compared to levels in the USA.

This volume addresses the lack of academic and practical research into corporate venturing by examining the role of this activity both as a form of large firm–small firm collaboration and as an alternative source of equity finance for small firms. These issues are explored through surveys of thirty-nine independent fund managers, seventy-three corporate executives and forty-eight technology-based firm directors. The book finds corporate venturing to be a valuable source of equity finance for early stage, technology-based firms, as well as for the institutional venture capital funds which specialise in investing in such ventures. Implications for both academic theorists and practitioners are considered.

Kevin McNally studied for his PhD at the University of Southampton, during which time he published his findings in a number of books, academic journals, trade publications and national newspapers. He is currently Head of UK Private Equity at Initiative Europe, the leading providers of publishing and research services to the European venture capital industry.

ROUTLEDGE STUDIES IN SMALL BUSINESS
Edited by David Storey

CORPORATE VENTURE CAPITAL

Bridging the equity gap in the small business sector

Kevin McNally

London and New York

First published 1997
by Routledge
11 New Fetter Lane, London EC4P 4EE

Simultaneously published in the USA and Canada
by Routledge
29 West 35th Street, New York, NY 10001

Typeset in Garamond by
J&L Composition Ltd, Filey, North Yorkshire

Printed and bound in Great Britain by
TJ International Ltd, Padstow, Cornwall

British Library Cataloguing in Publication Data

A catalogue record for this book is available from the British Library

Library of Congress Cataloging in Publication Data

A catalog record for this book has been requested

ISBN 0–415–15467–7

This book is dedicated to Mum, Dad, Nick and Lauren,
without whom it would not have happened.

CONTENTS

CONTENTS

FIGURES

FIGURES

TABLES

TABLES

xiii

FOREWORD

Nobody could describe the equity gap experienced by small firms as a new or inadequately investigated subject. The description of it in the Macmillan Report of 1931 still has a contemporary ring sixty-five years later. Moreover, the contention of the Radcliffe Committee in 1959 – that the equity gap had been largely closed by the establishment of the Industrial and Commercial Finance Corporation in 1945 – would now be regarded as highly optimistic, notwithstanding the important contribution made by 3i and the venture capital industry as a whole. It was certainly the view of the Bolton Committee in 1971 that the 'Macmillan Gap' still existed, and academic research and other investigations since have confirmed this view.

During the last few years, however, a number of developments have brought the subject of the equity gap increasingly to the fore. One has been simply the greatly increased focus on the economic contribution of small firms and the consequent importance of ensuring that their financial needs are adequately met. The very serious difficulties that emerged in the relationship between the clearing banks and their small business customers in the early 1990s prompted Eddie George, the Governor of the Bank of England, to take a direct initiative in the area of the financing of small firms. Relationships are now on a more constructive footing, with a strong emphasis on the importance of ensuring that finance is appropriate for the use that it is put to – whether it be bank debt, asset-based finance, or equity.

While much of the recent discussion about the financing of small firms has centered on debt finance and the role of the clearing banks, there has also been general acceptance that many smaller businesses in the United Kingdom continue to be under-capitalised. There have been a number of recent public policy initiatives aimed at ameliorating this: for example, the Enterprise Investment Scheme and Venture Capital Trusts. None the less, recent concentration on the particular needs of technology-based small firms has reinforced the point that small firms that are perceived to be in the high risk category – whether this perception is accurate or not – do not find it easy to raise risk capital, even in relatively small amounts. The Bank of England's report, 'The financing of Technology-based Small Firms'

(October 1996), made a number of recommendations aimed at improving the financing of this sector.

Two of the Bank's recommendations related to the broad subject of corporate venturing: one called for further research on the current extent of corporate venturing in the United Kingdom, while the other suggested that the CBI and others might act to increase awareness of the opportunities offered by corporate venturing and collaborative partnerships between larger and smaller firms. The Bank certainly regards corporate venturing as potentially a very important source of finance for technology-based small firms. Moreover, in the case of direct corporate venturing, the investee firm may also benefit from a high level of corporate investor involvement.

Against this background, Kevin McNally's book is both timely and stimulating, focusing as it does on corporate venture capital (CVC) as one particularly important manifestation of a wide range of forms of corporate venturing and collaborative partnerships. Dr McNally draws out very clearly the important distinction between direct and indirect CVC and suggests that the direct form is of particular interest for technology-based small firms. This is because the 'package' includes not just finance but also frequent contact between investor and investee firms, nurturing, and other collaborative links.

Dr McNally confirms the widely-held view that CVC is an under-developed corporate strategy in the United Kingdom, particularly when compared with the United States, although he also makes the point that some CVC activity probably takes place in the United Kingdom without recognition. He identifies two specific reasons for previously active investor companies withdrawing from CVC: poor investment experience in the past, and the trend towards concentration on core businesses.

Other aspects of the analysis in the book support the view that CVC, especially in the direct form, is potentially an important contributor to filling the equity gap for technology-based small firms. A typical CVC direct investment is for less than £300,000, and the pricing may well be more attractive than other forms of venture capital finance because corporate investors are strategically motivated. In other words, they are looking for more from the investment than a simple financial return.

Dr McNally's analysis merits careful consideration by both potential investor and investee companies, by public policy makers and by fellow researchers.

Adrian Piper,
Senior Adviser,
Business Finance Division,
Bank of England

PREFACE

This book is the product of a PhD thesis completed between October 1992 and September 1995 in the Department of Geography at the University of Southampton. 'Why geography?', you may ask, particularly given that the subject of the research appears, at least at first glance, to be more at home within a business school environment. By way of response I feel that it is important to stress that a thesis on this topic could have been researched and written within the context of any one of a number of academic or practitioner-based disciplines, and that to this extent it provides evidence of the typical interdisciplinary nature of research into small firms and entrepreneurship. Academic commentators in the fields of strategic management, industrial organisation, technology, economics, sociology and geography have contributed to the outcome of this thesis alongside practising venture capitalists, corporate executives and entrepreneurs. Whether their views and opinions were conveyed directly through face-to-face or telephone interviews, through more informal discussions or through their writings, I hope that my attempts to draw together, contrast and compare experiences from such a wide variety of sources have resulted in a rich and accurate insight into a field of inquiry which is becoming increasingly important to many people.

Small firms and entrepreneurship, and also the interrelated topics of company collaboration, networks and industrial districts, are all currently of particular interest to followers of contemporary economic geography. While geography, by definition, concerns itself primarily with a study of space, the inherent spacial dimension of many subject matters means that geographers are found in many places where they perhaps wouldn't be expected; many people would be surprised to see what is taught on a modern human geography degree course! As an undergraduate in Southampton I was first introduced to the various theoretical schools of thought underpinning the strategic alliance and entrepreneurship subject areas, as well as to the more practical issues concerning the start-up, growth and development of small companies. Attracted to this area, I decided to undertake an undergraduate dissertation looking at the problems faced by the UK's growing band of microbreweries. Having thoroughly enjoyed this research, not least because of the subject matter, but also because of the exposure it allowed me both to issues of small firm growth and to the science of methodological technique, I began to research the topic of small firm financing and inter-firm cooperation more thoroughly. It subsequently became clear that our knowledge both of the so called 'equity gap' for small companies and of the nature of specific forms of collaboration between large and small firms was incomplete, and that a study of corporate venture capital investment, or corporate venturing, grounded in these two areas of discussion would be of use not only to geographers, but also to academics and practitioners from a wide range of disciplines. I hope that the results of my efforts to this end, which extend far beyond the investigation of spatial patterns that might be expected from a 'geographer', will command the attention of the broad audience that I believe this subject matter deserves.

Kevin McNally

ACKNOWLEDGEMENTS

I am indebted to a large number of people without whom the completion of this research and the resulting book would have been impossible. I would therefore like to thank:

- My supervisor Colin Mason, whose enthusiasm, advice, support and patience during the course of my undergraduate dissertation and PhD were invaluable.
- The ESRC, for its financial support throughout the course of my studentship.
- All venture capital fund managers, corporate executives and small firm managers who agreed to participate in the research. I hope that my findings have been of use to them and their organisations and go some way to repaying them for their time and information.
- Everyone who has given me advice and guidance during the course of the research. In particular, I am grateful to William Bygrave, Kevin Caley, Richard Harrison, Ian MacMillan and Hollister Sykes for their ideas in the early days, to Maurice Anslow for a steady stream of up-to-date information on the venture capital industry, and to Gordon Murray, for numerous suggestions during the course of the research.
- My parents, for their endless encouragement and support in everything I do, and Nick, for being my best mate and helping me to see this through. Good luck in your own PhD!
- Lauren. Thank you for your love and support at all times. I wouldn't have made it without you.
- Finally, I would like to thank Taylor & Francis and MCB University Press, publishers of the journals *Entrepreneurship and Regional Development* and *International Journal of Entrepreneurial Behaviour and Research* respectively, for granting permission for material previously published in the above journals to be reproduced in this book.

Kevin McNally
October 1996

1

INTER-FIRM COLLABORATION

INCREASING LEVELS OF INTER-FIRM COLLABORATION

According to Dicken and Thrift (1992: 286), inter-firm collaborative relationships 'represent one of the major developments in the global economy of recent years . . . [and] have undoubtedly developed and proliferated dramatically. More than this, they are now central to the competitive strategies of virtually all large (and many smaller) corporations'. Emphasising this trend, Stiles (1994) suggested an increase in alliance formation in the European Union of approximately 400 per cent from 1990 to 1993, with similar trends in the USA and the Pacific Rim countries. This increase in the number and significance of inter-firm collaborative agreements during the 1980s and early 1990s has attracted considerable attention from researchers in various disciplines. Indeed, alliances have been of interest to writers in the fields of management (e.g. Miles and Snow, 1986; Pucik, 1988; Lewis, 1990; Powell, 1990; Shan, 1990; Stafford, 1994), industrial organisation (e.g. Ohmae, 1985; 1989; 1990; Contractor and Lorange, 1988; Hergert and Morris, 1988; Mowery, 1988; Gugler, 1992; Osland and Yaprak, 1993; 1995; Littler and Leverick, 1995), technology (e.g. Teece, 1986; Chesnais, 1988; Hagedoorn, 1993a; 1993b; 1995; Hagedoorn and Schakenraad, 1992; 1994; Segers, 1993; 1995), economics (e.g. Donckels and Lambrecht, 1995), sociology (e.g. Grabher, 1993) and geography (e.g. Cooke, 1988; 1992; Malecki, 1991; 1995; Sayer and Walker, 1992; Ahern, 1993a; 1993b).

Collaboration in industry is not new (Ohmae, 1985; Powell, 1987; Devlin and Bleackley, 1988; Pisano *et al.*, 1988; Shan, 1990; Sayer and Walker, 1992; Cooke and Morgan, 1993; Dodgson, 1993; Grabher, 1993) and its incidence may well be of a cyclical nature, corresponding to macro-economic cycles (Culpan and Kostelac, 1993). However, the most recent wave of relationships does exhibit certain distinguishing characteristics (Yoshino and Rangan, 1995). Differences include the diversity of companies involved today (Pisano *et al.*, 1988), the variety and complexity of organisational

1

forms (Chesnais, 1988; Borys and Jemison, 1989), the degree to which technological considerations now stimulate and facilitate collaboration (Dodgson, 1993), the unprecedented levels of sharing and commitment between firms (Kanter, 1988; Manardo, 1991; Mohr and Spekman, 1994), the active promotion of collaboration by governments (Dodgson, 1993) and the increasingly international orientation of relationships (Contractor and Lorange, 1988; Dodgson, 1993; Gugler and Dunning, 1993; Yoshino and Rangan, 1995).

Definitional issues

Despite widespread recognition of the trend towards collaboration, our understanding of exactly what this involves is confused by definitional inconsistencies (Saget, 1992; Hagedoorn, 1993a; Van Gils and Zwart, 1994; Yoshino and Rangan, 1995). Inter-firm collaboration can be broadly defined as a formal or informal agreement between two or more firms to perform or develop certain functional activities, each firm retaining its own legal status (Farrell and Doutriaux, 1994). However, Chesnais (1988: 55) recognised the 'high degree of flexibility in the definitions proposed by authors and in the range of agreements included in different studies'. He went on to suggest that this flexibility reflects the many different forms which relationships now take.

Many different terms have been used to describe inter-firm collaboration (Forrest, 1990; Morrison, 1993; Hara and Kanai, 1994; Brush and Chaganti, 1995). Within the alliance literature there is 'no standard terminology as yet, only a jostling of concepts' (Sayer and Walker, 1992: 129). Van Gils and Zwart (1994) point out that in order to indicate that firms are working together, the terms 'cooperate', 'cooperation', 'collaborative', 'contractual', 'strategic', 'corporate', 'joint', 'interfirm' and 'hybrid' have been used in combination with 'strategy', 'relationship', 'arrangement', 'agreement', 'alliance', 'partnership', 'venture', 'programme', 'linkage' and 'project' (e.g. by Mariti and Smiley, 1983; Harrigan, 1988; Hergert and Morris, 1988; Hull *et al.*, 1988; Borys and Jemison, 1989; Ohmae, 1989; Forrest, 1990; Shan, 1990).

One of the most commonly used terms is 'strategic alliance'. However, this can be misleading as it is often used inaccurately (Dodgson, 1993). An inter-firm collaborative relationship can be termed a 'strategic alliance' only when the arrangement offers actual or potential strategic advantage to at least one of the partners by focusing on issues important for the long-term development of a company and thus improving its competitive position (Hamilton, 1985; Harrigan, 1988; Olleros and MacDonald, 1988; Badaracco, 1991; Mytelka, 1991; Forrest and Martin, 1992; Teece, 1992; Bower and Whittaker, 1993; Parkhe, 1993; Segers, 1993; Osland and Yaprak, 1995; Shamdasani and Sheth, 1995). According to Morrison (1993: 8), strategic alliances 'serve a clear strategic purpose, and it is this strategic objective which distinguishes and separates strategic alliances from other forms of inter-firm co-operation'. These other forms of cooperation may be more concerned with cost-economising or indeed financial gain (Hagedoorn, 1993b) and, given their non-strategic orientation, are typically of shorter duration than strategic alliances (Perlmutter and Heenan, 1986; Powell, 1990; Lawton Smith *et al.*, 1991; Radtke and McKinney, 1991). Hagedoorn (1993b: 375) argued that 'although there is no strict correlation between organisational modes of cooperation and their strategic or cost-economizing content . . . some modes of cooperation [e.g. joint ventures and joint R&D] are more strategically motivated whereas others [e.g. customer–supplier relationships and one-directional technology flows] tend to be more oriented towards cost-economizing'. He went on to estimate that 85 per cent of collaborative agreements were strategically motivated, thus warranting the title 'strategic alliance'. However, some authors (e.g. Auster, 1987; Pucik, 1988) have chosen to avoid using terms such as 'alliance', 'collaboration' and 'cooperation' altogether since they 'suggest that the firms involved are working together to pursue common goals. In reality, goals may range from shared, to mixed, to conflicting, and the underlying relationships may range from cooperative to exploitative' (Auster, 1987: 3–4).

Forms of inter-firm collaboration

Collaboration manifests itself in a variety of approaches and contexts (Chesnais, 1988; Pucik, 1988; O'Doherty, 1990; Gordon, 1991; Brush and Chaganti, 1995; Littler and Leverick, 1995; Yoshino and Rangan, 1995), and can involve a broad range of functions, including research, product development, manufacturing and distribution (Pisano *et al.*, 1988; Kuhn, 1993). A particularly thorough review of the scope of 'collaboration' was offered by Dodgson (1993: 10):

> There is a plethora of definitions of collaboration . . . including a huge range of activities. They are formed by firms with other firms – suppliers, customers and, occasionally, competitors – and with higher education institutes and contract research organisations. Collaborations take place in the research, development, manufacturing and marketing functions, and can take a wide variety of forms. Vertical collaboration occurs throughout the chain of production for particular products, from the provision of raw materials, through all the manufacture and assembly of parts, components and systems, to their distribution and servicing. Horizontal collaboration occurs between partners at the same level in the production process.

Alliances therefore bring together partners that may be horizontally (Ohmae, 1989; Cooke and Wells, 1991) or vertically (Burdett, 1991; Collins and Doorley, 1991; Rothwell, 1992) related to each other, or may not be related to each other at all (Contractor and Lorange, 1988; Harrigan, 1988; Powell, 1990). They are often formed in an ad hoc fashion (Yoshino and Rangan, 1995) and can be concerned with concept generation, product development or product introduction (Gatewood *et al.*, 1995). Relationships can be of varying intensity and duration and involve large firm–large firm, large firm–small firm and small firm–small firm interchanges (Rothwell, 1989). Furthermore, universities, public research organisations and the state itself are also increasingly partnering with firms (O'Doherty, 1990; Houlder, 1995).

The three main alliance types are summarised in Figure 1.1. Much of the literature identifies two types of collaborative agreements, (i) contractual, non-equity arrangements and (ii) equity arrangements (Chesnais, 1988; Culpan and Kostelac, 1993). Contractual alliances include licensing agreements, distribution agreements, R&D contracts, joint marketing, supplier agreements, production sharing arrangements and technology exchange and training, or any combination of these (Lewis, 1990; Shan, 1990; MacDonald, 1991; Sayer and Walker, 1992; Culpan, 1993; Hagedoorn,

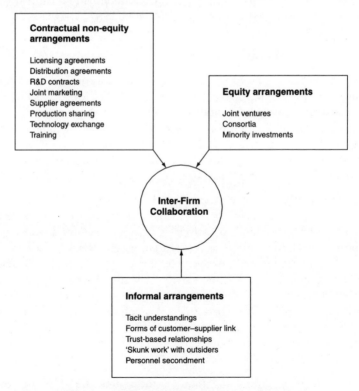

Figure 1.1 Main forms of inter-firm collaboration

4

1993a; 1993b; Osland and Yaprak, 1993; Yoshino and Rangan, 1995). Relationships that entail equity participation include joint ventures, consortia and minority investments (Ohmae, 1985; Lewis, 1990; Teece, 1992; Culpan, 1993; Hagedoorn, 1993a; 1993b; Bigbie, 1994).

A third category of alliances concerns far more informal arrangements. These are often difficult to identify because they involve a cooperative association between two or more firms in which trust is more important than formal contracts (Larson, 1990; Badaracco, 1991; Osland and Yaprak, 1993). Examples include tacit understandings among competitors in an oligopoly (Osland and Yaprak, 1993), customer–supplier relationships in which both parties take each other's interests into consideration (Håkansson and Johanson, 1988), and 'Skunk Work', which involves individuals who are performing undeclared work on company time collaborating with employees from other firms (Lawton Smith et al., 1991). Informal cooperation is often developed at the middle management level rather than on a higher management level as is the case with more formal collaboration. Although they receive less attention in the literature, the significance of these informal inter-firm linkages should not be underestimated (Lawton Smith et al., 1991). Indeed, one European study undertaken in the late 1980s found two-thirds of the cooperative relationships between firms in areas of technical development to be informal (Håkansson and Johanson, 1988).

Collaborative agreements are not specific to any particular type of organisation or industry (Perlmutter and Heenan, 1986; Pucik, 1988; Devlin and Bleackley, 1988; Lorange and Roos, 1992; Littler and Leverick, 1995). Their occurrence varies by industry according to three factors (Mowery, 1988): (i) the characteristics of the key competitive assets (i.e. technological, managerial, production, marketing, etc.) within an industry; (ii) the structure of the industry (age, entry barriers, etc.); and (iii) the characteristics of foreign markets for the products of an industry.

While they are evident in, and indeed between, many industrial sectors, alliances have tended to be concentrated in high technology industries and sectors that use more sophisticated technologies (Mariti and Smiley, 1983; Powell, 1987; 1990; Contractor and Lorange, 1988; Cooke, 1988; Pisano et al., 1988; Gordon, 1991; Bahrami, 1992; Teece, 1992; Dodgson, 1993; Grabher, 1993; Gugler and Dunning, 1993). These include micro-electronics, semiconductors (Gugler, 1992), computers (Wells and Cooke, 1992; Benassi, 1993), aeronautics, biotechnology, robotics, telecommunications (Devlin and Bleackley, 1988; Cooke and Wells, 1991; Morgan, 1991; Brown and Pattinson, 1995), automobiles (Devlin and Bleackley, 1988) and pharmaceuticals (Hergert and Morris, 1988; Lawton Smith et al., 1991; Lorange and Roos, 1992; Dodgson, 1993; Gugler and Dunning, 1993). Different industries tend to be associated with different forms of collaboration; for example, in the telecommunications and robotics sectors the focus of collaboration is typically product development; in automobiles it is the production process;

and in biotechnology and pharmaceuticals it is marketing and distribution (Dodgson, 1993). The reasons why alliances are concentrated in technology-based sectors are discussed later in this chapter.

Collaboration is a choice among several alternative ways of expanding a firm's capabilities (Devlin and Bleackley, 1988; Kogut, 1988; Kogut and Singh, 1988; Borys and Jemison, 1989; Culpan, 1993). Relationships between firms can be conceptualised along a continuum, ranging from infrequent 'arm's length' transactions to closer, long-term relationships to fully integrated relationships involving mergers, acquisition and internal business development (Lewis, 1990) (Figure 1.2). The new wave of collaborative relationships represents the middle ground of this continuum (Gertler, 1992; Sayer and Walker, 1992; Stafford, 1994). The traditional policy is the 'go-it-alone' strategy in which all activities are carried out 'in-house' or acquired by means of a market transaction (i.e. the target is reached through the hierarchy or the market) (Miles and Snow, 1992; Duijnhouwer, 1994; Gatewood et al., 1995). This concept of market versus hierarchy is having to be reconsidered with the increasing recognition that inter-firm agreements, which involve the externalisation of parts of the production process (Hamel et al., 1989; Anderson, 1993) but closer inter-firm linkages than arm's length relationships (Sayer and Walker, 1992), represent a mode of governance which is positioned between these two extremes (e.g. by Cooke, 1988; MacDonald, 1991; Hagedoorn and Schakenraad, 1992; Lorange and Roos, 1992; Pegg et al., 1992; Ahern, 1993a; Cooke and Morgan, 1993; Culpan, 1993; Dodgson, 1993).

A further form of business relationship that is sometimes considered to be a new form of collaborative agreement is subcontracting (e.g. by Hamilton and Singh, 1992; Van Gils and Zwart, 1994). However, the term 'subcontracting' is used to describe a broad range of relationships and therefore needs unpacking to reflect its diversity. Only forms of subcontracting that are *relational* (Sayer and Walker, 1992) (i.e. based on higher levels of integration in which relationships are semi-permanent and involve close coordination between firms) can be regarded as collaborative relationships (Miles and Snow, 1992; Esposito et al., 1993; Blenker and Christensen, 1994; McFarlan and Nolan, 1995). Other forms of

1	2	3	4	5	6
'One-off', 'arm's length' transactions	'Traditional' subcontracting	**Inter-firm collaboration**	Mergers	Acquisition	Internal business development

None <---> Total

Degree of integration

Markets   Hierarchies

Figure 1.2 Spectrum of firm growth strategies based on degree of integration

subcontracting involve the use of simple subsupplies with very low levels of inter-firm coordination (Collins and Doorley, 1991). Curran and Blackburn (1994) found the difference between these forms of subcontracting relationships and one-off market transactions to be negligible.

THEORETICAL CONSIDERATIONS: SOME EXPLANATIONS FOR INCREASING LEVELS OF COLLABORATION

Conventional alliance theories

The inter-firm collaboration literature has posited a number of theories in order to address the reasons why firms enter into closer business relationships (Borys and Jemison, 1989; Powell, 1987; 1990; Dodgson, 1993; Hagedoorn, 1993a; 1993b; Parkhe, 1993; McGee and Dowling, 1994; Mohr and Spekman, 1994; Ring and Van de Ven, 1994; Skjerstad, 1994). The three most frequently discussed approaches (e.g. by Kogut, 1988; Pegg *et al.*, 1992; Culpan, 1993) are as follows: *transaction-cost theory* (after Williamson, 1975), *strategic behaviour models* (otherwise known as strategic management, business strategy or competitive strategy theory – after Porter, 1980) and *resource dependence theory* (after Pfeffer and Salancik, 1978) (Table 1.1). Each of these will be considered in turn.

Transaction-cost theory

This states that firms will cooperate if it is the most efficient way to undertake an activity, minimising the sum of production and transaction costs (Kogut, 1988; Kogut and Singh, 1988; Ahern, 1993b; Culpan, 1993). Transaction and production costs are the costs that organisations incur

Table 1.1 Summary of main theoretical approaches to collaboration

Theory	Goal	Strategy
Transaction-cost theory (Williamson, 1975)	Efficiency	Organisations gain efficiency by reducing transaction costs; risk and uncertainty are major components of transaction costs
Strategic behaviour theory (Porter, 1980)	Effectiveness (control, profitability)	Organisations maximise profitability by improving their competitive positions
Resource dependence theory (Pfeffer and Salancik, 1978)	Effectiveness (power, control)	Organisations gain and maintain the resources they need by controlling their environment through the reduction of risk and uncertainty

Source: Adapted from Ahern, 1993a

when they seek to restructure, meet new challenges and implement new strategies (Ciborra, 1991). They include the cost of transforming inputs into products and services, search costs, monitoring costs, quality costs and extortion costs (Kogut, 1988; Thomas, 1988; Culpan, 1993). Transaction-cost theory predicts that these costs will determine whether transactions will occur internally through 'hierarchies' or externally through 'markets' (Williamson, 1975; Cooke and Morgan, 1993; McGee, 1994). It is argued that firms adopt hierarchies to internalise their transactions when the costs of external market transactions increase and become less efficient (Ahern, 1993a; McGee, 1994). The problems of 'entering into market transactions that involve uncertainty, the acquiring of transaction-specific assets, and the potential opportunistic behaviour on the part of the other party provide a strong incentive for firms to internalize their transactions through hierarchies' (McGee, 1994: 3).

According to Ahern (1993a), our understanding of the cooperation between firms can be aided by an extension of transaction-cost theory. It has been seen that cooperative agreements represent a middle ground between markets and hierarchies (Sayer and Walker, 1992; Cooke and Morgan, 1993). It is argued (e.g. by Kogut, 1988; Shan, 1990; Culpan, 1993; McGee and Dowling, 1994) that inter-firm collaboration may be more efficient than either markets *or* hierarchies for some activities. Indeed, an alliance can reduce costs by reducing uncertainties and forbearance and by increasing cooperation, commitment and trust between partners (Buckley and Casson, 1988; Culpan, 1993). A transaction-cost approach may also be useful in determining which forms of alliance are employed (Yoshino and Rangan, 1995).

Although transaction-cost theory contributes to an understanding of why firms cooperate, it does not offer a complete explanation (Ahern, 1993a). The theory tends to concentrate on vertical relations and either discusses them in general theoretical terms or analyses concrete developments in case studies from which generalisations are difficult to make (Hagedoorn, 1993b). A number of authors have recognised that cost minimisation is not the sole reason for cooperative behaviour (e.g. Kogut, 1988; Jarillo, 1989; Shan, 1990; McGee and Dowling, 1994) and that transaction-cost theory fails to adequately account for a firm's environment (Perrow, 1986; Ahern, 1993a). Indeed, as Grabher (1993: 5) notes, 'economic actors neither behave as atomized individuals outside a social context nor adhere slavishly to unchangeable habits or norms'. The next two approaches do consider the firm's external environment.

Strategic behaviour models

This approach considers the competitive strategies of firms (Culpan, 1993). Whereas transaction-cost theory focuses on cost minimisation, strategic behaviour suggests that a firm's decision to collaborate is based on the desire to maximise long-term profitability by improving the firm's competitive position and expanding its core competencies (Kogut, 1988; Shan, 1990; McGee, 1994; McGee and Dowling, 1994; Skjerstad, 1994). Strategic behaviour models therefore predict that firms engage in cooperative activities regardless of their effect on transaction costs (McGee and Dowling, 1994). Porter's (1980) theory of competitive advantage is based on five competitive forces: the threat of new entrants, the bargaining power of suppliers, the bargaining power of buyers, the threat of substitute products, and rivalry among other firms. An analysis of these factors should shape a firm's business strategy (Kanter, 1989; Culpan, 1993; Culpan and Kostelac, 1993), and Porter (1985) suggested that this strategy should involve low-cost leadership, product differentiation and focus. Inter-firm collaboration can provide competitive advantages of cost, deriving from economies of scale, differentiated products, because of superior technology or product quality, or segmented markets and appeal to only a limited number of customers (Culpan, 1993).

Resource dependence theory

This theory suggests that firms depend on other organisations within their environment to learn and acquire needed resources and competencies such as management skills, technical know-how, capital and even reputation (Pfeffer and Salancik, 1978; Teece, 1986; 1992; Parkhe, 1993; Culpan, 1993; Eisenhardt and Schoonhoven, 1994; Osland and Yaprak, 1995). According to Ahern (1993a), the survival and success of a firm are determined by its ability to acquire and maintain the resources that it needs, and thus exert control over its environment by reducing the risk and uncertainty that it faces. There are two sources of control: (i) the ability to respond and adapt to the external environment empowers firms, and (ii) firms gain control by modifying the environment to enhance their own performance (Ahern, 1993a). While transaction-cost theory suggests that cooperation will be used when this is cheaper than other forms of interaction, the resource dependence approach states that alliances will be used if they are perceived as being more appropriate for accessing the resources upon which the firm relies (Ahern, 1993b).

Compatibility of theories

The literature therefore suggests that transaction-cost, strategic behaviour and resource dependence considerations are important variables motivating firms to form collaborative relationships (Shan, 1990). As has been noted, some modes of cooperation may be more strategically motivated (relating to strategic behaviour and resource dependence theories, and seemingly warranting the title *strategic* alliance) while others will tend to be oriented more towards cost-economising (relating to the transaction-cost approach) (Hagedoorn, 1993b). Although transaction-cost theory is often thought to compete with the other two views, the three approaches are not mutually exclusive (Tyler and Steensma, 1995) and complement rather than contradict each other (Kogut, 1988; Shan, 1990; Ahern, 1993a). Assuming that firms pursue strategies that enable them to gain both control and efficiency, a combination of the three (and possibly other) theories is appropriate (Ahern, 1993a).

However, while the conventional alliance theories discussed do provide an insight into the possible reasons why firms cooperate, on their own they are inadequate for explaining why the number and form of alliances has increased rapidly since the early 1980s. As Dodgson (1993) and Osland and Yaprak (1995) note, changing business environments and systems of production, as well as the impact of technological change, have to be considered.

Macro-scale considerations in the modern business environment

Since the mid-1980s, companies have been increasingly confronted by a number of interrelated macro-scale developments and trends which have affected the nature of the business environment in which they operate (Ohmae, 1985; Venkatachalam and Weaver, 1989; Hitt *et al.*, 1991; Morgan, 1991; Mytelka, 1991; Cooke, 1992; Gertler, 1992; DTI/CBI, 1993; Duijn-houwer, 1994; Bahrami and Evans, 1995; Littler and Leverick, 1995; Osland and Yaprak, 1995; Shamdasani and Sheth, 1995; Tyler and Steensma, 1995; Yoshino and Rangan, 1995). As Boynton and Victor (1991: 53) noted, 'a change of historic proportion is occurring in today's competitive environment'. The four major developments affecting firms are as follows (after Henricks, 1991).

Increasing competitive intensity

Many companies have experienced increasing competition in marketing their products and services (Cooke, 1992; Lorange and Roos, 1992; Culpan, 1993; Jarillo, 1993). As Block and MacMillan (1993: 1) note, 'today's marketplace is characterized by fast-paced and unremitting competition'. Companies are therefore required to vigorously seek competitive advantage through innovation, product differentiation and superior product performance (Lawton Smith *et al.*, 1991; Rothwell, 1992; Ginsberg and Hay, 1993).

Increasing globalisation

Demand, supply and competition have expanded onto a global scale (Lewis, 1990; Shan, 1990; Lawton Smith *et al.*, 1991; Morgan, 1991; Gugler, 1992;

Culpan, 1993; Esposito *et al.*, 1993; Duijnhouwer, 1994; Pekar and Allio, 1994; Osland and Yaprak, 1995; Yoshino and Rangan, 1995), largely as a result of the convergence of consumer needs (but the retention of local preferences), technological advancement, the emergence of product systems and the promotion of world-wide standards (Ohmae, 1985; 1990; Collins and Doorley, 1991; Amin and Thrift, 1992; 1993; Gugler and Dunning, 1993; Van Gils and Zwart, 1994). Increasing globalisation also reflects the need to find new markets for mass-produced goods when existing markets become saturated in the face of rising industrial productivity (James and Weidenbaum, 1993). According to Cooke and Wells (1992: 61), 'globalization is probably the most powerful force affecting the practices of firms', and Collins and Doorley (1991: 5) emphasised that 'companies must take full advantage of international market opportunities if they are to achieve the scale economies needed to remain competitive'.

Shorter windows of opportunity/shorter product life-cycles

As customers demand products at increasingly greater speeds and technological advancements mean that product life-cycles are diminishing (Muzyka, 1988; Boynton and Victor, 1991; Gugler, 1992; Rothwell, 1992; Duijnhouwer, 1994; Van Gils and Zwart, 1994; Osland and Yaprak, 1995), the period of time during which a product remains profitable is becoming shorter and shorter, thus intensifying global competition. Shorter product life-cycles mean that continuous innovation is essential (McCann, 1991; Cooke, 1992; DTI/CBI, 1993; Bettis and Hitt, 1995; Garud and Kumaraswamy, 1995; Yoshino and Rangan, 1995) since firms must commercialise their R&D resources much faster than in the past (Morgan, 1991).

Rapidly changing technologies

Rates of industrial technological change and diffusion are rising and 'technological competition' is intensifying as firms seek competitive advantage through product differentiation and performance (Ohmae, 1985; Miles and Snow, 1986; Lewis, 1990; Collins and Doorley, 1991; Cooke, 1992; Gugler, 1992; Kodama, 1992; Rothwell, 1992; Van Gils and Zwart, 1994; Bettis and Hitt, 1995). Technological change is a major competitive force with strategic implications for individual companies and entire industries (Hamilton, 1985; Bettis and Hitt, 1995). The increasing complexities of technology make it much less likely that a single company will have all the skills and resources required for innovative R&D programmes (Ohmae, 1985; 1989; 1990; Collins and Doorley, 1991; Cooke, 1992; Lorange and Roos, 1992; Culpan, 1993; Gugler and Dunning, 1993; Gatewood *et al.*, 1995; Tyler and Steensma, 1995).

11

These four factors are clearly far from being mutually exclusive. Indeed, their highly interrelated nature was illustrated by Young (1988: 103):

> The recovery from the recession of the early 1980s has been characterised by increasingly competitive markets. This has to a large extent been due to the 'shrinking world' where markets, distribution and hence competition have moved to a global scale . . . Higher disposable incomes and the development of the consumer society have so fed the markets that for many products, saturation point has been reached. This in turn has generated a need for manufacturers to clearly differentiate their products . . . [There has also] been a dramatic reduction in product lifecycles, forced by the pace of technological innovation and more aggressive marketing.

The response of companies to macro-scale pressures

As Tom Peters' work entitled 'Get Innovative or Get Dead' in *California Management Review* (1990/1991) suggested, companies have recognised the need to respond to an increasingly competitive global economic environment. The responses of firms to increasing environmental pressures can be conceptualised within the notion of *flexibility* (Perlmutter and Heenan, 1986; Malecki, 1991; 1995; Morgan, 1991; Amin and Thrift, 1992; Gertler, 1992; Weinstein, 1992; Bettis and Hitt, 1995). According to Imrie (1994: 569), 'flexibility has become a watch-word for a variety of responses to new consumer demands and competition'. Flexibility is embodied in the shift from 'Fordism' (or 'Organised Capitalism') to 'Post-Fordism' (or 'Disorganised Capitalism' or 'Flexible Specialisation/Accumulation') (Piore and Sabel, 1984; Lash and Urry, 1987; 1994; Harvey, 1989; Lawton Smith *et al.*, 1991; Cooke, 1992; Malecki, 1995). Increasing macro-scale *disorganisation* at national and international levels, characterised by loss of control by countries over domestic and foreign markets, has encouraged greater *organisation* at the firm level as companies attempt to lessen the uncertainty that they face within a disorganised setting (Lawton Smith *et al.*, 1991). Firms have responded to increasing innovation risk, prolonged demand risk and the crisis of control over the labour process by moving away from monolithic and rigid organisational designs, geared for repetitive transactions and routine activities (Bahrami, 1992). They have moved towards becoming enterprises which exhibit flexibility and agility in the organisation of production, the utilisation of labour and the organisation of relationships with other firms (Shutt and Whittington, 1987; Gertler, 1992; Miles and Snow, 1992; Moye, 1993; Imrie, 1994; Garud and Kumaraswamy, 1995; Malecki, 1995; Yoshino and Rangan, 1995). Post-Fordist business organisation has been argued (e.g. by Cooke, 1992) to involve substantial dependence on networks of suppliers, a high degree of production flexibility,

12

more decentralised and less bureaucratic management structures, higher skill densities in workforces, more flexible working practices and an increased tendency towards inter-firm collaboration. Flexibility is therefore a multidimensional concept associated with change and innovation; coupled with robustness and resilience; implying stability, sustainable advantage and evolving capabilities and competencies (Collins and Doorley, 1991; Bahrami, 1992; Garnsey and Wilkinson, 1994).

As mentioned above, one aspect of increasing flexibility concerns heightened levels of inter-firm collaboration (Shutt and Whittington, 1987; Cooke, 1988; 1992; Morgan, 1991; Gertler, 1992; Miles and Snow, 1992; Blenker and Christensen, 1994; Curran and Blackburn, 1994; Imrie, 1994; Bettis and Hitt, 1995). Indeed, macro-scale considerations have played, and continue to play, key roles in motivating inter-firm cooperation (Chesnais, 1988; Devlin and Bleackley, 1988; Lewis, 1990; Badaracco, 1991; Mytelka, 1991; Botkin and Matthews, 1992; Ahern, 1993a; Grabher, 1993; Bidault and Cummings, 1994; Beamish and Inkpen, 1995). The recent emergence of new forms of inter-firm collaboration largely reflects competitive pressures which have arisen from fundamental changes in the process of production and in the form that competition now takes in the world economy (Perlmutter and Heenan, 1986; Pucik, 1988; Lawton Smith et al., 1991; Mytelka, 1991; Brouthers et al., 1995; Brown and Pattinson, 1995; McFarlan and Nolan, 1995) and which have forced firms to seek flexible organisational, strategic solutions and new rules of behaviour (Miles and Snow, 1986; Cooke, 1988; Borys and Jemison, 1989; Ohmae, 1989; Burdett, 1991; Lawton Smith et al., 1991; Morgan, 1991; Dollinger and Golden, 1992; Esposito et al., 1993; Pekar and Allio, 1994; Bettis and Hitt, 1995; Osland and Yaprak, 1995; Yoshino and Rangan, 1995). According to Gertler (1992: 261), collaborative relationships 'constitute one significant piece of evidence of the resilience of large firms in the face of external threats'.

The objectives of collaboration in the current business environment

Through collaboration firms can benefit in the following nine ways:

New development costs/cost sharing

Firms with higher costs lose market share, their profit margins erode and they have less capital for development (Badaracco, 1991). Particularly in areas of technological innovation, the costs of new product development are often too large for a single company to bear alone leading to collaboration with other firms (Lewis, 1990; Morgan, 1991; Wissema and Euser, 1991; Cooke, 1992; Dodgson, 1992; Culpan and Kostelac, 1993; Gugler and Dunning, 1993; Littler and Leverick, 1995).

Risk reduction/sharing

Business has become increasingly risky as a result of weakening profits, shortening product life-cycles, uncertainty and variable company incomes (Grabher, 1993; Brouthers *et al.*, 1995). Alliances allow firms to compete without committing significant amounts of resources (Mariti and Smiley, 1983; Chesnais, 1988; Contractor and Lorange, 1988; Badaracco, 1991; Culpan and Kostelac, 1993). They can also lead to product portfolio diversification and fixed cost dispersion/reduction (Contractor and Lorange, 1988; Gugler and Dunning, 1993).

Access to markets

Collaboration with firms that are established in other, often international, markets is particularly beneficial for firms seeking rapid market entry (Lewis, 1990; Gordon, 1991; Morgan, 1991; Dodgson, 1992; Culpan, 1993; Shamdasani and Sheth, 1995). Alliances can either enable a firm to sell a product quickly because its partner has the product available, or can increase a company's speed to market by widening its network of distribution outlets via its partner's local know-how (Ohmae, 1985; Badaracco, 1991; Beamish and Inkpen, 1995; Yoshino and Rangan, 1995).

Access to technologies

Companies can stay abreast of technological developments in other firms through collaboration (Littler and Leverick, 1995). Alliances allow firms to keep a 'watching brief' on developing technology without heavy investment (Powell, 1987; 1990; Ciborra, 1991; Gordon, 1991; Morgan, 1991; Dodgson, 1992; Culpan, 1993; Grabher, 1993; Hagedoorn and Schakenraad, 1994). In addition, companies can pool or swap technologies with other firms (Mariti and Smiley, 1983; Chesnais, 1988; Contractor and Lorange, 1988; Lewis, 1990). According to Teece (1992: 17), 'there is no arena in which uncertainty is higher and the need to coordinate greater than in the development and commercialization of new technology'. This helps to explain the tendency for collaboration to occur in technology-based industries.

Developing industry standards

New technologies can sometimes be commercialised only if the entire industry uses the same standard. Collaboration is an appropriate way for setting such standards (Wissema and Euser, 1991; Grabher, 1993).

Pooling of complementary resources/assets

The combining of complementary assets and strengths, both tangible and intangible, is a particularly important objective of collaboration (Powell,

14

1987; 1990; Pucik, 1988; Grabher, 1993; Brouthers *et al.*, 1995). Many alliances in the pharmaceutical and biotechnology fields, for example, have been built on this rationale (Contractor and Lorange, 1988). While one partner may contribute certain critical resources, such as technological skills and assets, another may provide finance, technical know-how or access to markets (Hladik, 1988; Badaracco, 1991). According to Henricks (1991: 48), 'a company decides to partner because it wants one or more of four things from an ally: marketing, manufacturing, technology or finance'. Alliances therefore help firms to deal with resource constraints (Borys and Jemison, 1989; Gugler and Dunning, 1993). As well as being a means of controlling a given stock of complementary assets, collaboration can also provide control over the optimal development trajectory of these assets (Lawton Smith *et al.*, 1991).

Economies of scale/scope

These are derived from the lower average cost from larger volumes and lower costs from using the comparative advantages of each partner (Mariti and Smiley, 1983; Powell, 1987; Contractor and Lorange, 1988). Given the increasing recognition that even large companies cannot 'go it alone' as the pace of technological change increases and product life-cycles shorten (Cooke, 1992), collaboration can enable firms to obtain economies of scope through the sharing of technical know-how and working skills (Storper and Harrison, 1990; Lawton Smith *et al.*, 1991).

Monitoring/blocking of competitors

Through alliances, firms can observe how, when and where their competitors are deploying newly created or recently acquired knowledge and skills (Badaracco, 1991). Alternatively, alliances can themselves reduce competition for partners, or increase costs and/or reduce market share for a third company (Contractor and Lorange, 1988; Badaracco, 1991; Culpan, 1993).

Vertical quasi integration

Closer linkages with suppliers and customers can aid access to materials, technology, labour, capital and distribution channels as well as developing brand recognition (Contractor and Lorange, 1988; Morgan, 1991; Culpan, 1993). It has been predicted (Cooke, 1992) that vertical collaboration is the most widespread form of inter-firm cooperation in the innovation sphere.

In the light of recent macro-scale pressures on companies, the main motives for collaboration can therefore be grouped into the following four categories (Lawton Smith *et al.*, 1991; Jarillo, 1993; Osland and Yaprak, 1993):

15

- Flexibility
- Market power
- Efficiency
- Competencies

This supports the transaction-cost approach, which suggests that firms employ alliances in order to seek cost efficiencies; the strategic behaviour approach, which outlines the need for firms to enhance their competitiveness in the marketplace; and also the resource dependence argument which emphasises the need for firms to develop competencies by accessing external resources (Bettis and Hitt, 1995).

Clearly, precise objectives are company specific and although the overall motivations for collaboration can be easily summarised the situation at firm level is very complex (Lawton Smith *et al.*, 1991). A company will pursue the form/s of alliance which it perceives will best meet its objectives. As Lorange and Roos (1992: 267) note, 'no particular type of strategic alliance is better or universally more correct than others; what matters is to make the appropriate choice of strategic alliance form, given the particular conditions at hand'.

Several authors (e.g. Benassi, 1993; Osland and Yaprak, 1993; Duijnhouwer, 1994) have considered the generic motives of alliances. According to Malecki (1991), the form of alliance employed will reflect a firm's decision to pursue any of three strategies:

- A *window strategy* will often take the form of research contracts or minority equity investments and allows firms to identify and monitor leading-edge technologies developed elsewhere.
- An *options strategy* may also take the form of research contracts or minority equity investments but can also involve joint ventures or licensing agreements. It is more selective than the window strategy, designating a small number of market or technical areas in which to participate.
- A *positioning strategy* may involve R&D contracts, licenses and joint ventures aimed at production. This type of strategy reflects a commitment to a product or technology for commercial exploitation.

Some authors (e.g. Lorange and Roos, 1992; Duijnhouwer, 1994; Yoshino and Rangan, 1995) have discussed the degree to which collaboration can be classified as 'offensive' or 'defensive'. When a firm collaborates in order to take advantage of the possibilities available, this is regarded as an offensive strategy. However, where a firm is not able to fend off the threat represented by a development on its own and consequently cooperates with another firm, this is a defensive strategy (Grabher, 1993; Duijnhouwer, 1994). Lorange and Roos (1992) took this a stage further by conceptualising four generic motives for alliances – as a defence, to catch up, to remain, or to restructure. These motives reflect both the strategic importance of the alliance in the company's portfolio and the firm's business's market position (Lorange *et al.*, 1992) (Table 1.2). According to Håkansson and Johanson (1988), firms with strong market positions (leaders) will tend to seek formal, 'visible' collaboration (either contractual or equity) with prestigious actors in networks that are considered important. In contrast, firms with less strong positions will try, at least initially, to develop more informal, 'invisible' collaborative agreements, thus establishing a position before it is made visible.

Alternative firm growth strategies

Collaboration is not the only response of firms in the current competitive business environment. Many companies, and particularly large firms, have used a range of different strategies in an attempt to become more flexible, enhance market power and expand competencies (Botkin and Matthews, 1992). Particularly in areas of new business development, companies have been supplementing conventional internal development, acquisitions and arms length policies with *intrapreneuring*, which is a company-wide, internally oriented strategy designed to promote an entrepreneurial environment within the corporate organisation, and *internal corporate venturing*, which involves the establishment of autonomous in-house new ventures (Scholl-hammer, 1982; Bailey, 1984; MacMillan and George, 1985; Littler and Sweeting, 1987a; Hall, 1989; Botkin and Matthews, 1992; Ginsberg and Hay, 1993; Schumann, 1993) (see Chapter 2 for full definitions and further discussion of internal corporate venturing).

Alliances are adopted as a result of a trade-off between the benefits and costs of alternative arrangements as firms select the most effective approaches for discovering and developing new areas of profitability (Peterson, 1967; Ciborra, 1991). Several authors (e.g. Mariti and Smiley, 1983; Chesnais, 1988; Lewis, 1990; Ciborra, 1991; Sayer and Walker, 1992; Teece, 1992; James and Weidenbaum, 1993; Jarillo, 1993; Stafford, 1994) have

Table 1.2 Generic motives for inter-firm alliances

		Firm's business/market position	
		Leader (contractual/equity collaboration)	*Follower (informal collaboration)*
Strategic importance in firm's portfolio	Core	Defend	Catch up
	Peripheral	Remain	Restructure

Source: Adapted from Lorange and Roos, 1992: 7

outlined the advantages of collaboration over other strategies, particularly in technology sectors. These benefits are illustrated in Table 1.3 in terms of the scope, control and risks associated with individual policies.

Various difficulties encountered by companies attempting to grow via traditional mechanisms have been identified (e.g. by Burrows, 1982; Muzyka, 1988; Rothwell, 1992; Grabher, 1993). Internal activities, if possible at all, often take too long and risks are taken alone. In the case of outright acquisition of firms which hold needed resources, the buyer shoulders all the risk burden. Acquisition often includes receipt of unnecessary activities, can be financially unfeasible for many companies (Stafford, 1994), and, in the case of large firms acquiring small firms, can destroy the speed of action and flexibility of the smaller firm (Powell, 1987; Doz, 1988; Baty, 1990; Hull and Slowinski, 1990; Dodgson, 1992; Forrest and Martin, 1992; Grabher, 1993). Arm's length transactions cannot add competitive strength and risks are taken separately. Furthermore, numerous authors (e.g. Hanan, 1976; Fast, 1981; Block, 1982; MacMillan et al., 1984; Elder and Shimanski, 1987; Sykes and Block, 1989; Sexton and Bowman-Upton, 1990) have identified structural and procedural obstacles to success in internal venturing. These are often related to conflict between the formal needs and policies of the established firm and the needs of the new internal ventures (Lerner, 1995).

In contrast, alliances have a number of potential advantages that mean that they are better suited than other strategies to the current demanding business environment (Miles and Snow, 1992; Littler and Leverick, 1995; Tyler and Steensma, 1995; Yoshino and Rangan, 1995). They involve 'loose coupling' (Grabher, 1993), that is they will mesh only those parts of each firm's culture and functions that are required to work together in order to

Table 1.3 Characteristics of firm growth strategies

	Internal activities	Acquisitions	Arm's length transactions	Strategic alliances
Scope	Core strengths	Closely related to core strengths	Cannot add competitive strength	Add competitive strength
		Need most of purchased firm	Limited by risks others willingly take alone	Most extensive access to outside resources
Control	Full	Full	Via initial terms	Ongoing mutual adjustments
Risks	Taken alone	Taken by buyer	Taken separately	Shared

Source: Lewis, 1990: 19

18

add competitive strength and access required resources (Lewis, 1990). They can help companies to share responsibilities and risks, react more quickly and benefit from the long-term planned security of a large, integrated company, but also help do away with coordinating bureaucracy and keep the entrepreneurial drive of independent firms (Sayer and Walker, 1992; Jarillo, 1993; Osland and Yaprak, 1995). Furthermore, alliances are typically easier to dissolve than internal developments or mergers because their sunk costs are smaller, commitments are less irreversible and inertia lower (Ciborra, 1991).

INCREASING LEVELS OF COLLABORATION BETWEEN LARGE AND SMALL FIRMS

Until the early 1990s, most of the alliance literature had focused on collaboration between large, established firms rather than small ventures (Storper and Walker, 1989; Dollinger and Golden, 1992; McGee and Dowling, 1994; Van Gils and Zwart, 1994). However, during the 1990s, research on alliances involving small firms has become more widespread (e.g. Forrest and Martin, 1992; Ahern, 1993a; 1993b; Dodgson, 1993; Golden and Dollinger, 1993; Slowinski et al., 1993; Ettington and Bantel, 1994; Van Gils and Zwart, 1994; Brush and Chaganti, 1995), reflecting increasing recognition of the relative significance of this form of collaboration (e.g. by Hamilton, 1985; Perlmutter and Heenan, 1986; Doz, 1988; Hergert and Morris, 1988; Baty, 1990; O'Doherty, 1990; Lawton Smith et al., 1991; Radtke and McKinney, 1991; Botkin and Matthews, 1992; Gugler, 1992; Lorange and Roos, 1992; Gugler and Dunning, 1993; Rothwell, 1993; Silver, 1993; Case, 1995; Segers, 1995). According to Powell (1987: 68), 'there appears to be a wholesale stampede into various alliance-type combinations that link large generalist firms and specialized entrepreneurial start-ups'. Indeed, Forrest (1990: 38) observed that while 'strategic alliances between large firms are quite a common occurrence . . . recently small firm/large firm collaborations have become more prevalent'.

Forms of large firm–small firm collaboration

Collaborative relationships between large and small firms (often termed 'strategic partnerships' – e.g. by Teece, 1986; Hull and Slowinski, 1990; Radtke and McKinney, 1991) can take a number of forms (Slatter, 1992). The main forms are shown in Table 1.4, although the list is not exhaustive, with the most frequent being marketing agreements, joint ventures and collaborative R&D (Case, 1995). It is evident from this table that, as is the case for inter-firm collaboration in general, large firm–small firm relationships can be contractual, equity or informal agreements, involving links with vertically or horizontally related companies.

19

Table 1.4 Forms of large firm–small firm collaboration

Collaborative relationship	Definition
Manufacturing relationships	One firm, usually the large, manufactures products for the other
Customer–supplier relationships	Long-term relationships with vertically related companies
Licensing agreements	One firm is granted access to the other's patents or technology for a fee
Client-sponsored research contract	The small company is paid to conduct research into particular products or processes for another company
Marketing/distribution agreements	Agreements whereby one firm markets and distributes the other's products
Collaborative R&D	An agreement to collaborate on the development of specific products or processes
Large firm–small firm joint ventures	Formation of an independent third enterprise– assets are contributed by both parties, who also share risks
Venture capital investments	Minority equity investment by the large company in the smaller firm
Venture nurturing	As well as finance, the large company provides the small with advice and expertise in areas such as marketing, manufacturing and research
Sponsored spin-outs	Minority equity investment by the large company in a small firm which originated within the large company
Personnel secondment	Informal collaboration involving swapping of personnel between firms
Learning opportunities	Informal agreements where companies educate each other about products, processes and techniques

Sources: Compiled from Contractor and Lorange, 1988; Forrest, 1990; Shan, 1990; Gilbert, 1991; Forrest and Martin, 1992; Sandham and Thurston, 1993; Rothwell and Dodgson, 1994

Potential benefits of large firm–small firm strategic partnerships

Large firm–small firm alliances have the potential to realise many of the benefits to firms of collaboration *per se* that were outlined earlier in this chapter (Forrest, 1990; MacDonald, 1991; Duijnhouwer, 1994). Moreover, these benefits may be enhanced as a result of combining the different organisational structures and complementary strengths of large and small firms (Ahern, 1993a; Grabher, 1993). Both large and small companies can therefore capitalise on the potential synergies arising from the sharing and transfer of resources while respecting each other's independence (Niederkofler, 1991; Botkin and Matthews, 1992; Sykes, 1993). Cooperation of this kind therefore has the potential to provide a sustainable source of competitive advantage for both large and small firms, resulting in higher levels of performance than either could have achieved alone (Hull and Slowinski, 1990).

The perceived complementarity between large and small firms is based on the premise that such firms possess different skills and are faced with quite different operational constraints (Lawton Smith *et al.*, 1991). Indeed, according to Hull and Slowinski (1990), large and small firms enter into partnerships with each other for different reasons – large firms are principally interested in technology, small firms in financing and marketing, and both are typically interested in manufacturing and managements. Large and small firm motivations will be considered in turn.

Large firm motivations

For many large companies, the key to competitive advantage, and indeed survival, is the re-creation of an entrepreneurial spirit within the firm (Schollhammer, 1982; Birley and Norburn, 1985; Glamholtz and Randie, 1993). Kanter (1989) suggested that giants (large companies) would have to 'learn how to dance' if they were to become more innovative and compete successfully in future. Therefore, many large firms have been forced to restructure and revitalise their business portfolios (Doz *et al.*, 1985; Littler and Sweeting, 1987b). In order to remain competitive in global markets, industrial corporations have become increasingly dependent on the successful development of new products and processes. For innovation purposes, most large firms rely on in-house development of new products, acquisition and merger, intrapreneuring or internal venturing (Littler and Sweeting, 1987b; Botkin and Matthews, 1992). However, as a result of their size most large firms are slow-moving, lack creativity, have high costs and experience difficulties moving innovations to market swiftly (Botkin and Matthews, 1992; McKee, 1992; Ahern, 1993a; Schumann, 1993).

Several authors (e.g. Olleros and MacDonald, 1988; Powell, 1990; Botkin and Matthews, 1992) have recognised a tendency for some large companies to externalise their search for an entrepreneurial injection and establish strategic partnerships with small companies. Instead of giants learning how to dance on their own, an increasing number are preferring to waltz with small, entrepreneurial partners (Bygrave and Timmons, 1992). This has been termed both the 'third wave of entrepreneurship' and 'extrapreneuring' by Botkin and Matthews (1992). The major advantages for large firms of collaboration with small firms are outlined in Table 1.5.

According to many commentators (e.g. Perlmutter and Heenan, 1986; Doz, 1988; Segers, 1993), partnerships offer large firms a channel to tap into the innovative and entrepreneurial potential of smaller firms. Unlike large companies, small firms are not as impeded by existing businesses which require lengthy bureaucratic decision-making processes. They can therefore specialise in particular areas of development and can respond to the changing demands of the market more quickly than many large corporations (Hull and Slowinski, 1990; Lawton Smith *et al.*, 1991). Their greater freedom from constraints therefore allows them flexibility, adaptability and enhanced communications (Rind, 1981). According to Mast

21

Table 1.5 Advantages of large firm–small firm collaboration

Advantages for large firms	Advantages for small firms
New product development opportunities	Access to finance
Increase/broaden company range	Access to management expertise
Provide customers with better service	Access to new markets for products
Financial gain	Increase size of distribution networks
Window on new technologies	Product development assistance/ access to technical expertise
Provide solutions to technical problems	Potential sales to partner
	Gain credibility
Window on new markets	Access to further funding from sources beside partners (e.g. EC)

Source: Based on Lawton Smith *et al.*, 1991: 462

(1991: 27), 'new opportunities that will later become of interest to large corporations are initially surfacing in market niches that are either too small to attract attention, or which are addressed by technologies that can only be exploited by specific people with specific skills that are not readily available to the corporation'.

Therefore, by forming an alliance with a small firm, large companies can gain an up-to-date window on new developments without having to attempt to research them in-house, an option which may not have been cost effective (Baty, 1990; Botkin and Matthews, 1992), and can become far more responsive to new developments (Olleros and MacDonald, 1988; Lawton Smith *et al.*, 1991). Partnering will often be quicker and less costly than internal development for the large firm since the small company will have already developed the idea or product to some extent. Risk and uncertainty are thus reduced. Collaboration with small entrepreneurial firms can also enable large companies to increase or broaden their range by providing access to new markets and customers (Baty, 1990). Alliances with firms based in other countries are becoming a popular way of gaining foreign market entry. Furthermore, if relationships are successful they can be expanded, providing the larger partner with low risk future expansion (Botkin and Matthews, 1992).

Small firm motivations

Small companies are typically more entrepreneurial, inventive and flexible than large firms, and are therefore often better able to cope in a dynamic business environment. However, small firms usually lack resources, most notably finance, marketing expertise, manufacturing know-how and management capabilities (Hisrich, 1986; Dickson *et al.*, 1990; Larson, 1990; Lawton Smith *et al.*, 1991; Botkin and Matthews, 1992; Brush and Chaganti, 1995; Segers, 1995). As a result, the promising products of many small firms often fail to reach commercialisation (Hull *et al.*, 1988; Teece, 1992; Hart *et al.*, 1995) unless a network of critical resource suppliers is established (Larson, 1992; Steier and Greenwood, 1995).

There are several reasons why partnerships with large companies are particularly desirable for the small firm (Roberts, 1980; Lawton Smith *et al.*, 1991; Stewart, 1993) (Table 1.5). Most of these reasons are concerned with access to the resources, both tangible and intangible, of the larger partner (O'Doherty, 1990; Larson, 1990; Henricks, 1991; Lawton Smith *et al.*, 1991; Radtke and McKinney, 1991; Forrest and Martin, 1992; Van Gils and Zwart, 1994; Belotti, 1995; Hart *et al.*, 1995). In terms of tangible resources, there are four areas of potential benefit for the small firm. First, large firms can provide access to new markets and distribution channels via their extensive support systems and advertising networks (Baty, 1990; MacDonald, 1991; McCann, 1991). According to Anderson (1993: 1823), 'collaborative relationships provide an essential strategy for survival and provide access to global markets, thus giving the small firms an opportunity to develop internally a more vertically integrated organisational structure without the huge amount of capital commitment, experience, and skills normally associated with such an undertaking'. Second, large companies can provide finance to their smaller partners (Baty, 1990; McCann, 1991; MacDonald, 1991; Dodgson, 1992; Segers, 1993; 1995). As Lawton Smith *et al.* (1991) note, small biotechnology firms often collaborate with large pharmaceutical companies as a means of gaining financial security and in order to finance the growth of the company. Third, small firms often lack the required business knowledge to commercialise their products and produce them efficiently (Forrest, 1990; Ahern, 1993b). Through partnerships, large companies can provide the required management expertise (Stewart, 1993). Fourth, collaboration can also be a means of obtaining grants to support innovation (Lawton Smith *et al.*, 1991). Small firms often find it easier to obtain grants through schemes such as Eureka and ESPRIT if they have a larger partner on which they can 'piggy-back'.

In addition to the above tangible benefits, close affiliation with a well-known corporate organisation can enhance the reputation and credibility of a small, lesser known firm (Baty, 1990; Larson, 1990; Henricks, 1991; MacDonald, 1991; Dodgson, 1992; Stewart, 1993; Belotti, 1995), help it to overcome the 'liabilities of newness' (Bahrami and Evans, 1995) and shield it from the survival pressures of the market (Skjerstad, 1994). According to Lawton Smith *et al.* (1991: 465), 'collaboration with major companies can lead to technical, professional and commercial visibility, particularly valuable to small firms'. Relationships with corporate partners enhance the attractiveness of small firms in an initial public offering prospectus and can be of particular value when approaching other prospective investors and negotiating business deals (Winters and Murfin, 1988). Ahern (1993b) recognised the importance of the credibility factor in motivating small Canadian firms to partner with large corporations, and Belotti (1995) reported similar findings for the wood-working industry in Sweden where the 'prestige' factor is considered by small firms to be of even greater value than more tangible technical or financial resources.

Collaboration with large firms therefore provides small firms with the opportunity to access a wide range of tangible and intangible resources vital for their growth and development while still remaining independent enterprises. Indeed, Teece (1992: 4) observed that 'in some circumstances cooperative agreements can enable smaller firms to emulate many of the functional aspects of large integrated enterprises, without suffering possible dysfunctions sometimes associated with large size'.

Concentration of large firm–small firm alliances in technology-based industries

As is the case with inter-firm collaboration in general, strategic partnerships are particularly common in technology-based industries (Hamilton, 1985; Powell, 1990; Niederkofler, 1991; Slatter, 1992; Bower and Whittaker, 1993; Segers, 1993; 1995; Farrell and Doutriaux, 1994; Belotti, 1995), marking what Rothwell and Dodgson (1994) term the 'Fifth Generation Innovation Process'. This reflects both the large firm's need to become an 'agile giant' (Bahrami and Evans, 1995) and stay abreast of new technological developments, and also the particularly severe resource constraints encountered by small technology-based firms (TBFs) (Gilbert, 1991; Forrest and Martin, 1992; Hamilton and Singh, 1992). Indeed, there is increasing recognition that global competition is based on technological innovation and within this environment not even the largest companies can maintain technological leadership in all areas. Furthermore, time-to-market is of critical importance in assuring business success (Anderson, 1993; Standeven, 1993; Farrell and Doutriaux, 1994). Consequently, alliances have become essential for most technology companies.

Collaboration can be particularly beneficial in technological sectors because of the complementary assets of small TBFs and large corporations (Silver, 1993; Belotti, 1995; Segers, 1995). Small firms can realise technological solutions more rapidly but often lack resources (Segers, 1993; 1995). The combination of large and small firms, and the exchange of the entrepreneur's technology for the corporation's resources, can therefore speed the innovation process and enhance growth (Hull *et al.*, 1988; Sommerlatte, 1990). In support of this, Rothwell (1993: 5) suggested that 'innovatory advantage is unequivocally associated with *neither* large *nor* small firms'. The advantages of large firms are mainly *material* – associated with greater

24

financial and technological resources – while the advantages of small firms are mainly *behavioural* – related to flexibility, dynamism and responsiveness (Rothwell, 1989; SBRC, 1992; Dodgson, 1993; Segers, 1993; Rothwell and Dodgson, 1994). The potential for mutually beneficial collaboration and 'dynamic complementarities' (Rothwell, 1983; Dodgson, 1993; Grabher, 1993) is therefore considerable as synergistic alliances can be formed that benefit both parties (Segers, 1993; 1995; Sykes, 1993). The behavioural advantages of small firms can help large corporations to improve their positions in terms of market and technological dynamism. In return, the large company's resources play an important role in the efforts of small firms to commercialise their products and technologies (MacDonald, 1991; Ettington and Bantel, 1994; Skjerstad, 1994). For young TBFs, technology therefore becomes an important exchangeable resource and competitive weapon – a 'coin of the realm' (Forrest and Martin, 1992; Eisenhardt and Schoonhoven, 1994).

Spatial patterns of large firm–small firm collaboration

Much of the literature which addresses large firm–small firm strategic partnerships, and indeed all forms of collaboration, has tended to ignore the spatial dimension of alliance formation (Cooke and Wells, 1991). However, some commentators (e.g. Anderson, 1993; Curran and Blackburn, 1994) have recognised that partnerships have an influential role to play in reconfiguring the spatial organisation of industries. What is not clear is the spatial scale involved. The field of economic geography has witnessed a constructive debate concerning the relationship between flexible inter-firm linkages and, on the one hand regionalisation/agglomeration, and on the other globalisation (Piore and Sabel, 1984; Hirst and Zeitlin, 1989; Storper and Scott, 1990; Amin and Thrift, 1992; 1993; Storper, 1995). Theories and empirical findings to date are somewhat contradictory since they appear to show both a decline in the importance of local economies in inter-firm relations *and* an increase in their importance for certain kinds of links (Chesnais, 1988; Cooke and Morgan, 1993; Curran and Blackburn, 1994; Storper, 1995). While it has been suggested (e.g. by Amin and Thrift, 1992; 1993) that local and global scales are not mutually exclusive but dialectical, considerable debate concerning the relative importance of different levels of spatial organisation does still exist.

Several current models of business interaction emphasise the importance of large firm–small firm strategic partnerships within delimited spatial boundaries (Crevoisier and Maillat, 1991; Curran and Blackburn, 1994), marking 'the transition to a new era of vertically disintegrated and locationally fixed production' (Amin and Thrift, 1992: 572). The Flexible Specialisation (Piore and Sabel, 1984) and Flexible Production (Storper and Scott, 1990) theses in particular suggests the significance of the 'industrial

25

district'. These districts are seen as ways in which local industrial societies can restructure and revitalise their economies in order to compete in international markets. Both cooperation and competition exist within the industrial district. It can be conceptualised as a particular type of agglomeration characterised by a localised thickening of inter-firm relationships (Malecki, 1991). It has been argued (e.g. by Storper, 1995) that agglomeration is an outcome of the minimisation of transaction costs and that without agglomeration the advantages of interdependence (e.g. flexibility and risk sharing) are reduced because of the increased costs and difficulties of transacting.

An alternative school of thought which has attempted to conceptualise the importance of regionalisation in the modern business environment concerns the notion of the 'milieu' (Camagni, 1991; Crevoisier and Maillat, 1991; Keeble, 1994; Maillat, 1995; Storper, 1995). 'The milieu is essentially a context for development, which empowers and guides innovative agents to be able to innovate and to coordinate with other innovating agents' (Storper, 1995: 203). The milieu, consisting of a dynamic ecosystem of institutions (protagonists), rules, practices, knowledge, know-how and a technical culture, is closely linked to the concept of collaboration and networks (Camagni, 1991; Bahrami and Evans, 1995; Maillat, 1995), and suggests that there is something intangible which permits and facilitates innovation within particular regions, or 'constructed territories' (Maillat, 1995). Leading on from this is the 'evolutionary paradigm' (Storper, 1995) which posits that regional economies, and the networks of firms within them, constitute nexuses of 'untraded interdependencies'. In other words, it is suggested that the region is a key element in the supply architecture for learning, or 'becoming', and innovation (Storper, 1995).

Theorists of industrial districts, milieux and regions in general therefore put great emphasis on spatial proximity in large firm–small firm collaboration, and indeed collaboration *per se* (Brusco, 1982; Aydalot and Keeble, 1988; Rothwell, 1989; Sabel, 1989; Grabher, 1993; Garnsey and Wilkinson, 1994; Vatne, 1995). According to Aydalot and Keeble (1988: 16), 'to a considerable extent, the local environment is the material expression on the ground of inter-firm functional relationships'. Proximity and common cultural identity may reduce transaction costs and facilitate information exchange and learning through well-functioning relations among suppliers and users of products and services (Camagni, 1991; Amin and Thrift, 1992; Gertler, 1992; Bahrami and Evans, 1995; Vatne, 1995).

However, a counter-argument suggests that inter-firm relationships are not limited by location (Ohmae, 1985; Anderson, 1993; Clark, 1993; Garnsey and Wilkinson, 1994; Malecki, 1995). As Gordon (1991: 180) stresses, 'there is no necessary reason why firms with specialized linkages should operate in close proximity', and indeed the relations between large and small firms appear now to be less close geographically than many previous views have implied (Curran and Blackburn, 1994). Clark (1993) described the 'chain-of-links' firm which competes globally by establishing a network of subcontracting and collaborative linkages on a world-wide scale. This trend towards the 'global network corporation' (Yoshino and Rangan, 1995) largely reflects new sophisticated production, information, communication and transportation technologies that have enabled spatially diverse firms to link up effectively with each other (Anderson, 1993). This provides support for the argument that technological advancement has resulted in a shift in the scale of competition from the regional to the global (Cooke and Wells, 1991). Many observers believe that the pressures for a more global orientation of business activities will overwhelm the trend toward regionalisation during the 1990s (James and Weidenbaum, 1991). Even Storper (1995), a supporter of the regionalisation school, concedes that transaction-cost constraints on the spatial dispersion of collaborative relationships quickly disappear in many industries as inputs become standardised and are produced at higher output levels, and also that untraded interdependencies are not necessarily regionalised. Also, Camagni (1991) noted that collaborative relationships with organisations outside local milieux are vital if 'entropic death', which threatens closed systems, is to be avoided.

Potential problems of strategic partnerships

Despite the potential benefits of strategic partnerships, such alliances can be problematic, particularly for the small firm (Perlmutter and Heenan, 1986; Dickson *et al.*, 1990; McCann, 1991; Miles and Snow, 1992; Sayer and Walker, 1992; Dodgson, 1993; Eisenhardt and Schoonhoven, 1994; Farrell and Doutriaux, 1994; Beamish and Inkpen, 1995). Many of the potential problems facing small firms when collaborating with large companies are common to all collaborations. However, they are often much more serious for small ventures which are typically financially constrained and have limited market strength (Dodgson, 1993). Doz (1988: 337) even described the obstacles facing small entrepreneurial firms in strategic partnerships as 'formidable'. While all collaborative forms have their own specific problems (Beamish and Inkpen, 1995), Botkin and Matthews (1992) identified five general, somewhat interrelated, issues that could be problematic in *all* forms of large firm–small firm collaborative relationships: these largely relate to the different operating structures and cultures of large and small firms.

Trust and liability

An important aspect of collaboration should be increasing firm inter-dependency. According to Aoki (1984) and Brouthers *et al.*, (1995), max-imum gains can come only from mutual trust, reciprocity and compatible goals, and not from the competitive two-player game which characterises most commercial activity. However, development of the collaborative interface between large and small firms is often constrained by the traditional competitive model of business interaction, which reflects the cultural and institutional rigidities inherent in large companies (Baty, 1990; Lawton Smith *et al.*, 1991). Small firms are often sceptical about the aims and hidden agendas of large partners, the fear of unequal treatment and a lack of trust (Mariti and Smiley, 1983; Chesnais, 1988; Steward, 1993). An atmosphere of distrust and domination by the large firm can therefore jeopardise the stability of a collaborative relationship (Perlmutter and Heenan, 1986).

Large companies can be vulnerable to the actions of smaller partners even when the entrepreneur's intentions are good. For example, large companies that partner with smaller firms are prone to challenges in court by third parties seeking retribution and redress for real or imagined actions of the smaller partner (Botkin and Matthews, 1992). An example cited by Botkin and Matthews (1992) refers to a small firm partner of Kodak which drew attention from angry consumer groups. As Botkin and Matthews (1992: 147) explain, 'had Kodak not been the parent, the groups probably would not have gone to court because the small company had few assets worth pursuing. But when the parent is a major corporation with financial reserves, its legal exposure is magnified'.

Control and failure

The need for control, order and predictability underlies the corporate strategy of integration. However, the need for control can be a pitfall in developing strategic partnerships since entrepreneurship is notoriously unpredictable and opportunistic (Ginsberg and Hay, 1993) because it has to cope with unpredictable outcomes. This dichotomy often results in large companies treating their smaller partners as subordinates rather than equals (Botkin and Matthews, 1992). Indeed, as Van Gils and Zwart (1994: 10) note, 'in a partnership with a large enterprise it's usually the strategy of the large enterprise that determines the direction of the alliance'. This intensifies the entrepreneur's fears of losing their independence and of an unwelcome take-over (Chesnais, 1988; Duijnhouwer, 1994; Garnsey and Wilkinson, 1994). According to Oakey (1993), large companies form partnerships with small firms as a first step towards acquisition – a process he has termed 'predatory networking'. Indeed, Lawton Smith *et al.*, (1991) also found large firms to have a reputation of behaving in a predatory manner towards small firms.

As well as problems caused by the large firm's desire *for* control, too little control and commitment can also present difficulties. Some large companies do not offer the commitment necessary to overcome the inevitable conflicts of cultures between firms (Stewart, 1993) and further difficulties may arise relating to differing management styles or the 'not invented here' (NIH) syndrome. The latter occurs when technical employees of the large company are unwilling to accept innovations from external sources (Lawton Smith *et al.*, 1991). In addition, a lack of commitment, communication and coordination can result in differing priorities of each firm, For example, a large company may not deploy sufficient resources to develop a new product which the smaller firm regards as potentially important (Lawton Smith *et al.*, 1991).

Entrepreneurial businesses are inherently risky and have to accommodate failures. However, large firms attempt to minimise risk and the chances of failure (Botkin and Matthews, 1992). There different attitudes towards failure present a serious potential pitfall for partnerships. Entrepreneurship cannot be discussed without considering failure, and corporate executives who cannot tolerate failure or use it as a positive learning mechanism are probably not well suited to strategic partnerships (Botkin and Matthews, 1992).

Perceptions of time

Many entrepreneurs and corporate executives have differing perceptions of time (Mamis, 1995). Most large corporations work within strict, short-term (usually quarterly) time horizons with regard to performance, growth and delivery (Botkin and Matthews, 1992). In contrast, entrepreneurs tend to have longer-term horizons. This reflects their recognition that new businesses often take a long time to grow and mature (Botkin and Matthews, 1992), and therefore require multi-year business plans. The problems related to these differing perceptions may be magnified if entrepreneurs promise their large partners more than they can deliver in set time periods in an attempt to impress. The time dimension can also create conflict on a daily basis. Botkin and Matthews (1992) noted that employees of large companies often make a clear distinction between work and personal time. Many entrepreneurs, however, tend to merge their business and personal time, often working long and odd hours. While they recognise this to be a generalisation, Botkin and Matthews (1992) highlight this issue as a further area of potential conflict.

Value and compensation

In terms of value, corporate executives with a management power orientation are unlikely to find satisfaction through strategic partnerships – they take a disproportionate amount of time but add very little to the manager's power base (Botkin and Matthews, 1992). In contrast, entrepreneurs are not concerned with their power base or company politics. Indeed, the desire to avoid company politics is a major reason why entrepreneurs start their own businesses. These differences can be a source of conflict between executives and entrepreneurs. A further difference concerns compensation, and in particular the fact that executives earn consistent monthly salaries while many entrepreneurs share in unpredictable cash results (Botkin and Matthews, 1992).

Cultural differences

One aspect of increasing levels of collaboration has been the rising number of alliances between companies in different countries (Contractor and Lorange, 1988; Hergert and Morris, 1988; Hladik, 1988; Pucik, 1988; Lorange and Roos, 1992; Culpan and Kostelac, 1993; Dodgson, 1993; Gugler and Dunning, 1993; Bidault and Cummings, 1994; Kanter, 1994). Cultural differences between countries cannot be dismissed when considering international collaboration (Perlmutter and Heenan, 1986; Pucik, 1988; Hara and Kanai, 1994; Beamish and Inkpen, 1995; Brouthers *et al.*, 1995; Shamdasani and Sheth, 1995). According to Botkin and Matthews (1992), motivations and the definition of success vary by nationality. Not all entrepreneurs value the same things and not all large company executives look for the same results from small firms. This has obvious implications for cross-border alliances. However, despite previous work indicating cultural differences between nationalities (e.g. by Hofstede, 1980), the increasing globalisation of the modern world prompts questions about the continuing importance of cultural differences and whether they will deteriorate in the light of economic change and cross-cultural contact (McGrath *et al.*, 1992).

SUMMARY AND CONCLUSIONS

The purpose of the discussion in this chapter has been twofold: first, it has provided a context for this book. It has outlined the increasing significance of inter-firm collaboration in international business, identified the new forms that cooperation is taking and examined the theoretical and macro-level considerations that attempt to explain alliance formation and organisation. Of particular significance for this study is the increasing propensity for large and small companies to collaborate and form strategic partnerships. While the underlying causes are similar to those for all types of collaboration, the potential complementarity and synergistic possibilities of large and small firms is particularly high given their respective material and behavioural assets. However, such relationships are often plagued by constraints relating to the different organisational structures of large and small companies.

Second, this chapter has illustrated the general and, largely as a result, complex nature of discussions concerning inter-firm collaboration. Increasing levels of collaboration have generated a great amount of interest from academics and practitioners from many disciplines. Discussion and debate have led to a recognition of the wide range of alliance types and motivations for collaboration that exist. Most researchers and theorists have therefore attempted to simplify their discussions by taking an holistic view of alliances and considering the motivations for, advantages of, and problems associated with many different collaborative forms together. However, as a result research to date has been largely inconclusive (Brush and Chaganti, 1995; Yoshino and Rangan, 1995), and important distinctions between different forms have often been overlooked. Indeed, according to James and Weidenbaum (1993: 12), alliances are now 'set up in so many combinations and permutations that it is difficult, and often misleading, to generalize'. Although some authors have attempted to concentrate their research on particular forms of alliance (most notably joint ventures – which themselves are variously used for patent licensing, manufacturing, subcontracting, product sharing, leasing, shared R&D, marketing, etc. (Kukalis and Jungemann, 1995; Shaughnessy, 1995) – or technology alliances), their discussions have often centred around more general accounts of collaboration *per se*. As Yoshino and Rangan (1995: 4) note, 'writers who treat alliances as glorified joint ventures shed little light on the subject. The notion of strategic alliances, like entropy, is much talked about but little understood'.

Therefore, it is argued that in the light of the complexity surrounding inter-firm collaboration, there is a need for the research emphasis to become more focused on individual forms of inter-firm collaboration. This need is particularly great in the case of large firm–small firm alliances. As Stewart (1993: 168) noted, 'the dynamics of an alliance between a small . . . enterprise and a larger partner may differ from that of comparably sized organisations. Consequently, more research is required on alliances of this type'. Similarly, Belotti (1995) recognised the need to 'dedicate more attention to the interests and motives of small firms for developing relationships with other firms and to better understand – and thereby encourage – the kind of complementarity that may exist between large and small firms'. A more focused approach will help to clarify our conceptualisation of the collaboration process, enable a more accurate classification of alliance forms than has been seen to date, and assist and inform the decision-making processes of practitioners.

Furthermore, looking specifically at the UK, the number of studies focusing on inter-firm collaboration involving UK firms has been limited. This may reflect a lack of alliances involving UK companies. Indeed, several authors (e.g. Lawton Smith *et al.*, 1991; Botkin and Matthews, 1992) have found that many UK companies have not been interested in collaboration. Traditionally, British industry has been organised into separate firms dealing with each other at arm's length. This legacy has constituted a major factor in inhibiting inter-firm collaboration. However, there are indications that increasing numbers of UK-based firms, particularly in technology-based sectors, are collaborating with others on a national and international basis (Lawton Smith *et al.*, 1991; DTI/CBI, 1993; Gourlay, 1995a). Research which examines collaboration in the UK context is therefore particularly timely and much needed.

This book examines one particular form of collaboration between large and small firms that has remained largely ignored in discussions of collaboration, namely the minority equity stake, or *corporate venture capital* (CVC) investment. The process of large companies taking minority equity stakes in small firms is often also known as *corporate venturing*. Several authors (e.g. Klein, 1987; Chesnais, 1988; Ormerod and Burns, 1988; Baty, 1990; Hull and Slowinski, 1990; Collins and Doorley, 1991; Henricks, 1991; MacDonald, 1991; Manardo, 1991; Radtke and McKinney, 1991; Hagedoorn, 1993a; Rind, 1994; Case, 1995) have identified CVC as a form of large firm–small firm alliance, although very few detailed studies have been undertaken which look specifically at CVC. Indeed, no such studies have been undertaken in the UK. Chapter 2 therefore provides a detailed review of the CVC literature and addresses definitional issues as well as identifying the extent of this form of collaboration world-wide. The chapter also provides a more detailed review of the book's aims and objectives.

2

CORPORATE VENTURING AND CORPORATE VENTURE CAPITAL

Definitions, potential benefits, evidence and justifications for research

INTRODUCTION

The focus of this chapter, and indeed of the book as a whole, is on corporate venture capital investment. In order to introduce this form of large firm–small firm collaboration, this chapter first attempts to define the CVC process, highlighting the distinctions between CVC and corporate venturing, terms which are often incorrectly used interchangeably. It then discusses the objectives and potential benefits of CVC, before identifying the levels of this activity world-wide. In the light of this discussion, the chapter concludes with a detailed research rationale followed by an account of the research aims, questions and methodology.

CORPORATE VENTURING AND CORPORATE VENTURE CAPITAL: SOME DEFINITIONS

> The term 'Corporate Venturing' is rather vague, tending to mean different things to different people
>
> (Ormerod and Burns, 1988: 80)

It was noted at the end of Chapter 1 that *corporate venture capital* investment is often known as *corporate venturing*. However, like so many other venture capital buzzwords, the real meaning of the term *corporate venturing* is hazy (Dawkins, 1986) because it has been used to describe a variety of somewhat different corporate activities (Block and MacMillan, 1993). Major definitional problems plague researchers seeking comparability across, and even within, corporate venturing studies (MacMillan, 1986), and failure to distinguish between the various possible corporate venturing modes can cause great confusion (Vesper, 1984). In an attempt to overcome this potential confusion, it is therefore important at the outset to recognise the range of activities described as corporate venturing and to outline the definition of corporate venture capital used in this study.

The corporate venturing spectrum

Corporate venturing encompasses a variety of techniques used by large companies seeking business growth and expansion (Block, 1982; *European Venture Capital Journal*, 1990a). Several attempts have previously been made in the literature to classify a *spectrum* of corporate venturing activity in order to aid clarification (e.g. Hanan, 1969; Rothwell, 1975), and although slight variations are seen in the conceptualisations of individual authors, the major characteristics are reasonably constant.

Perhaps the best known corporate venturing spectrum is that of Roberts (1980) which he termed the *Spectrum of Venture Strategies* (Figure 2.1). This encapsulates a number of alternative strategies for the development of new ventures. These range, on a scale of increasing risk and corporate commitment, from venture capital investment through venture nurturing, spin-offs and joint ventures to internal corporate venturing (Roberts, 1980; Pinchot, 1985; Oakley, 1987). Roberts's spectrum provides a reasonable summary of the range of corporate venturing activities discussed in the literature. However, the spectrum is by no means exhaustive, and many subdivisions of the various 'bands' of corporate venturing have been suggested (e.g. by Block, 1982). However, for the purposes of this study, the above typology can be regarded as adequate.

Figure 2.1 illustrates that the spectrum of corporate venturing activities can be generally divided into 'internal', 'in-house' strategies and 'external' strategies involving links with other independent firms (i.e. forms of inter-firm relationship). Miller and Camp (1985: 88) refer to the two as 'cousins'.

1	2	3	4	5	6
Venture capital	Venture nurturing	Venture spin-off	New style joint venture	Venture merging and melding	Internal venture

low corporate involvement/ risk   --->   high corporate involvement/ risk

| --------------------- External --------------------- | Internal

Key
1 Large firm investment of capital in stock of small company
2 As above but also incorporates managerial assistance for the small firm
3 Large company spins-off a new business as a separate firm with financial support
4 Large and small firms enter jointly into new ventures
5 Combinations of venture strategies described so far
6 Development of an 'in-house' entrepreneurial unit

Source: adapted from Roberts, 1980: 136

Figure 2.1 Spectrum of venture strategies

Such a division is suitable for the purposes of this discussion, and both 'internal' and 'external' strategies shall be considered in turn.

Internal corporate venturing (ICV)

Corporate strategy which is labelled 'Internal Corporate Venturing' (ICV) is generally understood to refer to a 'formalized entrepreneurial activity within existing business organisations which receive explicit organisational sanction and resource commitments for the purpose of initiative, corporate endeavors – new product developments, product improvements, new methods or procedures' (Schollhammer, 1982: 211). According to Block and MacMillan (1993: 14), ICV

- involves an activity *new* to the organisation
- is initiated or conducted *internally*
- involves significantly *higher risk* of failure or large losses than the organisation's base business
- is characterised by *greater uncertainty* than the base business
- will be *managed separately* at some time during its life

Internal corporate venturing involves an individual ('intrapreneur') or group being provided with total responsibility for a product within a corporation, and then given the freedom to run this division in an entrepreneurial manner in isolation from the rest of the corporation (Hall, 1989). The intrapreneur is 'an employee with the space to function as a free market entrepreneur within the limits agreed upon by himself and the corporation' (Bailey, 1984: 361). There may be many 'intrapreneurs' within a company who have significant entrepreneurial skills but are reluctant to leave the corporation in order to exploit them (Winters and Murfin, 1988). Ron Lord, once management training director of accountants Arthur Young, described the ICV process as the 'igniting of a small business spark within a large business environment' (cited Povey, 1986).

Internal corporate venturing has been variously named in the literature (Lorenz, 1993) as 'internal entrepreneurship', 'intra-corporate venturing', 'intrapreneurship', 'corporateurship' (Vesper, 1984), 'venture management' (Burrows, 1982) and 'intra-corporate entrepreneurship programs' (ICEP) (Susbauer, 1978). Distinctions between intrapreneurship and internal corporate venturing were drawn in Chapter 1; intrapreneurship has been described as a company-wide, internally oriented strategy designed to promote an entrepreneurial environment within the corporate organisation, while internal corporate venturing involves the establishment of autonomous in-house new ventures (Schollhammer, 1982; Burgelman, 1983; Bailey, 1984; MacMillan and George, 1985; Pinchot, 1985; Hall, 1989; Botkin and Matthews, 1992; Ginsberg and Hay, 1993). However, despite these distinctions, the majority of the literature does not distinguish between intrapreneurship and internal corporate venturing.

The management style and objectives of a particular company will help determine whether the intrapreneurial 'New Venture Division' (Fast, 1978) takes the form of a task force, a venture department or a subsidiary (Burrows, 1982), and whether it is developed on a large scale (macro) or a small scale (micro) (Fast, 1978). Whatever the strategy employed, the unit's primary functions remain the investigation of potential new business opportunities, the development of business plans and the management of the early commercialisation of ventures (Fast, 1978).

First popularised by 3M and DuPont in the late 1960s, ICV strategies have since been employed by Hewlett-Packard, Merck, Motorola, Johnson and Johnson, Corning, General Electric, Wal-Mart, Monsanto, IBM, Texas Instruments, Union Carbide, Rank Xerox, Levi and General Motors, as well as a significant number of other major corporations, particularly in the USA. ICV is one way in which these companies have attempted to develop new, innovative businesses and a more entrepreneurial 'in-house' climate (Fast and Pratt, 1981; Block and MacMillan, 1993) in response to the competitive pressures (i.e. increasing global competition, rapid technological change and shorter product life-cycles) that were identified in Chapter 1.

The importance of innovation for the modern business organisation cannot be overemphasised. According to Rothwell (1983) there is a growing acceptance of the key role played by innovation in the stimulation of economic growth, and the enhancement of competitiveness. Schollhammer (1982) recognised that in a corporate context, a firm's price discrimination power and its profit potential are enhanced by innovation, while entrepreneurship is the key element for gaining competitive advantage and greater financial rewards. Therefore, confronted by the pressures of the modern business environment as well as the continually declining attractiveness of traditional avenues of corporate growth and diversification such as outright acquisition and research and development (Roberts, 1980; Burrows, 1982; *Chemical Week*, 1992), many large corporations have decided upon the internal corporate venturing option. According to Ginsberg and Hay (1993: 3),

> to become properly entrepreneurial . . . it is not enough for large corporations to invest heavily in research and development; instead they need to instil a climate in which employees are encouraged to develop innovations that would be transformed into fast-growth new business lines within the existing corporate structure.

While an understanding of these general motivations is important, at the micro-economic level a range of motives driving corporations to consider the ICV option has been recognised. Taurins (1992) identified ten possible objectives of ICV, including the diversification and growth of the business, introduction of competitive pressure onto internal suppliers, divestment of non-primary activities, and spreading of the risks and costs of innovation. In addition, ICV can allow additional synergies to be discovered in the large resource combination constituted by firms (technological and human), as well as providing a means for advancing corporate capabilities (Burgelman, 1983).

Large firm environments often militate against innovation and are hostile to change (Hanan, 1969), but ICV attempts to reduce the associated risks by making innovation more predictable and less random. By employing such an entrepreneurial approach, a large firm combines the advantages of the small, independent business (singleness of purpose, simplicity of communication, and direct accountability) with its own size advantages (Peterson, 1967).

External corporate venturing and corporate venture capital

The terms *external corporate venturing* and *corporate venture capital* are definitional minefields. According to NEDO (1986), external corporate venturing involves a structured relationship between large, established companies, and smaller, unquoted, usually innovative firms. This broad definition has also been adopted by several other authors (e.g. Ormerod and Burns, 1988; Hall, 1989; Dunn, 1992) and the term *external corporate venturing* is often used – particularly in the USA – to describe all forms of strategic partnerships between large and small companies (Baty, 1990; Rind, 1994).

Although external corporate venturing does usually involve the provision of equity finance to complement the strategic relationship (regardless of whether this relationship is formal or informal) (Block, 1983), in its broadest sense it does not have to (Teece, 1992). Equity investments may allow the small company to commit the necessary resources to fulfil the contractual agreement, may foster closer working relationships and more open information flows, and allow the large company to share in the increased valuation of the smaller partner resulting from the collaboration (Radtke and McKinney, 1991).

However, the term *corporate venture capital* is used to describe instances only where an equity stake has been taken by a large corporation in a small, unquoted company, whether it is coupled with further strategic relationships or not. NEDO (1986) refers to the large firm as the 'sponsor' and the smaller firm as the 'investee'. In contrast to external corporate venturing, the specific corporate motives for corporate venture capital investment may not be strategic at all, but may be related instead to financial gain or even social responsibility (Honeyman, 1992). Clearly, this has implications for when corporate venture capital investments warrant the title *strategic alliance*.

CORPORATE VENTURE CAPITAL: NATURE AND FORMS

Corporate venture capital investment can take two main forms (ACOST, 1990; Sykes, 1993): externally managed (indirect) investment, when investments are made via externally managed venture capital funds which in turn reinvest in small firms, and internally managed (direct) investment, when investments in individual independent ventures are selected and managed by the corporation itself. Both forms of investment are associated with different corporate organisational structures, investment vehicles and investment characteristics (Figure 2.2).

	Corporate Venture Capital			
Type of investment	**Externally managed (indirect)** (investment via independently managed venture capital fund)		**Internally managed (direct)** (direct subscription for minority equity stakes)	
Investment vehicle	Independently managed fund ('pooled'/ 'multi-investor')	Independently managed *captive* fund ('client-based'/ 'dedicated')	In-house corporate managed fund	Ad hoc/ one-off investments
Investment characteristics	Funds reinvest in small, innovative companies Corporate investors may play a hands-on role or establish further *strategic partnerships* with investee companies (e.g. customer, supplier, licensing, research contracts, joint production/ marketing, etc.)		As well as finance, relationships may be hands-on and involve *venture nurturing* – managerial assistance in marketing, production, R&D, etc.; and/or formation of further *strategic partnerships* Investments may be alongside independently managed venture capital funds (*parallel investments*)	
Corporate organisational structure	Corporate investment may be coordinated by a separate subsidiary (fully or partially owned) or an in-house department/operating division/function. In each case, externally and/or internally managed strategies may be the focus. An integrated, in-house venture capital programme may be established combining several CVC vehicles as well as other corporate development strategies.			

Figure 2.2 Corporate venture capital strategies

Externally managed (indirect) CVC

Externally managed CVC involves a non-financial company investing as a limited partner in an independent venture capital fund which is usually closed and managed by experienced venture capitalists (Honeyman, 1992).[1] This form of investment represents the simplest form of corporate commitment. There are two main forms of externally managed CVC investment: pooled funds and client-based funds.

Pooled funds

Corporations may invest in 'pooled', 'balanced' or 'multi-investor' venture capital funds, as they are variously called. The corporation will typically invest in two to five funds (total cost of approximately £2 million to £5 million) many of which will be 'focused' in that they specialise in making investments in particular industry sectors. The fund will then go on to reinvest this and other monies (typically raised from institutional investors such as pension funds and insurance companies) in small, usually unquoted, companies (Oakley, 1987). The corporate investor receives reports on portfolio companies as well as a monthly listing of all deals received (Honeyman, 1992).

Client-based funds

Alternatively, companies may invest in 'client-based' funds which are often referred to as 'captive' or 'dedicated'. These involve an established venture capital firm taking an investment from a large corporation, and then building for it a portfolio of small companies relevant to its strategic development. Thus a large company is the only limited partner in a specific fund targeted at a particular corporate development sector. Although client-based funds are clearly externally managed and therefore distinct from direct CVC, the corporate investor does have much more of an active role than when it invests in pooled funds, defining its key areas of interest and gaining right of first refusal on any deals identified (*European Venture Capital Journal*, 1990a). The 'cherry picking' approach of client-based funds can often lead to companies establishing direct, internally managed CVC programmes (ACOST, 1990).

Internally managed (direct) CVC

As with the externally managed strategies, direct CVC can be divided into two forms: corporate managed venture capital fund and ad hoc/one-off investments.

Corporate managed venture capital fund

This is a variant of the captive, client-based fund investment theme but involves *internal* management. A large company establishes its own venture capital fund which is often in the form of a subsidiary, and enjoys its own autonomous management, thus guaranteeing operational independence. Such a fund operates in a similar way to an independent venture capital fund; it identifies and evaluates investment opportunities, makes minority equity investments in firms of interest and often occupies a seat on the board of portfolio companies (Honeyman, 1992). This approach usually involves large capital outlays.

Ad hoc/one-off investments

These represent an unstructured approach to CVC undertaken by companies that form CVC relationships on an opportunistic basis. Independent ventures are identified by corporate divisions who typically refer the investment decision to corporate head office. A study by Siegel *et al.* (1988) in the USA found that almost half of their sample companies had made CVC investments only on an ad hoc basis. In Chapter 1 it was noted that the majority of *all* collaborative alliances are formed in an ad hoc fashion (Yoshino and Rangan, 1995). 'Spin-offs' can be included as ad hoc CVC investments, although in rare cases they may be managed by more formal internally managed funds. 'Spin-offs' involve the exploitation of ideas which have arisen in the R&D laboratory of a large company, but which are unsuitable for internal exploitation (Rothwell, 1975; Collins and Doorley, 1991), as they do not fit the mainstream interests of the large firm. Corporations want to achieve some return on the accumulated investment that they have made over time in developing these technologies, and therefore such 'on the shelf' projects may be 'spun-off' as separate companies in which the parent corporation may receive an equity position (Smollen, 1978). Often, one or more independent investors provide additional finance for the spin-off, and the new company then seeks to gain market and operational experience in a new field (Roberts, 1980).

The literature suggests that direct CVC investments are sometimes made alongside established venture capital firms (e.g. Sykes, 1993). Such 'parallel' investment is sometimes known as 'piggy-backing' (NEDO, 1986). Indeed, Bleicher and Paul (1987: 64) observed a trend for 'establishing focused corporate venture capital programmes in co-operation with an external venture capital organisation'.

Corporate investors may be 'hands-on' whereby directors take seats on the board of investee firms and hence influence management decisions. In addition, CVC investments may be complemented by a certain degree of *venture nurturing* (Roberts, 1980). This involves the provision by the investing company of a certain degree of managerial and technical assistance to the investee firm in areas such as R&D, production, marketing and distribution (Rothwell, 1975; NEDO, 1986; Allen, 1992; Honeyman, 1992). Furthermore, both direct and indirect investments may provide opportunities for the establishment of further contractual business relationships between investor and investee firms (Allen, 1992). Such relationships may involve manufacturing collaboration, when the larger firm makes products on behalf of the smaller one, licensing deals, or marketing liaison, with exploitation of the larger company's distribution networks and sales outlets by the smaller firm. Doz (1988) also recognised research contracts, loans, and other financial arrangements between the large firm and the smaller venture.

Companies that wish to make venture capital investments often establish fully or partially owned subsidiaries for this purpose (Warren and Kempenich, 1984). Siegel *et al.* (1988) describe CVC subsidiaries as being either 'pilots' or 'co-pilots', depending upon their degree of autonomy in relation to the corporate parent. 'Pilots' have far greater authority to make investment decisions than 'co-pilots', who enjoy significantly less independence. Alternatively, a company may coordinate its investment through an in-house operating division. In both cases, the programme focus may be oriented towards direct or indirect investments, or indeed both.

Corporations may integrate all their venture capital investment activity in one in-house programme. Such a programme may involve the holding and monitoring of a portfolio of investments in venture capital funds, the operation of a venture capital subsidiary, and the management of ad hoc investments (*European Venture Capital Journal*, 1990a). Such a 'company within a company' (Myrick, 1986: 34) would therefore aim to invest in a large number of venture capital projects and may also be involved with the development of other business research and development strategies such as non-equity strategic partnerships, contract research agreements and acquisitions (Winter and Murfin, 1988).

THE POTENTIAL BENEFITS OF CORPORATE VENTURE CAPITAL INVESTMENT

The potential benefits for large firms

For the large firm the fundamental reasons for making CVC investments, either directly or indirectly, are the same as for ICV. Companies are motivated by the need for flexibility along with an 'entrepreneurial injection' to stimulate innovation and hence aid growth and diversification in times of strong global competition and shorter product life-cycles (Dunn, 1992; Silver, 1993). Mast (1991) explained that the corporation's main aim is to manufacture and sell existing products, while attempting to stay ahead of the competition in the development of new ones. Like ICV, CVC is one 'tool' which can help achieve this (Klein, 1987; Hegg, 1990).

Moreover, the process of externalising the search for innovation via inter-firm relationships such as CVC may have some inherent advantages over internal venturing (Block, 1983; Bleicher and Paul, 1987; Ginsberg and Hay, 1993). Indeed, many of the advantages for large companies of 'waltz-ing with entrepreneurial partners' (Bygrave and Timmons, 1992) rather than 'dancing on their own' (Kanter, 1989) were discussed in Chapter 1. The key concept of CVC, as a form of inter-firm collaboration, is that each company provides something which the other does not have (Henricks, 1991). Indeed, NEDO (1986: vi) saw CVC as offering an 'opportunity to combine the different strengths of large and small companies in order to generate opportunities for business development which might not other-wise be fully exploited'.

In terms of the specific objectives of companies for making CVC investments, Winters and Murfin (1988: 210) noted that 'the rationale for a corporation becoming a participant in the venture capital process is frequently confused or ill perceived'. While the principal goals of CVC strategy are usually considered to be concerned with the attainment of flexibility and innovation for growth, several authors have considered large company objectives in more detail. For example, Greenthal and Larson (1983) suggested that corporations pursue one or more of three goals when participating in venture capital. They seek to acquire new businesses, gain access to new technologies, and/or obtain attractive returns on invested funds. Warren and Kempenich (1984) also considered diversification into unrelated high-growth fields to be an important motivation. Baty (1990), Collins and Doorley (1991), Mast (1991) and Rind (1994) all emphasised similar objectives, noting that CVC relationships can provide a window on new opportunities, can help plug product/technology gaps, can help accel-erate strategic changes within the corporation and provide opportunities for the establishment of further business relationships as well as being finan-cially rewarding.

The most recent empirical data based on large firm motivations were obtained during a study of approximately 100 corporate venture capitalists in the USA (Silver, 1993). Listed below, in order of importance, are the sixteen CVC motivations outlined in the US survey:

- To incubate and reduce the cost of acquisitions
- Exposure to possible new markets
- To add new products to existing distribution channels
- A less expensive form of research and development
- To expose middle management to entrepreneurship
- Training for junior management
- Utilise excess plant space, time, and people

- To mesh the activities of several departments
- To generate capital gains
- Investigation: develop antennae for new technologies
- Income generating
- Group therapy for senior management
- Good public relations
- The competition may be doing it
- To retain a stake in spin-off companies
- To encourage new company formation in the community

There appears to be a general agreement that large firm motivations for making CVC investments can generally be classified as either *strategic* (i.e. enabling large companies to assess new markets, tap new talent, diversify, acquire windows on technology, establish further business relationships with investee firms, etc.), *financial* (i.e. for the principal purpose of obtaining an attractive return on investment),[2] *social responsibility related* (whereby a company invests to be seen to be aiding economic well-being, particularly in regions in which it has made considerable redundancies), or even simply concerned with *educating* the investing company about venture capital investment (Rind, 1981; MacMillan *et al.*, 1986; Siegel *et al.*, 1988; Sykes, 1990; Honeyman, 1992; Block and MacMillan, 1993; Gompers, 1994; Abbott and Hay, 1995).

However, there is debate concerning which motivations are most important. According to many authors (e.g. Rind, 1981; Baty, 1990; Collins and Doorley, 1991; Mast, 1991; Crackett, 1992; Block and MacMillan, 1993; Pratt, 1994), most corporations involved in CVC have primarily strategic objectives. *Chemical Week* (1992) suggested that CVC investments were being used increasingly for strategic purposes rather than in order to gain financially. However, George Hegg (1990: 29), Vice-President of Strategic Planning Services at 3M in the USA, suggested that the motives were more complex, noting that 'good strategic rewards will also provide good financial rewards'. Similarly, Winters and Murfin (1988) stated that the high returns to be obtained from venture capital investment are the main reason why many corporations are attracted to this field. Despite these comments, the *European Venture Capital Journal* (1990a) questioned the compatibility of financial and strategic objectives together.

Specific forms of CVC activity have been perceived as being more suitable for particular objectives:

- *Indirect CVC* Through investment in a venture capital fund a corporate can gain access to a far larger portfolio of investee companies than would be the case with direct investment (Collins and Doorley, 1991; MacDonald, 1991), as well as enjoying greater diversification by geographic region, investment stage and field of interest (Winters and Murfin, 1988). Corporate investors can benefit from the venture capitalists' screening process and experience in picking winners, and have more opportunities for earning attractive returns on investment (Sykes, 1990; MacDonald, 1991; Block and MacMillan, 1993). Investment in a number of pooled funds can lead to the establishment of contact with numerous funds and their portfolio companies as a result of a wider spread of capital invested. However, such multi-investor funds may not provide the significant strategic focus or contact with investee firms which is possible with more client-based funds that are specifically oriented towards the areas of interest of the corporate investor.

- *Direct CVC*   Direct, internally managed investments have the potential to provide greater strategic benefit than indirect investments (Sykes, 1990). Rather than providing advantages in the form of deal flow and return on investment, the establishment of internally managed venture capital funds or ad hoc investments allow much closer interaction between large and small partners, especially when a more 'hands-on'/ nurturing approach is employed by the larger firm (Block and MacMillan, 1993). However, some disagree that direct strategies provide greater strategic benefits than indirect strategies. For example, the late Paul Bailey, formerly a venture capitalist with Baring Venture Partners in London, stated in 1985 that 'involvement with the international venture capital community (externally managed CVC) is by an overwhelming margin the most productive mechanism a corporation can have for providing the corporation with useful numbers of prefiltered business opportunities' (P. Bailey, 1985: 11). He went on to suggest that a corporation's optimal approach to venture capital is to invest in independently managed funds, or at least alongside them in parallel deals.

Particular organisational structures within the large company may be more appropriate for specific objectives. For example, Mast (1991) suggested that if the primary aim of the CVC programme is diversification then a centralised operation may be more suitable than a decentralised one, which might be more successful if the support of existing business areas is the objective. However, the optimal structure of a CVC programme is company specific and does not only depend upon corporate objectives. For certain companies, such as those new to venture capital, dedicated, externally managed programmes may be appropriate, while companies with narrower business interests may find that ad hoc investment works better (Mast, 1991). Each specific CVC strategy requires a certain level of corporate resources, and has the potential for satisfying particular aims (Bleicher and Paul, 1987), and it must be recognised that the desired strategy may not always be possible, as implementation relates to availability of these resources.

It may be that some industrial sectors tend to employ particular strategies more often than others. Mitton (1991), Dodgson (1992) and Bygrave and

Timmons (1992) have all noted the concentration of ad hoc investments in the biotechnology industry, allowing large firms to maintain a 'watching brief' on developing technology. On a larger scale, it has been suggested by Hurry *et al.* (1992) that Japanese CVC investment in general is far more strategically biased than, for example, US investment, which gives greater emphasis to financial motives.

Given that CVC investments, and particularly those made directly, are often strategically motivated, it is reasonable to suggest that this form of inter-firm relationship warrants the title *strategic* alliance. Indeed the role of CVC as a business development strategy has been recognised (e.g. by *UK Venture Capital Journal*, 1985; Littler and Sweeting, 1987a; Oakley, 1987; Baty, 1990; Sykes, 1993), and Hardymon *et al.* (1983: 115) described CVC as a 'middle route to diversification' between acquisition and internal development. CVC investment therefore has the potential to be a viable complementary strategy to these more traditional corporate development options.

The potential benefits for small firms

The potential benefits of CVC strategy for small firms can, as with large firms, generally be divided into two broad categories – financial and strategic.

Financial benefits

The acquisition of capital has long been considered a critical factor for success in new ventures (Sargent and Young, 1991). According to Roberts (1990: 81), 'money provides "the grease", the wherewithal to make it happen', and without capital the new venture cannot succeed.

The financing needs of technology-based firms (TBFs) are distinctive because of the high costs associated with technological product and process development (Manigart and Struyf, 1995). The amount of finance required in order to develop and launch a technology-based product on the market is often between ten and twenty times greater than the initial R&D investment (Standeven, 1993). Furthermore, the amount of finance required for the development of technology-based products has increased since the mid-1980s and is likely to increase further (Standeven, 1993). This has led Standeven (1993: 11) to predict that 'the availability of financing will become a more crucial issue for the success of new technologies'.

Several studies have recognised that the TBF founder's savings, as well as the assets of family and friends, are often the foundation of seed capital (e.g. Bruno and Tyebjee, 1984; Oakey, 1984; Roberts, 1991; Murray, 1994a; 1995). However, while financing requirements do vary by sector (Roberts, 1991; Mason and Harrison, 1994), for the majority of TBFs internal equity and profits alone are insufficient to meet the high capital requirements for development and progression to the next growth stage (Baty, 1990). Therefore, while they are still in the very early stages of development many TBFs are forced to seek external investment capital (Oakey, 1984). Not surprisingly, the firms that most vigorously seek external capital tend to be growth-oriented companies (Oakey, 1984).

For many TBFs, external equity finance is more appropriate for their financing needs than debt finance (Standeven, 1993; Mason and Harrison, 1994; Manigart and Struyf, 1995). A major problem associated with the financing of TBFs concerns the cyclical nature of both product sales and R&D expenditure. As Oakey (1984: 240) notes, 'the growth and subsequent decline of sales over time from an initial or subsequent new product implies that the profits will not be uniform'. This cyclical revenue detracts from the TBF's security and credibility with lenders and limits its ability to repay debt. Banks are therefore typically cautious of lending to technology-based ventures, and particularly those in the early stages of development. This reluctance to invest also reflects the problems of distinguishing between good and bad technology businesses (Mason and Harrison, 1994), the lack of expertise of banks in these sectors and also the limited collateral of TBFs (Baty, 1990; Moore, 1994; Philpott, 1994).

Therefore, many TBFs have to turn to sources of external equity finance if their businesses are to survive beyond the seed stage (Baty, 1990; Slatter, 1992; Standeven, 1993; Mason and Harrison, 1994; Moore, 1994) even though it means diluting the entrepreneur's ownership and control (Burns, 1992; Buxton, 1995; Manigart and Struyf, 1995). There are a wide variety of sources of external equity finance potentially available to fund the technology-based company's capital requirements through its successive stages of growth (Roberts, 1991);[3] these include funding from family and friends, government sources, informal and institutional venture capital and public markets. The stage of development of a company (Roberts, 1991) as well as its growth orientation (Standeven, 1993) both strongly influence the types of capital that are required and potentially available.

However, despite the range of potential sources, most TBFs, and indeed small firms in general, face unique financing problems at virtually every stage of their development (Walker, 1989; Murray, 1994a). These problems are particularly severe in the early stages when firms typically have limited collateral (Murray, 1994a; 1995; Murray and Lott, 1995), unproven products and technologies (Murray, 1995), but insufficient funds with which to finance projects themselves (Gompers, 1994). Many of the traditional sources of finance for firm growth are unavailable to small companies as a result of imperfections in the debt and equity markets (Walker, 1989).

A shortage of funds has been seen as a major barrier to the growth of small businesses in the UK (ACOST, 1990). The difficulties encountered by small firms in raising capital for start-up and growth have been discussed periodically in government inquiries (e.g. HM Government 1931; 1959; 1971; 1979; ACOST, 1990) and the academic literature (e.g. Hall, 1989; Mason and Harrison, 1991a; 1992; Binks, 1993; Boocock *et al.*, 1993; Murray, 1994b) since the early 1930s. A number of studies (e.g. Mason and Harrison, 1992; 1995; Murray, 1993) have drawn particular attention to the obstacles faced by small enterprises seeking *equity* finance. This 'equity gap' is often associated with a shortage of finance in tranches of less than £250,000, although there is debate concerning the exact amounts involved.

ACOST (1990) highlighted the particular importance of venture capital as a finance source for small firms and suggested the recent rapid growth of the industry to be 'ample testimony to the fact that it meets a capital market gap not previously covered by more traditional, passive investment institutions' (p. 35). The emergence of a venture capital industry in the UK has indeed reduced the size of the equity gap (Mason and Harrison, 1992). The UK venture capital industry was created in a period of sustained economic growth throughout the 1980s during which time it experienced quite dramatic growth (Abbott and Hay, 1995; Murray, 1995). In 1981, thirty venture capital organisations committed £66 million to 163 investee firms (Murray, 1995). By 1994 the British Venture Capital Association (BVCA) had 114 full members, 111 of which invested £2.07 billion world-wide (£1.67 billion in 1,101 firms in the UK) in that year (BVCA, 1995a).

However, despite the rapid growth of the UK venture capital industry, its contribution to overcoming barriers to growth in small firms has been limited for two main reasons. First, the venture capital industry has increasingly failed to provide equity finance for start-up and early stage firms (Murray, 1991a; 1992a; Murray and Lott, 1995). This form of investment has been termed *classic* venture capital by several authors (e.g. Bygrave and Timmons, 1992; Abbott and Hay, 1995; Murray and Lott, 1995), and is distinct from investments in later stage deals which have become collectively known as *development* or *merchant* capital. While there has been a general trend away from classic venture capital towards development capital in both the USA and Europe, this trend has been most marked in the UK (Abbott and Hay, 1995; Mason and Harrison, 1995). While seed, start-up and other early stage deals accounted for 24 per cent of 1993 disbursements in the USA, the corresponding figure for the UK was 6 per cent (BVCA, 1994; Venture Economics, 1994). Despite a 10 per cent rise in the total amount invested in early stage deals in 1994, this masks a 25 per cent decrease in the number of early stage financings during the year as only £76 million of the £1.67 billion invested in the UK that year was devoted to early stage firms (BVCA, 1995a).

Later stage deals, especially management buy-outs and buy-ins (MBOs and MBIs), now dominate the contemporary UK venture capital industry (Scottish Enterprise, 1993; Abbott and Hay, 1995; Murray, 1995; Murray and Lott, 1995). This shift to development capital reflects three main factors. First, investments in early stage firms often involve small amounts and it has been argued (e.g. by Mason and Harrison, 1995) that the high evaluation and monitoring costs associated with venture capital investment mean that it is often uneconomical for funds to make small investments. Second, UK fund managers have been placed under increasing pressure by institutional investors who are seeking higher returns in shorter time periods (discussed in greater depth later in this chapter in the section 'The potential benefits for independent venture capitalists'). Start-up and early stage deals tend to be higher risk, have often performed poorly in the past and have therefore been 'crowded out' by later stage investments (Murray and Lott, 1995; Weyer, 1995) as more and more funds turn their focus to development capital. Third, fund managers are increasingly concerned about their remuneration. This is obtained from annual fees from limited partners (usually 2 per cent of total capital committed) and a percentage (probably 20 per cent) of realised capital gains. It might be expected that fund managers would prefer to invest in early stage deals given the potential higher capital gains. However, because of the recent poor performance of such investments, managers are increasingly attempting to raise larger amounts for investment in later stage deals due to the higher fee income associated with larger funds (Abbott and Hay, 1995). While it is important not to assume that if funds stopped investing in development capital and MBOs they would automatically start investing in start-ups (Murray and Lott, 1995), it is clear that the two forms of investment do compete with each other for the available capital (Weyer, 1995), and the recent preference for later stage deals has been to the detriment of classic venture capital (Abbott and Hay, 1995).

The second major barrier to small firm growth is concerned with the failure of the venture capital industry to provide funding for TBFs (Moore, 1994). The three most frequently discussed sources of external equity finance for growth-oriented TBFs at various stages of their development are venture capital funds, business angels and public markets. They will be considered in turn.

Venture capital funds

Venture capital funds are often considered to be the dominant source of post start-up equity finance for growth-oriented TBFs (Freear and Wetzel, 1990) and their role in providing finance for start-up companies has also been identified (e.g. by Rosenstein et al., 1989; Freear and Wetzel, 1990). Several authors have noted that US venture capital fund activity has been largely defined within a technology focus (Bygrave and Timmons, 1992; Murray, 1993; 1995; Standeven, 1993; Abbott and Hay, 1995). Indeed, Rizzoni (1991: 39) even suggested that 'the problems concerning the financing of high-risk initiatives involving long-term profitability – such as innovative science-based projects – have been overcome in the USA by means of venture capital development'. While this may be an overexaggeration, the importance of venture capital funds for the financing of TBFs in the USA is widely acknowledged (Murray and Lott, 1995).

In contrast to the USA, UK venture capital funds tend to be reluctant to invest in TBFs (Mason and Harrison, 1992; Scottish Enterprise, 1993; Standeven, 1993). This is largely the result of the perceived high-risk nature of technology investments, which in turn reflects the innovativeness of the products and processes concerned (Bygrave and Timmons, 1992; Murray, 1995; Murray and Lott, 1995). Venture capitalists are also wary of the size of capital inputs required, the financial inexperience of the founders and the attitudes, practices and imperfections in the capital market (Oakey, 1984; Sweeting, 1991a; Moore, 1994; Murray and Lott, 1995). The more rigorous investee selection process required for technology financing is a further relevant factor (Murray, 1995), although it is not clear whether this represents a cause or effect. On the one hand, venture capitalists may be reluctant to invest in TBFs *because* of the rigorous selection process required, while on the other, this rigorous selection process and the consequent higher 'hurdle rates' set for the acceptance of TBFs may *result* in fewer firms meeting the venture capitalist's standards (Murray and Lott, 1995).

While these factors have relevance on a world-wide basis (Standeven, 1993), there is particular recognition of shortfalls in the provision of venture capital to TBFs in the UK (ACOST, 1990; Sweeting, 1991a; Murray, 1993; Moore, 1994). It has been argued (e.g. by Weyer, 1995) that this reflects both the UK investment culture, which is often considered to be risk averse and short-termist, as well as the lack of high-calibre TBFs in the UK. This reluctance to invest in TBFs has increased since the mid-1980s (Sweeting, 1991a; 1991b) (Table 2.1). Indeed, Murray (1995) calculated that the proportion of funds allocated to TBFs more than halved in the nine years to 1993. This has largely been because of the high failure rates and poor performance of TBFs during this period (Sweeting, 1991a), and therefore the preference of fund managers and their institutional

Table 2.1 Percentage numbers and value of technology investments (excluding MBOs/MBIs) in the UK, 1984–93

	1984	1985	1986	1987	1988	1989	1990	1991	1992	1993
Technology – % no. total investments	42.3	37.6	33.9	31.4	24.4	31.8	32.7	27.4	25.8	29.4
Technology – % value total investment	42.0	41.5	32.5	34.9	20.5	32.0	30.2	29.2	25.7	32.9

Note: Figures for 1994 not available since method of classification was altered in this year rendering comparison impossible
Source: Murray, 1995

investors for less risky medium- or low-technology deals. The trend is also linked to the move away from early stage deals, which have often involved TBFs (Abbott and Hay, 1995). Despite the need for external equity finance by TBFs during the early stages of their development (Sweeting, 1991a; Moore *et al.*, 1992; Scottish Enterprise, 1993; Mason and Harrison, 1994; Murray and Lott, 1995), an increasing proportion of the technology-based companies that are successful in attracting venture capital finance are at the expansion stages of their development or are MBOs or MBIs (Cookson, 1994).

Technology investing has become a specialist activity undertaken by a minority of venture capitalists (Sweeting, 1991a; 1991b; Cosh and Hughes, 1994; Weyer, 1995). Standeven (1993) described a similar trend in Canada. If MBOs and MBIs are omitted, 84 per cent of total annual disbursements in the USA between 1986 and 1991 were in technology-related projects, compared with only 30 per cent in the UK (Murray and Lott, 1995). Similarly, in 1993 technology deals accounted for 78 per cent of the total number of investments made in the USA, while the figure for the UK was only 29 per cent (see Table 2.1). According to Murray and Lott (1995), UK venture capital funds' annual investment in technology-based deals averaged only 14.1 per cent of total investment for the eight years 1984–91.

Business angels

The majority of investment in TBFs at the seed and start-up stages of development has been provided by informal investors or *business angels* (Freear and Wetzel, 1990; 1991; Roberts, 1991; Standeven, 1993). Business angels are wealthy individuals who invest relatively small amounts of equity capital in small firms primarily in order to gain financially but often also to participate in the growth of young ventures (Roberts, 1991). The role of angels declines sharply, however, at later stages of firm development when larger sums are typically required (Freear and Wetzel, 1990; 1991). Most informal investors in the USA have a preference for investing in high technology enterprises (Haar *et al.*, 1988). Conversely, Mason and Harrison (1994) noted the much more limited involvement of business angels in the financing of such firms in the UK. In addition, business angels in the UK are less likely than their US counterparts to finance start-ups (Mason and Harrison, 1994). Gaston (1989) found 56 per cent of informal venture capital investments in the USA to be at the start-up stage while Mason and Harrison (1994) found the figure for the UK to be just 27 per cent.

Public markets

The public markets have been proposed as a source of finance for expansion stage, growth oriented TBFs (Roberts, 1991; Standeven, 1993). However, two factors combine to make this source inaccessible to most firms.

First, the significant fixed costs involved in raising finance on the public market, including underwriting and accountancy fees and printing costs, make it uneconomic for TBFs to raise small amounts of finance from the public markets (Mason and Harrison, 1994). Hutchinson and McKillop (1992) suggested that it is uneconomic to raise sums of less than £10 million via public markets. Second, in order to meet the criteria for listing, companies must have reached sufficient size and have a trading record. This therefore excludes early stage TBFs (Smith, 1994).

The opportunities for going public are greater in the USA than in the UK (Abbott and Hay, 1995). This reflects the differing role of 'Junior' stockmarkets in these countries. The UK, and indeed Europe in general, does not have a market to match NASDAQ in the USA. NASDAQ offers a single, homogenous market specifically set up to deal with the particular needs of small firms (Fassin and Lewis, 1994). It is the strongly preferred market of issuers and underwriters for independent public offerings (IPOs), and the keys to its success are its market-makers and electronic trading system (Urry, 1995). The attraction of NASDAQ has led many European TBFs to seek a listing in the USA rather than in Europe (Bennett, 1995; Gourlay, 1995b). However, an Alternative Investment Market (AIM) has recently been launched by the London Stock Exchange, and there is continuing debate about the prospects of the EASDAQ market in Europe, which could perform a similar role to NASDAQ.

ACOST (1990), Murray (1991b; 1995), the European Commission (see Duhamel et al., 1994) and Abbott and Hay (1995) have all emphasised both the need for research to focus on ways of stimulating the supply of risk finance in various forms and the importance of 'a new class of investors, prepared to make long term investments in R&D based companies' (ACOST, 1990: viii). ACOST (1990) identified corporate venture capital investment to be a potentially important alternative source of equity finance for small firms. Indeed, Ormerod and Burns (1988) reported that more and more small companies are finding that funding from corporate venture capitalists can be a viable complement, or possibly even an alternative, to more conventional venture capital sources.

Corporate venture capital investment has the potential to help address the problems facing young firms, and particularly TBFs, seeking external equity finance (ACOST, 1990; Rind, 1994). Four factors make corporate equity finance a potentially beneficial source of funding for such firms: amount invested, sector of investment, stage of investment and lower costs.

Amount invested   Although the amount invested depends largely upon the CVC strategy employed, large firms tend to provide smaller amounts than independently managed venture capital funds, and greater amounts than business angels. Thus, CVC has the potential to bridge this aspect of the equity gap.

Sector of investment The fact that many investing companies have strategically oriented motivations, and in particular may be seeking windows on new technologies (MacDonald, 1991; Roberts, 1991; Hurry *et al.*, 1992), implies that TBFs, or fund managers that specialise in making investments in TBFs on behalf of their limited partners, will be popular targets for these companies (Winters and Murfin, 1988; Kotkin, 1989; Collins and Doorley, 1991; Roberts, 1991; Manigart and Struyf, 1995). This suggests that CVC may be a valuable alternative funding source for the very firms which experience most difficulties in obtaining venture capital finance.

Stage of investment It is reasonable to suggest that a further consequence of the corporate desire to obtain a window on *new* technologies, products, processes and markets will be a concentration of investment in *early* stage firms. Indeed, Taylor (1989) noted that companies involved in making CVC investments have traditionally been active in investing in early stage ventures in the USA. As Collins and Doorley (1991: 29) note, 'one of the primary objectives of any industrial company must . . . be to identify and monitor key technologies early in their development'. As well as making early stage investments to ensure windows on the most recent developments, the corporate sector can also provide a source of follow-on finance during the development stages of the small firm (Roberts, 1991).

Lower costs The strategic rather than financial orientation of many CVC investments suggests that entrepreneurs will benefit from higher valuations and less dilution of their equity than would be the case with more conventional investment sources (Silver, 1993; Rind, 1994; Mamis, 1995). In other words, the smaller company receives more for its share capital (Henricks, 1991) as the corporate offers 'cheap capital' in the hope of receiving strategic benefits (*Journal of Applied Corporate Finance*, 1992; Timmons and Sapienza, 1992). Furthermore, corporate investors are typically less concerned with short-term financial returns and exits than many other investors, and have a greater level of patience and understanding of business issues (Timmons and Sapienza, 1992).

Strategic benefits

Small companies often have the opportunity to benefit strategically from the 'value-added' provided by their equity investors. Once a venture capital investment has been made it is in the interests of the investors, whether they be funds or business angels, to do everything they can to ensure that their investee companies succeed in order to maximise their financial returns (Sweeting, 1991b). Various forms of managerial activity on the part of the equity investor can help to add value to a firm (Klein, 1987;

Pratt, 1994). This is particularly important in the case of TBFs where there is often a mismatch between the entrepreneur's technical competence and business skills (Bailey, 1985; Forrest, 1990; Landström, 1990; Murray, 1993; 1994a; Standeven, 1993; Stewart, 1993; Abbott and Hay, 1995). Technology-based firms are therefore increasingly seeking external equity investors who can offer more than just finance (Roberts, 1991; Bygrave and Timmons, 1992; Deger, 1994; Onians, 1995). Venture capital has come to mean the provision of funding *and* business development support (Young, 1985; Bygrave and Timmons, 1992), and has even been described as a form of collaborative relationship (by Steier and Greenwood, 1995).

There are several ways in which venture capital fund managers can add value to a company (Steier and Greenwood, 1995). Bygrave and Timmons (1992) grouped the forms of venture capitalist involvement into three distinct categories. First, the venture capitalist's role can be *strategic*; it can act as a sounding board to management, assist with the development of corporate strategy, management recruiting, obtaining alternative sources of finance and managing short-term problems (MacMillan *et al.*, 1988; Gorman and Sahlman, 1989; Rosenstein *et al.*, 1989; Sweeting, 1991a; 1991b; Fredriksen *et al.*, 1992; Pratt, 1994; Abbott and Hay, 1995; Bahrami and Evans, 1995; Steier and Greenwood, 1995). Second, the venture capitalist can provide a *social* or *supportive* role, acting as a mentor or confidant. Third, the venture capitalist can provide access to a *network* of other venture capitalists, tax experts, lawyers, patent agents, grant agencies, prospective customers and suppliers, etc. (Bailey, 1985; Jarillo, 1989). As the venture capital arena has become more competitive some venture capitalists have stressed that value-added is their most distinctive competence (Rosenstein *et al.*, 1989; Timmons and Sapienza, 1992; Gourlay, 1994a). Sapienza *et al.* (1992) identified differing levels of value-added provided by fund managers with nationality. In a comparative study of four countries they found US, Dutch and UK fund managers to be highly involved with investee firms, although in the UK they are not particularly responsive to the individual and specific needs of firms and do not vary their involvement greatly with circumstances. However, Abbott and Hay (1995) noted that with the shift to later stage financings since the late 1980s, many fund managers have become far more hands-off, offering little value-added.

Business angels also typically provide more than just money for investee firms (Mason and Harrison, 1992; Standeven, 1993; Ehrlich *et al.*, 1994; Wetzel and Freear, 1995). Indeed, studies conducted by Ehrlich *et al.* (1994) in the USA and by Harrison and Mason (1992) in the UK have found that angels are involved in similar value-added activities to institutional venture capitalists such as serving as a sounding board, formulating business strategy, monitoring financial and operating performance and obtaining alternative sources of finance. Standeven (1993) considered the level of expertise provided by business angels to even surpass that provided by venture capital funds.

While the value-added provided by formal and informal venture capital providers is often very beneficial to investee firms (Bailey, 1985; ACOST, 1990; Bygrave and Timmons, 1992; Flynn, 1995; Mason and Lumme, 1995; Steier and Greenwood, 1995), there are some areas of company operations for which assistance cannot easily be provided by these investors. This is particularly true for TBFs. Investors in such companies require a thorough knowledge of the specific sector/s in which they invest, including a famil-iarity with the specific technologies, processes and markets involved if they are to be effective hands-on investors (Bygrave and Timmons, 1992; Duhamel *et al.*, 1994). However, venture capitalists do not often possess this knowledge (Murray, 1993; 1995). Reporting on a survey of 227 UK venture capital executives, Abbott and Hay (1995) found only 19 per cent of fund managers to have technology-related backgrounds compared to 50 per cent with a background in finance. Therefore, venture capitalists will often not be able to provide TBFs with the industry-specific technical, production and marketing expertise and facilities which are vital for their success (Young, 1985; Hull *et al.*, 1988; Murray, 1993; Farrell and Doutriaux, 1994). Indeed, many empirical studies from various countries (e.g. Mac-Millan *et al.*, 1988; Landström, 1990; Sadtler, 1993) have found that venture capitalists' value-added activities are most frequently financially oriented, whereas technological, production and marketing issues receive the least venture capitalist involvement. This is problematic since Moore (1994) recognised a crucially important constraint facing the TBF, distinguishing it from more conventional small firms, to be the dearth of marketing and sales skills. Furthermore, Slatter (1992) highlighted a lack of technical resources as one of the most significant barriers to growth for such companies.

Corporate venture capital investment has the potential to provide inves-tee firms with the much needed value-added assistance that they require (Hobson and Morrison, 1983; Bailey, 1985; NEDO, 1986; ACOST, 1990; Baty, 1990; Honeyman, 1992; Pratt, 1994; Rind, 1994). Indeed, as a result of the typically strategic motivations of investing companies, and specifi-cally their desire to gain a closer look at the new developments within entrepreneurial firms, it is likely that investees will be nurtured by their corporate partners and thus receive more than just finance in return for their equity (Connell and Phillips, 1988; Kotkin, 1989; Henricks, 1991; Roberts, 1991; Hurry *et al.*, 1992; Abbott and Hay, 1995; Manigart and Struyf, 1995).

CVC can provide investee firms with the opportunity to benefit from the hands-on investment approach of large companies whereby corporate executives take seats on the board of investee firms and assist in their planning and strategy formulation (Lerner, 1995). Corporate investors are likely to have a greater understanding of the requirements, realistic growth rates and risks involved in the development of products, and can therefore provide far more appropriate support than an institutional investor (Baty, 1990). Particularly in the case of direct CVC, companies can also nurture investee ventures by providing practical assistance such as access to an existing marketing network, production or development facility, and also less tangible advantages including enhanced credibility in the marketplace (Roberts, 1980; Bailey, 1985; NEDO, 1986; Ormerod and Burns, 1988; SBRT, 1989; ACOST, 1990; Mitton, 1991; Allen, 1992; Honeyman, 1992; Rind, 1994; Bahrami and Evans, 1995; Buxton, 1995; Lerner, 1995; Mamis, 1995). Furthermore, both direct and indirect investments may provide opportunities for the establishment of further contractual business relationships such as research, sales and marketing or licensing agreements between investor and investee firms (Pratt, 1994).

CVC relationships can therefore provide 'small companies with the flexibility needed to compete in an increasingly global and competitive market' (Henricks, 1991). Indeed, several authors (e.g. Burstein and Hofmeister, 1985; Kotkin, 1989; ACOST, 1990; Hull and Slowinski, 1990; Murray, 1993; Mamis, 1995) have suggested that the value-added provided by non-financial companies that invest in venture capital makes them a more valuable source of finance than the institutional venture capitalist for TBFs. Roberts (1991) considered the value-added aspects of CVC investment to be potentially more valuable to investee firms than the finance itself if resources can be accessed and utilised effectively by the small firm.

The potential benefits for independent venture capitalists

It has already been noted that during the early 1990s, venture capitalists have experienced increasing pressure to realise higher returns in shorter time periods (Timmons and Sapienza, 1992; Gompers, 1994). Consequently, many fund managers have shifted their focus from relatively risky early stage technology-based deals to safer later stage financings in an attempt to prevent institutional investors from losing faith in venture capital, and in particular their funds (Abbott and Hay, 1995).

The pressures on fund managers that specialise in making start-up, early stage and technology investments have been particularly great in the UK. Indeed, the UK venture capital industry appears to be in a state of some considerable uncertainty (Murray, 1992b). Murray (1991a) identified widespread doubts among members of the BVCA that the industry would continue to sustain the growth rates of the 1980s during the first half of the 1990s. The longer-term availability of funds was reported to be the single most important concern, particularly with the 'increasing ambivalence of institutional investors to venture capital activity [which has been illustrated by] the growing difficulties experienced by venture capitalists seeking to raise new funds, particularly after 1989' (Murray, 1991a: 73). Murray (1991b) reported expectations of a 'shake-out' in the industry, as poorly performing independent venture capitalists, and those specialising in riskier, early stage and technology financing, are left particularly vulnerable to the increasing bargaining power of the institutional investors who increasingly favour investments in less risky development capital and MBO/MBI funds (Timmons and Sapienza, 1992). Murray (1991b: 19) further suggested that 'if the industry loses the confidence of the institutional investors . . . then the industry has no long term future in the absence of substantial alternative funding sources'.

These predictions have been confirmed with the early 1990s witnessing the most difficult fund-raising environment in the brief history of the UK venture capital industry (Murray, 1994b). The total amount of funds raised by independent UK venture capital firms fell from a high of £1.68 billion in 1989 to £400 million in 1991 (*Financial Times*, 1992) and then to £347 million in 1992 (BVCA, 1993), before increasing to £479 million in 1993 (BVCA, 1994). In 1994, the figure rose significantly to £2.551 billion. However, this has largely benefited only a small number of MBO/MBI funds.[4] This is reflected in a breakdown of the investment figures which show that two-thirds of the total capital invested in the UK by members of the BVCA in 1994 went into MBOs and MBIs. Independent funds specialising in early stage technology deals are still encountering difficulties in fund raising, evidence of which is provided by the venture capital company Korda and Co. which failed to find backing in 1995 for a new European technology fund and consequently pulled out of venture capital (Gourlay, 1995c).

Non-financial companies have the potential to be an important alternative source of finance for independent venture capital funds specialising in making investments in early stage and technology-based firms at a time when the amount received from institutional sources is declining. Gompers (1994: 2) noted that 'the future health of venture capital depends upon measures that will align the incentives of venture capital investors (i.e. those who invest in venture capital funds), venture capitalists and entrepreneurs who seek money to finance their projects'. In the light of this statement, if venture capitalists can succeed in convincing corporates that investment in their funds would be beneficial to them, there is scope for the venture capital community to tap additional capital resources (*European Venture Capital Journal*, 1990a). In addition, the corporate may possess a repository of technical industry-specific knowledge which can bring added value to a venture capital deal (*Canadian Venture Capital*, 1990; Collins and Doorley, 1991). It may be able to afford to commission investigations into patent validity and market size, etc., which no venture or venture capitalist could ever afford (Bailey, 1985), can contribute its marketing skills and networks to enhance the attractiveness of ventures which otherwise lack competitive advantage, and can provide an exit route for the venture capitalist (Hobson and Morrison, 1983; Bailey, 1985).

Summary

CVC investment therefore has the potential to be a particularly beneficial strategy for both investor and investee companies as well as venture capitalists. For large companies, CVC can provide an opportunity to gain either financially, strategically or by learning about the venture capital process. For investee firms, and particularly those in the early stages of development operating in technology-related sectors, CVC can provide a valuable source of funds as well as value-added benefits in the form of nurturing. Finally, for venture capitalists, and particularly those specialising in making investments in early stage TBFs, non-financial corporations are a potentially important alternative source of funding and industry expertise. Given this potential, the following section documents the history and current scale and trends in CVC world-wide. In particular, it identifies the extent to which CVC has been utilised and developed in the UK in comparison with the USA.

EVIDENCE AND TRENDS IN CORPORATE VENTURE CAPITAL INVESTMENT

Empirical studies

While CVC strategy has frequently been discussed in the context of inter-firm collaboration (e.g. by Doz, 1988; Hull and Slowinski, 1990; Collins and Doorley, 1991; MacDonald, 1991; Forrest and Martin, 1992), venture capital finance (e.g. by Timmons and Gumpert, 1982; Freear and Wetzel, 1990; 1991; Roberts, 1991; Gupta and Sapienza, 1992) and corporate new business development strategies (e.g. by Block, 1982; Littler and Sweeting, 1983; 1985; 1987a), very few studies have focused specifically on CVC. Those that have looked at CVC in more detail have tended to simply be anecdotal discussions of the activity (e.g. Fast and Pratt, 1981; Rind, 1981; Bleicher and Paul, 1987; Klein, 1987; Oakley, 1987; Winters and Murfin, 1988; *European Venture Capital Journal*, 1990a; 1990b; Mast, 1991; Dunn, 1992; Block and MacMillan, 1993) or, as Block and MacMillan (1993) noted, accounts based on detailed case studies (e.g. Hardymon *et al.*, 1983; Bailey, 1985; Piol, 1985; Sykes, 1986a; 1986b; Kotkin, 1989; Hegg, 1990; Corrigan, 1992; Lerner, 1995). While the importance of such studies should not be understated, there is a need for more comprehensive empirical data concerning the extent, nature, and particularly the motives for and benefits of CVC activity. Such data will enable analysis of the value of CVC strategy for participating companies (Block and MacMillan, 1993). In support of this recommendation, Siegel *et al.* (1988: 246) emphasised that 'further study is needed in order to determine how corporate venture capitalists successfully integrate financial and strategic considerations, and which benefits are most likely to be achieved'.

The larger-scale empirical studies that have been undertaken have originated in the USA. These include:

- Greenthal and Larson (1983) – a survey of twelve corporate venture groups in the USA
- *Journal of Accountancy* (1984) – a study of forty-four US senior managers with CVC experience
- Siegel *et al.* (1988) – a study of the objectives, investment criteria, organisation and experiences of fifty-two corporate venture capitalists in the USA
- Sykes (1990) – analysis of thirty-one US corporations involved in CVC
- Hurry *et al.* (1992) – a comparison of US and Japanese CVC investments in the USA
- Silver (1993) – interviews with approximately 100 executives responsible for the CVC operations of US companies

By comparison, there has been only one large-scale study of CVC in the UK. This was undertaken by the National Economic Development Office (NEDO, 1986) and involved interviews with 107 small firms and 228 large companies. This survey, the findings of which will be discussed later in this chapter, was designed to establish the attitudes and experiences of UK companies with respect to CVC. The CVC activities of European (including UK) companies have also been identified in Venture Economics' surveys (e.g. as reported in *European Venture Capital Journal*, 1990a), but the author is unaware of any further large-scale studies either in Europe or elsewhere in the world.

Levels of CVC activity world-wide

CVC in the USA

The levels of both direct and indirect corporate venture capital investment have, to date, been greatest in the USA. During the late 1980s and early 1990s, large US corporations have become an important source of venture capital for entrepreneurial companies (ACOST, 1990; MacDonald, 1991; Roberts, 1991; Honeyman, 1992; *Journal of Applied Corporate Finance*, 1992; Block and MacMillan, 1993; Silver, 1993; Rind, 1994). According to Collins and Doorley (1991: 186), CVC is now a 'well-established and widely accepted tool of corporate strategy in the United States'.

The first corporate venture capitalist was probably DuPont. It took a 38 per cent stake in General Motors in 1919 (one of its customers at the time)

(Rind, 1994). Many companies became active investors during the 1960s, typically seeking windows on new technology at a time of increasing competition. However, stock market declines in 1970, 1974 and 1975 led to the exit of many of these corporations including Alcoa, Dow, DuPont, Ford, General Dynamics, Mobil, Monsanto, Singer and Union Carbide. Many of these companies have since re-entered the field (Rind, 1994) in a renewed effort to access new technologies. In 1978, Smollen identified twenty US corporations active in venture capital, and by 1981 the list included Exxon, General Electric, Johnson and Johnson, 3M, AT&T, IBM and Lubrizol (Rind, 1981). Between 1982 and 1985 there was a steady growth in the number of corporations making CVC investments, particularly for strategic purposes (Rind, 1994) following a number of favourable legislative and tax-related measures (Abbott and Hay, 1995). Hardymon *et al.* (1983) noted that of the $3.5 billion managed by the US venture capital industry at the time, $400 million (11.4 per cent) was provided by non-financial companies. The early 1980s have been referred to as a 'transition' phase (*European Venture Capital Journal*, 1990b), during which time several companies changed their approach to CVC and many of the pioneering programmes were restructured. Having learnt about the venture capital process from indirect investments, numerous companies began to experiment with their own internally managed programmes. During the second half of the 1980s, a renewed interest in CVC was evident (*European Venture Capital Journal*, 1990b; Pratt, 1994) in the light of increasing competitive and technological pressures on companies as well as changing legal structures. However, after record levels of CVC investment in 1989, the early 1990s witnessed an overall decline in US CVC as companies reduced their exposure to venture capital due to recession (Dickson, 1993) paralleling an overall decline in US venture capital fund raising (Abbott and Hay, 1995).

In the USA, CVC has most recently moved from being a diversification vehicle to a development activity focused on supporting existing business units. This largely reflects the poor performance of previous diversification programmes. Companies have also become less concerned with acquisition and more focused towards strategic collaboration via CVC. They have become more comfortable collaborating with small firms and less motivated by control (Mast, 1991). Large companies are also tending to become involved earlier in the life cycles of emerging firms, but often try to develop contractual strategic relationships before making equity investments (Mast, 1991). Most CVC investment in the USA is in high technology industries, with particular growth in communications and medical and health care industries since the late 1980s.

According to Block and MacMillan (1993), approximately half of the US companies that have made CVC investments have used the direct approach, while the other half have invested indirectly. However, there appears to be an increasingly phased approach to corporate venture capital investment in the USA. Companies tend initially to invest in externally managed funds in order to learn about the venture capital business, and then move to direct investments later (Mast, 1991). Despite this, general fluctuations in the relative popularity of both externally and internally managed CVC activities are evident and appear to be of a cyclical nature.

Externally managed CVC

There was a steady increase in capital committed to externally managed, multi-investor venture capital funds by corporations between 1979 and 1986 in the USA. In 1987, Oakley estimated that over 100 US corporations were involved in indirect CVC, and corporations were still significant fund investors in 1988 (Winters and Murfin, 1988). However, US corporate investors have tended to move away from indirect investment; $483 million was invested in 1989, accounting for 20 per cent of all funds raised that year, whereas in 1992, corporates invested only $84 million, or 3 per cent of the total capital raised (Venture Economics, 1993). According to Abbott and Hay (1995: 52), corporate investors 'have been particularly badly hit by the recent recession'. The corporate contribution has since started to rise again ($341 million/9 per cent in 1994), and with anticipation of the continuing recovery of US venture capital (Gourlay, 1994b; Pratt, 1994) some experts have predicted renewed interest in CVC in the near future (Vachon, 1993).

The number of dedicated, client-based externally managed funds grew rapidly during the 1980s and early 1990s (Mast, 1991; Rind, 1994). This was largely because of dissatisfaction with the amount of strategic benefit gained from investment in 'standard' venture capital funds. It has already been noted that dedicated funds tend to be more focused and often corporations second employees to the fund to learn venture capital disciplines. The ACOST report of 1990 stated that the number of client-based funds in the USA had grown from 31 in 1982 to 102 in 1987. Monsanto, the US chemicals group, had invested $50 million in nine funds around the world before 1986 (Dawkins, 1986), and venture capital firm Advent International manage fourteen dedicated funds for large multinationals including RJR Nabisco, ALCOA and Apple Computer (*European Venture Capital Journal*, 1994; Gourlay, 1995d).

Internally managed CVC

Indirect, externally managed investments are being increasingly complemented by more direct investments which bypass funds, but are often made alongside independent venture capitalists (Rind, 1994). The internally managed fund approach has been common in the USA (Collins and Doorley,

1991). In 1987 only twenty-eight internally managed programmes existed (*European Venture Capital Journal*, 1990b). This number increased considerably to seventy-six in 1988 (Winters and Murfin, 1988), eighty-five in 1989 (Venture Economics, 1993), ninety-two in 1990 (*European Venture Capital Journal*, 1990b) and ninety-five in 1991 (MacDonald, 1991). However, the dropout rate among companies making such investments was high during the early 1990s (Pratt, 1994; Rind, 1994; Abbott and Hay, 1995), and by 1992 only sixty-nine companies operated captive CVC funds (Venture Economics, 1993). Nevertheless, it is estimated that there are currently more than seventy-two US and twenty-seven foreign corporations that directly invest over $500 million annually via internally managed funds in US ventures (Rind, 1994). Examples of companies that have used this form of CVC investment are Monsanto, Exxon, General Electric, W.R. Grace, ABB, AT&T, Intel and SmithKline Beecham (Pratt, 1994).

The 1980s and early 1990s witnessed a dramatic increase in the number of ad hoc direct CVC investments made by US companies. Winters and Murfin (1988) reported that two or three times as many corporations were involved in ad hoc venture capital investing as had internally managed funds. Collins and Doorley (1991) estimated that several hundred ad hoc investments are made in the USA each year. Corporations including Exxon, Lubrizol, National Distillers, Digital Equipment, EG & G, Analog Devices, Diamond Shamrock Chemicals Company and Compaq are all examples of companies which have employed this strategy, while Apple, Wang Laboratories, Datapoint and Genentech have all received ad hoc direct venture capital investment from large corporations (Hamilton, 1985). The use of ad hoc CVC investments has become increasingly popular in high tech sectors such as computers, telecommunications and biotechnology (Faulkner, 1989; Kotkin, 1989). For example, Bygrave and Timmons (1992) noted that 167 minority equity strategic alliances were formed in the US biotechnology industry in 1990, compared to 37 in 1986, and similarly Mitton (1991) found strategic partnerships, including minority equity investments, to be the largest contributor of funds to the biotechnology industry in San Diego. Furthermore, the five largest US electronics companies and the ten largest pharmaceutical companies have all made ad hoc direct CVC investments in the early 1990s (Rind, 1994).

Some corporations have used venture capital funds to spin-out internally-developed technologies (Mast, 1991). Monsanto attempted this with Kinetek Systems and Invitron, as did Alcoa with Biotage. Spin-off strategies have also been employed by companies such as EG & G, Teradyne, Unitrode, Battelle and Bolt, Beranek and Newman. Apple Computer is a well-documented example of a company established as a spin-out, and Apple itself has spun-off General Magic, which is led by some of Apple's original founders (Kehoe, 1993). In 1990, an entire portfolio was spun-out by Alcan Corporation in a deal with Ampersand Ventures. Xerox Corporation's Xerox

Technology Ventures and General Electric's Technical Ventures Group are examples of venture capital subsidiary companies established with the sole purpose of investing in ventures that are spun-out from the large parent corporation (Lerner, 1995).

In terms of the internal organisation of direct CVC in the USA, there appears to be a growing trend for investment to be via an in-house operating division rather than a separate subsidiary company. This relates to the 'autonomy versus control' dilemma facing corporations involved in corporate venturing emphasised by Ginsberg and Hay (1993). This recent trend for CVC programmes to exist *within* the organisation can be seen as an attempt to enhance the strategic fit of those programmes with the company's existing business (Mast, 1991). However, there are numerous examples of venture capital subsidiaries established to concentrate specifically on venture capital investment. Examples include Exxon Corporation (Sykes, 1986a; 1986b), Cooper Industries (Silver, 1979), Xerox (Xerox Technology Ventures), General Electric (GEVENCO), Lubrizol (Lubrizol Enterprises), Koppers (Kopvenco) and Tenneco (Tenneco Ventures) (Hardymon *et al.*, 1983; Warren and Kempenich, 1984; Burstein and Hofmeister, 1985).

There is growing evidence of a trend towards the internationalisation of US corporate venture capital investment (Mast, 1991; Honeyman, 1992). US corporations are increasingly investing directly in foreign-owned companies and establishing foreign, externally managed, client-based venture capital funds. Examples are Monsanto, DuPont, 3M, IBM and Apple's European venturing in partnership with Advent International (*Venture Capital Journal*, 1990). While the volume of innovative technology development is still greatest in the USA, US companies are recognising that exciting opportunities are developing rapidly in Europe and the Far East (Mast, 1991). However, because of the exploratory nature and different objectives of international CVC investment, such programmes are often structured differently from those in the USA. For example, Apple's CVC programme in the USA is an internally managed activity within the corporate business development group, while the company's European programme is a dedicated, externally managed fund investment. Since the mid-1980s there has been an increase in the number of non-US companies engaged in CVC in the USA. In the USA, the number of CVC programmes operated by US companies is declining as a percentage of the total. The significant growth in US-based programmes operated by non-US companies has been led by the Pacific Rim and Japan, whose shares grew from 3 per cent in 1983 to 12 per cent in 1989 (Mast, 1991). Externally managed programmes have been popular with these companies given their lack of knowledge of the US market.

CVC in Japan

In Japan, venture capital investment by non-financial companies is a more recent phenomenon than in the USA (Collins and Doorley, 1991), and really became noticeable only in 1982 when the Japan Associated Finance company (JAFCO) established the country's first venture capital fund. A number of western companies have made investments in JAFCO in order to gain access to Japanese technology (Collins and Doorley, 1991). Honeyman (1992) and Hurry *et al.* (1992) noted substantial increases in venture capital investing by Japanese firms, a trend which is exemplified by the increase in Japanese investment in the USA. According to MacDonald (1991), Japanese industrial corporations made minority investments in sixty small US companies in 1989, with investments totalling $370 million. In the same year, Japanese companies invested $63 million in sixteen US venture capital funds. Several authors have drawn attention to the indirect CVC activities of giants such as Mitsubishi, Mitsui & Co. and Fujitsu. However, many Japanese companies, including Canon, Kyocera, Nippon Steel and Kobe Steel, seem to be more interested in making ad hoc direct investments (Collins and Doorley, 1991), often in vertically related firms as part of their close-knit *Keiretsu* business networks.[5]

CVC in continental Europe

Large continental European companies have tended to be more cautious about venture programmes than those in North America and the Pacific region (Collins and Doorley, 1991; *European Venture Capital Journal*, 1991). However, the *European Venture Capital Journal* (1990a) identified 138 corporate investors in European venture capital funds, of which 72 are among the top 500 European corporations. Furthermore, MacDonald (1991) recognised that several European industrial corporations had in-house venture capital operations, and additionally, several corporations have developed ad hoc approaches to CVC (*European Venture Capital Journal*, 1990a). A Venture Economics survey, reported in the *European Venture Capital Journal* in 1990, listed 48 continental European corporations or Europe-based corporate operations and their activities in CVC (Table 2.2).

CVC in the UK

A very marked difference between the UK and the US venture capital industries has been the extremely low level of involvement of major corporations in the UK in CVC (*UK Venture Capital Journal*, 1987). As was noted in Chapter 1, the majority of large UK corporations exhibit a lack of interest in partnering with small companies (Botkin and Matthews, 1992). This reluctance to collaborate has been reflected in the particularly

Table 2.2 Companies active in CVC in continental Europe

		Ind CVC	Dir CVC	CVC subsid
	Asea Brown Boveri (ABB)	•		
	Agfa Gevaert	•		
	Alfa Laval AB	•		
	Akzo NV	•		
	Barilla SpA	•		
	Bayer AG	•		
	Robert Bosch GmbH	•		
	BMW	•	•	•
	Bongrain SA	•		
	BSN	•		
	Ciments Français	•		
	Daimler-Benz AG	•	•	
	Electricité de France (EDF)	•		
	SN Elf-Aquitaine	•	•	•
	Sanofi Elf Bio Industries	•		
	Fiat SpA	•		
Indigenous	France Telecom	•		•
continental	Havas	•		
European	Hoffman La Roche & Co	•	•	
corporations	Générale Sucrière	•	•	
	Hoechst AG	•		
	Institut Mérieux/Biomérieux	•	•	
	Lafarge	•		
	Louis Vuitton-Moët Hennessy	•		
	Mannesmann	•		
	Messerschmitt Boelkow Blohm	•		
	Michelin	•		
	Neste Oy	•		•
	Nestlé	•		
	Nippon Steel	•		
	Nixdorf Computer AG	•	•	
	Olivetti SpA	•	•	
	Pernod Ricard	•		
	Philips	•		
	Rhône Poulenc	•	•	
	Saint-Gobain	•		
	Siemens	•	•	•
	Thomson CSF	•	•	•
	Orkem	•		
	Volkswagen	•		
	Volvo	•		
	Apple Computer	•	•	
European	General Electric	•		
subsidiaries	IBM Corp	•	•	
of US	Johnson & Johnson	•		
corporations	3M	•	•	
	Monsanto	•	•	
	RJR Nabisco	•		

Source: European Venture Capital Journal, 1990a

low levels of CVC. Despite the fact that the UK can boast the most developed venture capital industry in Europe, large firms had played very little part in the development of this industry by the mid-1980s (*UK Venture Capital Journal*, 1985). In spite of increasing corporate interest in CVC during the second half of the decade, levels of both indirect and direct strategies were still low by 1990 (Pratt, 1990). Indeed, in the same year ACOST acknowledged there to be 'an almost complete absence of corporate venture capital in the UK' (ACOST, 1990: 41).

Externally managed CVC

As far as indirect, externally managed CVC is concerned, non-financial companies have provided only a relatively modest proportion of the total finance committed to UK venture capital funds (Abbott and Hay, 1995). According to Oakley (1987), no UK corporation undertook this approach to CVC until 1984, when a modest start was made with £17 million committed. Between 1984 and 1986, the average annual figure was £13 million (Oakley, 1987). In 1988, Ormerod and Burns tentatively suggested that eighteen companies had committed over £30 million to UK venture capital funds, although Oakley (1987) stated that only four UK venture capital groups were known to have raised capital from non-financial corporations.

Table 2.3 illustrates the total and percentage capital committed to independent funds by industrial corporations between 1986 and 1994, according to the BVCA. This indicates an absolute increase in the capital committed to venture capital funds by corporations until an initial peak of £62 million in 1989 (although still only 4 per cent of the total capital committed from all sources that year). Following this, a decline is evident in real terms, paralleling the overall decline in funds raised by the venture

Table 2.3 Capital committed to independent funds by non-financial corporations in the UK, 1986–94

Year	Total capital committed by industrial corporations (£m)	Percentage of total capital committed
1986	11	4
1987	21	3
1988	34	6
1989	62	4
1990	17	2
1991	20	5
1992	50	15
1993	37	8
1994	424	17

Source: British Venture Capital Association (BVCA), 1987–95

capital community. Indeed, the £20 million committed by non-financial companies in 1991 is actually a greater percentage of the total (5 per cent) than the £62 million committed in 1989 (4 per cent). The 1992 BVCA annual review reported an absolute increase in indirect CVC from £20 million invested in externally managed funds in 1991 to £50 million in 1992, at a time when the total amount raised from all sources fell (BVCA, 1993). This represents an increase in the percentage of funds raised from 5 per cent to 15 per cent. The corporate commitment fell back to £37 million (8 per cent of total funds raised) in 1993 (BVCA, 1994), but increased significantly to £424 million (17 per cent of the total funds raised) in 1994. These figures suggest that the levels of indirect CVC may be increasing in the UK, albeit from a very small base. Indeed, a comparison of the venture capital fund raising figures in the UK and the USA indicate that non-financial corporations were a more far more significant source of funds in the UK than in the USA during 1994 (Figures 2.3 and 2.4).

Many of the companies that have invested indirectly in the UK have been of foreign parentage. By 1985, the *UK Venture Capital Journal* reported that the only major corporations known to have invested indirectly in independent UK-based venture capital funds were Monsanto (in Advent Eurofund and Advent Capital), Air Products UK and American Hospital Supplies (in Alta-Berkeley Eurofund), Baker International, Elf Aquitaine and the Molson Companies (in Alta-Berkeley Limited Partnership), Johnson and Johnson (in Transatlantic Capital's Bio-Sciences Fund), and Siemens, BP and GKN

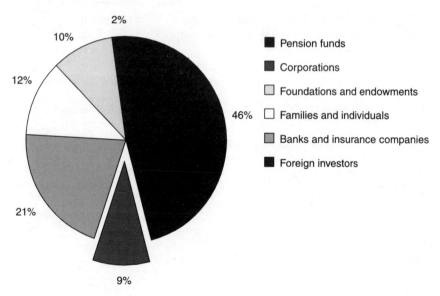

Figure 2.3 US venture capital: funds raised by source, 1994 (new funds: $3.76 bn)
Source: Venture Economics, 1995

CORPORATE VENTURING AND VENTURE CAPITAL

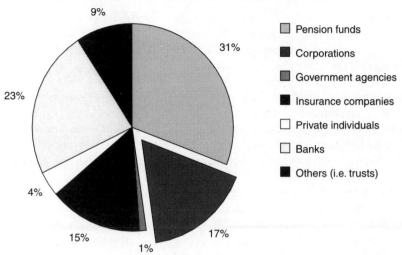

Figure 2.4 UK venture capital: funds raised by source, 1994 (new funds: £2.55 bn)
Source: British Venture Capital Association, 1995a

(in Advent Capital). Only the last two are UK corporations. Perhaps the best documented externally managed CVC fund established by a UK company is BG Ventures, a dedicated fund managed for British Gas by Innvotec. BG Ventures is a £15 million fund established in 1990, and represents the core of British Gas's CVC activities. Its investment focus is small innovative companies which are developing products or markets of strategic interest to the businesses of British Gas (Corrigan, 1992; Rudman, 1993). Some UK companies have established international indirect CVC programmes. For example, British Petroleum is one of a number of European multinationals to have invested in independent US venture capital funds, along with Hickson International, which has been linked with the US Columbine Venture Fund.

Internally managed CVC

The available evidence suggests that the levels of direct CVC investment are particularly low in the UK. First, there are only a few internally managed venture capital funds. One good example is Pilkington's Rainford Venture Capital Fund, which had £2.5 million invested in about ten companies in 1987 (Batchelor, 1987a). Second, while ad hoc investments in independent small firms were made by companies such as BOC, ICI, Pilkington and Shell in the 1970s, these ventures frequently met with very mixed results (Batchelor, 1987a). Since then, a small number of other corporations, such as British Aerospace (European Silicon Structures), Ferranti (Lattice Logic and Edinburgh Instruments), Plessey (Imperial Software Technology),

Cambridge Electronic Instruments, Micro Business Systems and British Tar Products, have all made ad hoc investments, some of them alongside independent venture capitalists (Ormerod and Burns, 1988) (investee companies in parentheses). Skapinker (1992) also noted several large groups in the music industry (e.g. Sony and Polygram) taking minority stakes in smaller record labels for strategic purposes. Companies which have used spin-off strategies in the UK include ICI's chemical and polymers group (Marlborough Biopolymers), ICI's agricultural division, Kodak UK, Ferranti (Libera Developments), Cookson Group (Cranfield Moulded Structures) and Sector Group (Microscribe) (spin-off companies in parentheses).

As in the USA, those companies which have undertaken direct CVC investment in the UK have often done so by establishing a subsidiary to coordinate investments. BP (BP Ventures), British Telecom (Martlesham Enterprises) and ICI (Marlborough Technical Development) have all established the separate companies named in parentheses for the specific purpose of supervising spin-off programmes and the financing of independent ventures. Johnston Group, a mechanical and civil engineering company based in Redhill, Surrey, formed Johnston Development Capital to pursue the aims of corporate venturing (Oates, 1987).

As with indirect CVC, a large proportion of the companies engaged in internally managed CVC in the UK are subsidiaries of foreign corporations that have experience of venture capital investment in their own countries. Examples include Johnson and Johnson, Monsanto, DuPont and 3M (Collins and Doorley, 1991). Thus the number of UK-owned corporations involved in venture capital is even smaller than it may initially appear (Povey, 1986). Again, some UK companies have established international programmes. For example, Oxford Instruments has made ad hoc investments in venture backed companies in the USA, while Ferranti and Thorn EMI have both used internally managed, US-based venture funds providing them with a window on technology-based developments to enhance their positions in European markets (Oakley, 1987).

The underdeveloped nature of UK CVC

During the mid–late 1980s there was recognition of both the importance and the underdeveloped nature of CVC in the UK. In 1984 the Venture Economics/Arthur Andersen conference on 'New Opportunities in Corporate Venturing' drew an encouraging attendance. In September 1986, NEDO conducted their survey of UK corporate venturing. According to their findings, only ten small companies had any CVC experience although two-thirds expected to have an interest in the future, and one-third of large firms indicated that they had tried corporate venturing, suggesting that other studies had underestimated the extent of the activity. NEDO suggested the development of a 'marriage bureau' service to help link large and small companies. In 1987, interest seemed to be stirred as NEDO drew together executives from around forty industrial companies for a day-long seminar on the subject (Batchelor, 1987a; 1987b), before establishing the NEDO Corporate Venturing Centre in 1988. This centre initially attempted to act as a broker for potential investor and investee companies by creating a Corporate Venturing Register and a network of financial consultants, bank managers and accountants. The centre was privatised in 1989 and bought by BASE International Consultants.

However, such efforts appear to have been in vain. The number of large and small businesses subscribing to the BASE Corporate Venturing Register has declined steadily, and while the centre still exists, it is no longer a major part of the work of BASE International. ACOST (1990: 38) reported that 'corporate venturing appears to us to be a greatly underdeveloped aspect of the UK venture capital market'. Apart from the above-mentioned BVCA figures indicating relatively high levels of indirect CVC activity, there is no evidence to suggest that the extent of CVC has increased since 1990.

It is possible to suggest five possible, somewhat interrelated, reasons why the levels of CVC are underdeveloped in the UK.

Lack of motivation of large companies

Large UK companies may simply not be interested in making venture capital investments. There are three possible interrelated reasons for this. First, companies may prefer to use alternative strategies to pursue their objectives. Botkin and Matthews (1992: 200) drew attention to the comments of Alan Hughes, Director of the Small Business Research Centre at the University of Cambridge, who acknowledged that 'large company executives are acquisition-minded. They want 100 per cent of a successful small company or nothing'. This is supported by the observation made in Chapter 1 that large UK corporations have not been interested in forming collaborative relationships of any kind because of a preference for more traditional growth strategies such as arm's length transactions and organic growth. Second, it is possible that some UK companies have little interest in innovation and obtaining windows on technology, products and markets. This is particularly likely to be the case during recession when companies tend to concentrate on core business activities (Honeyman, 1992). Indeed, it has been recognised (e.g. by PA Consulting Group, 1991; DTI/CBI, 1993) that UK companies are lagging behind many of their foreign counterparts in terms of innovation and technological development. Third, Povey (1986) considered the main reasons why UK corporations do not get involved with venture capital to be associated with their organisation, structure and culture. Both Botkin and Matthews (1992) and Honeyman (1992) have drawn attention to the particularly high levels of 'not

69

invented here' syndrome in the UK, while Hirst and Zeitlin (1989) have considered the general unwillingness of UK companies to adopt flexible strategies.

Lack of motivation of small firms

The desire for CVC finance may not exist from the small firm perspective. Again, there are three possible reasons for this. First, entrepreneurs may not be aware of the CVC finance option. Second, small firms may prefer to seek equity finance from other sources. This is supported by the suggestion made in Chapter 1 that small firms fear collaboration with large companies because of the possible loss of identity or acquisition (Chesnais, 1988; Botkin and Matthews, 1992; Oakey, 1993; Duijnhouwer, 1994; Garnsey and Wilkinson, 1994). Third, entrepreneurs may wish to retain maximum ownership and control of their firms and so gear their companies' operations to minimise the need for equity finance from external sources (Mason and Harrison, 1994; Murray, 1995), including large companies. According to Botkin and Matthews (1992), many UK entrepreneurs are reluctant to part with even 10 per cent of their equity.

Lack of perceived investment opportunities/entrepreneurs

It is possible that large companies are interested in the prospects of CVC, but believe there to be a shortage of suitable small innovative firms and hence a lack of investment opportunities. Indeed, Ormerod and Burns (1986: 108), commenting on the UK, noted that 'even the largest companies, with sophisticated intelligence-gathering networks, can find it difficult to identify a large enough stream of suitable potential corporate venturing partners'. A long-running theme concerns the reluctance of experienced individuals in the UK to sacrifice the security of working for a large company (because of tax benefits and stock option deals available in large companies) (BVCA, 1995b; Weyer, 1995). Dawkins (1985) suggested that the incentives for individuals to stay with large corporations were greater in the UK than in the USA, implying that there will be fewer spin-off firms in which large companies can take CVC stakes. Furthermore, the increasing concentration of the UK venture capital industry on buyout funds, which are not generally of interest to non-financial companies, suggests a possible reason for the low levels of externally managed CVC in the UK.

Information gap

The low levels of CVC in the UK may be related to a lack of information, advice and support made available to large companies, small firms and venture capitalists. One implication from the three factors outlined so far is that executives, entrepreneurs and fund managers in the UK may simply be unaware of the possibilities of CVC. The *UK Venture Capital Journal* (1985: 14) reported that 'there is still very little understanding among corporate development executives in the UK of how corporate venture capital can be used as a corporate development tool'. In the absence of measures designed to encourage CVC in the UK (notwithstanding the efforts of NEDO) it is likely that little has changed since the mid-1980s. If CVC investment does occur in the UK it is certainly not well publicised, and therefore there is a lack of role models for other large and small companies (Ormerod and Burns, 1986; Honeyman, 1992).

Withdrawal from CVC

It is possible that some companies in the UK have withdrawn from CVC activity. There are two possible reasons for this. First, companies may have returned to a concentration on core business areas during recession, as has been seen in the USA (Dickson, 1993). Such a change in corporate philosophy was exemplified by BP which sold its ten corporate venture holdings worth $15 million in 1992 as part of its return to a focus on core business areas (*Venture Capital Journal*, 1992). Second, companies may have become disillusioned with CVC strategy as a result of a failure to meet objectives in the past. A failure to meet objectives may result from either unrealistic objectives and expectations, poor original choice of strategy to meet given objectives, internal organisational problems or mismanagement (Fast, 1981; Rind, 1981; 1994; MacMillan *et al.*, 1984; MacMillan, 1986; Ormerod and Burns, 1986; 1988; Siegel *et al.*, 1988; Winters and Murfin, 1988; Sykes and Block, 1989; Sykes, 1990), all of which are likely given the shortage of training and advice available to companies in the UK. Indeed, Littler and Sweeting (1987a) believed it to be doubtful whether many UK corporations possessed 'the requisite expertise not only to perform it [CVC] effectively but also to capitalise on any opportunities that it may yield' (p. 130).

SUMMARY, RESEARCH AIMS AND METHODOLOGICAL OVERVIEW

Summary

This chapter has provided a detailed discussion of corporate venture capital (CVC) investment. As well as considering definitional issues, it has identified the various forms which CVC can take and the potential motivations for, and benefits of, the strategy. It has also reviewed evidence of the scale of CVC activity world-wide.

Corporate venture capital investment has often been referred to as *corporate venturing*. However, the term *corporate venturing* has been widely used in the literature to describe a variety of business growth strategies. Several authors have conceptualised a spectrum of corporate venturing activities which can generally be divided into internal and external strategies. Internal corporate venturing (ICV) involves the promotion of entrepreneurial activities within the corporation to stimulate innovation for growth and diversification. External corporate venturing involves the establishment of strategic partnerships between large, established companies and small entrepreneurial ventures.

This book is concerned with corporate venture capital investment. This involves corporate investment in smaller, unquoted, usually innovative businesses. It may be *indirect* investment (via an externally managed venture capital fund) or *direct* investment (internally managed and either in the form of an internal venture capital fund or an ad hoc investment). Corporate venture capital investments may be made via a separate subsidiary or an in-house operating division. For the larger firm, external strategies may provide not only financial gains associated with equity investment, but also numerous strategic benefits such as windows on new technology and markets. For the smaller company, CVC can provide a much needed source of external equity capital, as well as tangible and intangible strategic advantages arising from the nurturing that is often provided by corporate investors. CVC has the potential to be particularly valuable for technology-based firms and the venture capital funds that specialise in investing in such companies, both of which experience difficulties raising finance from more conventional sources.

The available evidence indicates that, despite its potential benefits, CVC is largely underdeveloped in the UK, particularly when compared to the USA and to a lesser extent western Europe and Japan. Various hypotheses have been formulated in an attempt to explain why the levels of CVC are low in the UK. It is possible that UK companies do not wish to make CVC investments or receive finance from this source. Alternatively, the development of CVC activity may be hindered by a perceived lack of investment opportunities. The small number of companies that have made CVC investments may have withdrawn from this activity either as a result of a strategic shift to concentrate on core business areas or because of unfavourable experiences with CVC. All of these hypotheses are related to some degree to the lack of information, advice and guidance available to companies in the UK.

Research rationale

The discussion in this chapter suggests a rationale for research in the field of corporate venture capital. The justifications for this study are fourfold.

Lack of academic study

Chapter 1 highlighted the current interest in new forms of inter-firm collaboration that is evident in the management studies, economics and economic geography literatures. In particular, it discussed the increasing amount of attention being paid to large firm–small firm alliances with the realisation that multinational companies and small ventures possess highly complementary assets and competencies. Within this debate, Chapter 1 also emphasised the need for research to focus on particular alliance types in order to develop an understanding of the individual characteristics and roles of each form of collaboration in the modern globally competitive business environment. Chapter 2 has outlined the lack of academic attention that has been paid to the subject of CVC, particularly within the context of inter-firm collaboration. Those empirical studies which have been undertaken have focused on the USA, have typically been based on detailed case study information, and have been largely practically based and designed for practitioners rather than academics. This omission has resulted in a notable gap in our knowledge of how and why large firm–small firm equity alliances are formed. Thus, there is a clear need for research which focuses on CVC within the context of inter-firm collaboration theory. Indeed, Steier and Greenwood (1995: 355) emphasise 'the need for further studies to examine collaborative relationships, particularly relationships established among founders and investors'.

Inconclusive evidence of the levels of UK CVC

There is a particular lack of empirical research on the topic of CVC in the UK which may well reflect the underdeveloped nature of this activity. Conversely, the belief that corporate involvement in venture capital is relatively insignificant in the UK may simply reflect the lack of empirical study. There is reason to believe that the levels of UK CVC may be higher than is often believed to be the case. If one accumulates all the anecdotal reports of CVC in the related literature and press, the resulting list of examples of the strategy in the UK is longer than that provided in any one report. Littler and Sweeting (1985), reporting on new business development in mature companies in the UK, noted that while acquisition was the most popular strategy among surveyed companies, corporate venturing (including all the forms described in Roberts's (1980) spectrum) was second, with venture capital methods alone employed by nineteen companies. This figure indicated a considerably higher level of CVC than was believed to exist at that time. Also, it has already been noted that the NEDO (1986) survey discovered that almost eighty (one-third) of the large company respondents had tried CVC. Furthermore, as has also been noted, the amount of finance raised by venture capital funds from non-financial corporations increased to £424 million in 1994 compared to £37 million in 1993. While it is important not to overstate the importance of a single year's investment figures, such a significant increase does suggest the growing interest of large companies in venture capital.

Several authors (e.g. Oakley, 1987; Hall, 1989) have suggested that a question mark must hang over the accuracy of past estimates of the levels of CVC in the UK. In 1990, the *European Venture Capital Journal* (1990a) suggested that a significant amount of CVC activity does take place, although the low-key approach of many corporate participants may contribute to the impression that the activity is less important than it really is. 'Venture' is considered to be a 'naughty' word by many companies (*European Venture Capital Journal*, 1990a: 4) because of a perceived disassociation between venture capital and science and technology. These companies may well be involved in making venture capital investments, but because of their desire to distance themselves from the term, their activities may be overlooked when seeking to identify a universe of corporate venture capitalists. Philippe Villaeys, Corporate Development Manager with IBM Europe in Paris, explained in 1990 that IBM refused to call its corporate development programme 'corporate venture capital' or even 'corporate venturing' because this would mean that it would be associated purely with a financial return objective, which was not the case (*European Venture Capital Journal*, 1990a). Therefore, in the opinion of the *European Venture Capital Journal*, a large number of corporations are, or have been, involved in CVC, whether externally or internally managed, but do not publicise their investments. While this comment was made within the Europe-wide context, there is certainly a need to investigate the possibilities of a similar situation in the UK. It is possible that what we are witnessing is a 'tip of the iceberg' phenomenon, as many CVC activities, and particularly those undertaken in an ad hoc fashion, go unrecognised and only a small number of the firms involved in venture capital are included in surveys (Honeyman, 1992). Therefore, the inconclusive evidence concerning the true extent of CVC activity in the UK renders empirical study appropriate and timely in order to investigate in more detail the significance of this strategy.

The potential benefits of CVC for participating companies

Even if it is established that CVC is still underdeveloped in the UK in comparison to the USA and elsewhere, the literature review and discussion in this chapter has clearly highlighted the potential role of this form of investment. Since NEDO (1986) noted corporate venture capital to be another useful weapon in the battle for innovation, growth and long-term profitability, several authors have commented on the importance of CVC strategy for large companies. In 1990 Beat Fischer, President of ABB

Venture Capital Ltd, observed that many transnational European corporations are interested in venture capital programmes focusing on their specific corporate needs. He believed the development of such programmes to be 'a prime task for European venture capital in the '90s!' (*European Venture Capital Journal*, 1990b). Similarly, ACOST (1990) noted that CVC could be considerably significant for the growth prospects of smaller firms, and a report in *Chemical Week* (1992) recognised CVC as a 'very cost-effective way of developing products and technologies – if it works' (p. 25). CVC can provide investee firms with access to vital funding as well as the 'value-added' benefits associated with the nurturing provided by corporate investors. Non-financial companies could also be an important alternative source of funds for venture capitalists making early stage, technology-based investments at a time when they are experiencing difficulties in raising finance from institutional investors.

Taking the importance of the strategy into account, NEDO (1986), ACOST (1990) and the European Commission (see Duhamel *et al.*, 1994) have recognised a need both to increase awareness of the potential benefits of CVC and to tackle the fears and practical difficulties which inhibit collaborative relationships between large and small firms. ACOST recommended that the 'DTI investigates ways in which corporate venturing activity may be stimulated in the UK both directly, and through linkages with the institutional venture capital industry' (p. 38). The Department of Trade and Industry has not acted upon this challenge. Empirical study is required to access the opinions of those who would be involved with CVC, namely venture capitalists, corporate executives and entrepreneurs, in order to develop an understanding of the needs and motivations of all parties.

Potential for overcoming barriers to development

According to Ormerod and Burns (1986), much could be done to encourage CVC activity, and thus enable its real and substantial potential benefits to be appreciated. As has been suggested, many of the possible reasons for the low levels of CVC in the UK could be overcome by increasing the levels of training and advice available to large and small companies, via venture capitalists, accountants, consultants, policy makers, etc. The stimulation of CVC should concentrate on increasing the number of companies interested in the strategy, as well as improving the chances of success once venture capital relationships are established. The only way to understand the most appropriate mechanisms by which CVC strategy may be stimulated and encouraged in the UK, is to obtain the opinions and suggestions of venture capitalists and large and small companies alike.

Research aims and questions

Chapters 1 and 2 have outlined several issues of interest to both academics and practitioners that warrant further investigation. Based on the implications of these two chapters the main aims of this book can be summarised as follows.

CVC and inter-firm collaboration theory

CVC has been identified as a form of inter-firm relationship between large and small companies. However, as has been emphasised, this form of collaboration has been largely neglected in the academic literature. Given the need to focus research on specific forms of collaboration, and in particular large firm–small firm alliances (emphasised in Chapter 1), this study aims to examine the relevance of the various alliance theories in explaining the formation and nature of CVC relationships. The research therefore considers the pressures on companies to either make or seek CVC investments and relates them to conventional alliance theories and debates concerning flexibility. The objectives of companies are identified in an attempt to clarify confusions regarding the extent to which CVC investments are strategically oriented and can be considered to be *strategic* alliances. In addition, the role of CVC alongside other forms of collaboration is considered. The study also addresses the debate concerning the geography of alliance formation by examining the spatial scale of CVC relationships, and in particular the tendency for investments to be made within industrial districts. Finally, the levels of this form of collaboration are considered relative to alternative firm growth strategies, and the significance of any problems which have been encountered is examined.

CVC and the 'Equity Gap'

This chapter has emphasised the potential importance of CVC investment as a source of finance for early stage TBFs and the venture capitalists that specialise in investing in such firms. In this sense, it can be argued that CVC may be an important mechanism for helping to bridge the equity gap. This book therefore aims to examine the extent to which CVC has actually benefited small firms and venture capitalists, and also to identify any problems which have been experienced. Particular emphasis is placed on the significance of CVC investors as providers of nurturing for investee firms. The research therefore focuses on the nature of CVC relationships and considers whether any distinctions need to be made between direct and indirect investment forms. Despite its potential importance, CVC is widely believed to be an underdeveloped strategy in the UK. This book re-examines the levels of CVC investment and considers the most appropriate strategies for the encouragement of this activity.

In order to fulfil these aims the book addresses the following questions:

- What evidence is there of CVC activity in the UK (both externally managed/indirect and internally managed/direct)?
- What are the objectives of CVC strategy from large firm, small firm and venture capitalist perspectives?
- What are the characteristics of CVC investment (in terms of the typical forms it takes, investment processes, decision making, post investment relationships, organisational structures, sectors of industry, firm sizes, investment sizes, etc.)?
- What have been the post-investment experiences of (i) investing companies, (ii) investee companies and (iii) venture capitalists?

If it is established that CVC is still underdeveloped in the UK in comparison to the USA and elsewhere, then

- Why is CVC strategy underdeveloped in the UK? Are there specific barriers which limit involvement and success? Are companies involved in other business strategies instead of CVC? If so, why? Is CVC appropriate only in particular business environments? Are smaller companies obtaining adequate equity finance from other sources?
- How can CVC be stimulated and developed in the UK at both micro and macro-economic levels?

Research methodology

The research consisted of three distinct nationwide surveys. These surveys involved interviews with (i) corporate executives from UK-based companies known to have made, or at least considered making, CVC investments, (ii) UK-based venture capital fund managers, and (iii) representatives from UK-based technology-based firms that are known to have raised CVC finance. Table 2.4 summarises the main aims and issues that arise from each of these surveys. For the first two surveys, a mixture of face-to-face and telephone methods was employed. Survey three involved just telephone interviews. Interviews were conducted using a semi-structured questionnaire which contained a selection of closed and open format questions, the latter designed specifically to provide more qualitative data concerning the respondents' opinions of CVC strategy.

The choice of research techniques in this study reflects careful consideration of the suitability of particular methodologies and their implications for the reliability and validity of the data obtained as well as the influence of the interviewer on data collection. Given the amount of data required in this survey, and also its commercially sensitive nature, interviews were

Table 2.4 Summary of survey aims

Survey	Survey aims/issues	Chapter
Executives from seventy-three large companies that have made, or at least considered making, CVC investments	• Types of companies that have made CVC investments • Objectives of investing companies related to the use of particular forms of CVC • Degree to which CVC complements other strategies • Internal organisation of CVC • Investee/venture capital fund selection criteria • Characteristics of investments • Degree to which relationships involve nurturing • Performance of CVC investments • Constraints on performance • The decision not to make CVC investments • Future levels of CVC investment • Levels of CVC investment in comparison with the USA	3 and 4
Thirty-nine venture capital fund managers	• Significance of corporate sources for independent/affiliated venture capital funds • Characteristics of, and suspected motivations behind, corporate investments • Characteristics of venture capital funds which have raised finance from corporate sources • Advantages and disadvantages of CVC for venture capitalists • Current levels of indirect CVC and possible future trends	5
Directors from forty-eight TBFs that have raised CVC finance	• Financial histories of TBFs that have raised CVC • Significance of CVC *relative* to other sources at particular stages of firm development • The decision to seek CVC • The process of seeking and raising CVC • Form of the CVC relationship • Benefits of CVC for the TBF (including the hands-on/nurturing role of corporate investors) • Problems that have arisen for the TBF	6

considered to be the most appropriate survey technique. It was felt that a combination of face-to-face and telephone interviews would also increase the chances of obtaining a satisfactory sample size. Both methods can help to ensure that respondents are the most suitable individuals within organisations to be interviewed (Healey and Rawlinson, 1993), and allow clarification of complex issues and probing of inconsistencies, as well as assistance with interpretations, language and meaning (Schoenberger, 1991). It is therefore argued that the interview-based approach can allow 'a coherent representation of how and why particular phenomena came to be' (Schoenberger, 1991: 188).

Semi-structured questionnaires involving a mixture of structured and open-ended questions were considered particularly appropriate for this study given the combination of quantitative and qualitative data required. It was anticipated that this approach would increase the chances of obtaining reliable and valid data. As Schoenberger (1991: 182) notes, 'the questionnaire design really controls the interview'. In terms of *control*, two extreme scenarios exist, neither of which is desirable for the interviewer. First, there is a risk that respondents will impose their own agendas on interviews and not provide *relevant* information. Second, in highly structured interviews, lack of intellectual engagement or complete knowledge may mean that respondents simply adapt their responses to the questionnaire's categories, thus providing less accurate information (Schoenberger, 1991). According to Schoenberger (1991: 182), 'the goal should be collaborative dialogue that engages the respondent in working through the research problem'. Therefore, a combination of standardised, structured questions, which tend to be more reliable, and open-ended questions, which typically force respondents to think things through, thus resulting in a higher degree of accuracy and validity, was deemed most appropriate for this study. Great importance was placed on the need to interest respondents in the topic of the interview, and therefore all were given the option of receiving a copy of the survey findings. In a further attempt to ensure high levels of reliability and validity the interviewer stressed the confidentiality of all information provided.

A further issue concerns the influence of the interviewer on the data collected. It is inevitable that social interaction will impinge on the data collected (Oakley, 1981) and all researchers must be aware of their 'positionality' (McDowell, 1992) and take a self-critical stance towards their research (Schoenberger, 1992). Academic researchers are inevitably influenced by both personal beliefs and backgrounds and the beliefs of their discipline (Gibb, 1992; Schoenberger, 1992). Furthermore, the social characteristics of the interviewer, for example their age, race, sex and social status are important since they 'evoke different cultural norms and stereotypes that influence the opinions and feelings expressed by respondents' (Herod, 1993: 308). While race and sex were not considered to have a significant impact in this study, age and student status were important. Respondents may consider a young researcher relatively inexperienced in business to lack understanding of certain issues, and hence simplify their responses and omit important details. Alternatively, respondents may be particularly 'open' in their responses, providing highly confidential information because of the 'distance' of the researcher from their companies. In order to minimise these problems, the interviewer was well informed about companies before interview, thus reassuring respondents that he understood the issues under discussion (Schoenberger, 1991). Good preparation may also make the interview more interesting for the interviewee and allow the researcher to assess accuracy and validity to some extent.

Given the differing circumstances of each of the three surveys, a more specific description and justification for both the sample selection and the methodology used in each case is provided in the relevant chapters of the book. Chapters 3 and 4 are both based on the findings of a survey of executives from seventy-three large corporations that have made or considered making CVC investments. Chapter 3 considers why companies make CVC investments. It identifies the diversity of objectives of CVC strategy from the perspective of the corporate investor and examines why some companies prefer to use alternative strategies. Chapter 4 examines CVC from the perspective of the equity gap, and in particular considers the stages of development and industrial sectors which receive the most CVC finance. It also investigates in detail the nature of the CVC relationship and the post-investment experiences of investing companies. Chapter 5 is based on a survey of thirty-nine venture capital fund managers and is concerned with their experiences of corporate investors in their funds. Chapter 6 discusses the findings of a survey of forty-eight technology-based firms, all of which were known to have raised CVC finance. The chapter examines the relative importance of CVC finance for these firms compared to other sources, particularly at the early stages of firm development, and considers the 'value-added' nurturing aspect of CVC investment and any benefits experienced by investee companies. Finally, Chapter 7 provides a summary of the research findings as well as a discussion in the light of the main research aims. The implications for academics, venture capitalists, corporate executives, entrepreneurs and policy makers are considered, before an agenda for further research is proposed.

3

CORPORATE VENTURE CAPITAL INVESTMENT IN THE UNITED KINGDOM

A survey of corporate objectives

INTRODUCTION

Chapter 1 discussed the dramatic growth in the number of new forms of collaborative, inter-firm relationship that have been seen since the beginning of the 1980s. While inter-firm agreements are nothing new, this current wave involves a much wider and more flexible range of relationships than has previously existed (Chesnais, 1988), with collaboration occurring for a wide variety of reasons and manifesting itself in a number of forms (Dodgson, 1993). Various theories have been posited in an attempt to account for this trend towards collaboration, and it has been argued that a major cause has been the intensification of external pressures on companies within the contemporary marketplace (Collins and Doorley, 1991). To survive in this environment firms have needed to seek greater efficiency, greater flexibility and a reduction in uncertainty (Mytelka, 1991; Ahern, 1993a; Block and MacMillan, 1993), and collaboration has been viewed by many companies as a way of achieving these objectives and hence improving their ability to compete (Skjerstad, 1994). Alliances formed between large and small companies have the potential to be particularly beneficial to both partners due to the complementary characteristics of such firms, not least in areas of innovation (Hull and Slowinski, 1990; Rothwell, 1993).

The review of the collaboration literature in Chapter 1 highlighted the lack of research into individual alliance forms. It was argued that there is a need for such research in order to improve our understanding of the motivations and objectives of companies for establishing particular types of alliance. Corporate venture capital (CVC) investment has been identified as a form of inter-firm collaboration between large and small companies which has been largely neglected in the literature. The available evidence suggests that it is an underdeveloped activity in the UK. This chapter examines the reasons why some companies make CVC investments, and the reasons why other companies do not. It presents the results of a series of interviews conducted with senior corporate executives at a number of UK-based corporations. After considering the research aims and methodology in more detail, this chapter proceeds by describing the characteristics of the survey sample and reconsidering the levels of CVC in the UK based on the survey evidence. A detailed analysis of the objectives of investing companies is presented, followed by an investigation of the reasons why some companies do not make investments. The chapter ends with a discussion of the potential future levels of CVC in the UK in this era of increasing inter-firm collaboration.

RESEARCH AIMS AND METHODOLOGY

Research aims

This survey is aimed at both academic and practitioner audiences. From an academic perspective, it examines both the corporate objectives for making CVC investments and also the reasons why some companies prefer to employ other strategies rather than this particular form of collaboration. The findings will help improve our understanding of the role of CVC in the context of flexible, collaborative inter-firm relationships, and in particular the relevance of alliance formation theories for this form of collaboration. From a more practical point of view, the survey aims to provide existing and potential corporate venture capitalists with an insight into the motivations and strategies of their peers, and help venture capitalists and entrepreneurs seeking finance to better understand the needs and motivations of the corporate sector. It also seeks to analyse the degree of complementarity between CVC and other corporate activities and to examine both the levels of CVC investment in the UK in comparison with the USA and the potential future levels of this activity.

This survey therefore addresses the following questions:

- What types of companies are making CVC investments?
- What are the objectives of companies making CVC investments?
- Are specific forms of CVC investment more appropriate for particular objectives?
- To what extent do CVC investments complement other corporate strategies?
- Why do some companies choose not to make CVC investments and what alternative business development strategies do they use?
- Is CVC activity underdeveloped in the UK in comparison with the USA?
- What are the future levels of CVC likely to be in the UK?

Methodology

Because of the low levels of CVC investment in the UK it was inappropriate for the purposes of this survey to take a random sample of large corporations. Such an approach could not guarantee the identification of sufficient companies engaged in corporate venture capital activity which is vital given the nature of the research questions. The sample therefore consisted of indigenous UK companies and UK-based subsidiaries of foreign corporations that were reported in the business literature or the press, or identified during numerous conversations with experts in the venture capital and corporate fields, either to have made CVC investments or to have considered doing so. In addition, several subsidiaries of foreign companies were included because their foreign parents were known to have made CVC investments, and given the international outlook of many modern CVC programmes (Mast, 1991) the possibility that such subsidiaries would have invested themselves was considered to be high. This sample was chosen because it would include both a significant proportion of the UK-based companies that have made CVC investments (including some with 'lower-profile' CVC investment programmes), as well as a number of companies that have chosen not to invest. Both types of companies were important given the nature of the research questions. However, it cannot be claimed that the survey sample is representative of the entire population of UK-based companies that have been involved in CVC.

This sample selection procedure resulted in the identification of a hundred and nine corporate organisations, of which seventy-one were UK companies and the remaining thirty-eight were subsidiaries of foreign corporations. All firms were contacted by introductory letter and follow-up telephone calls. Initial contact was made with the Chief Executive of a company. It was anticipated that executives within the appropriate corporate functions would be more inclined to agree to participate in the survey if the letter requesting assistance had been passed down from the Chief Executive. A total of seventy-three companies agreed to participate in the survey (67 per cent response rate). Forty-seven (64 per cent) of the participating companies were UK firms and the remaining twenty-six (36 per cent) were foreign owned.

The survey design involved semi-structured questionnaires administered via face-to-face and telephone interviews. The advantages of these methods were discussed in Chapter 2. Either a face-to-face *or* telephone interview was conducted with a director from each of the seventy-three participating companies. Face-to-face interviews were necessary for most companies which had made CVC investments because of the quantity of information required. In contrast, telephone interviews were suitable for companies which had not made any investments as such interviews required a much smaller volume of statistical information, and much of the discussion was concerned with general opinions of the CVC process.

NUMBERS AND CHARACTERISTICS OF
INVESTING COMPANIES

The survey findings confirm the suggestion forwarded in Chapter 2 that CVC activity is only on a limited scale in the UK but contradict ACOST's view that there is a complete absence of this form of investment. Over one-third (28/38 per cent) of the seventy-three sample companies had made corporate venture capital investments, nineteen of which were indigenous UK companies and nine were subsidiaries of foreign corporations. While sixteen of these twenty-eight firms – over half the total (57 per cent) – had made only direct, internally managed CVC investments, five (18 per cent) had made just indirect, externally managed investments and seven (25 per cent) had made both direct and indirect investments. A total of £58 million had been invested indirectly, while £68.7 million had been invested directly by the sixteen companies for which data were available.

Although the survey sample comprised only companies known to have invested, or considered doing so, these figures nevertheless do indicate that CVC investment is an activity undertaken by a number of major corporations in the UK. However, of the twenty-three companies that had made direct CVC investments, nineteen described the investments they had made as 'ad hoc' or 'one-off', as opposed to being made via a formal, internally managed fund. This propensity for investments to be made in an ad hoc manner suggests that previous studies and reports may have failed to recognise this form of CVC and consequently underestimated the levels of the activity, and also implies that CVC is not a deeply rooted key strategy in many companies.

The companies that had made CVC investments represented a broad spectrum of industries (Figure 3.1). Among the twenty-eight companies were six utilities firms, five computer/electronic firms, four engineering companies, three gas/oil companies, two organisations from the transport and distribution sectors, and two involved with the manufacture of iron and steel. The remaining companies were active in quite diverse fields ranging from the manufacturing of toys and plastics to the manufacturing of iron and steel, and several were highly diversified companies. While Mast (1991) highlighted the significance of CVC in the US computer and electronics sectors, he also found many deals in the healthcare and chemical industries which are not evident in this survey. However, the abundance of utility companies identified in this survey as having made venture capital investments suggests this sector to be more active in CVC in the UK than in the USA. Several of the twenty-eight companies operated in industrial sectors which could be described as high technology, although just as many were in medium or low technology industries, supporting Honeyman's (1992) suggestion that CVC is not exclusive to high technology corporations as its principles are just as applicable in low-tech or even no-tech industries.

84

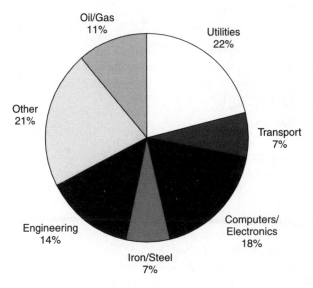

Figure 3.1 Industrial sectors of investing companies

The average size of the companies that had made CVC investments was approximately 29,000 employees, although it ranged from 137 employees in the case of a UK subsidiary of one Japanese company to 171,000 employees for one major UK corporation. Indeed it would appear that companies of all sizes have made CVC investments, although it must be noted that the smallest of these companies are subsidiaries of sizeable foreign corporations.

CORPORATE OBJECTIVES FOR MAKING CVC INVESTMENTS

It was noted in Chapter 2 that a debate exists concerning the rationale for a corporation becoming a participant in the venture capital process. While several writers (e.g. Mast, 1991; Rind, 1981; Block and MacMillan, 1993) believe corporate venture capital activities to be undertaken largely for strategic reasons, others (e.g. Winters and Murfin, 1988; Hegg, 1990; Honeyman, 1992) have commented on the importance of financial or social responsibility related objectives in some cases.

Objectives of survey companies

The results of this survey show the main macro-level considerations of companies for making CVC investments to be as follows (listed in descending order of importance):

- The need to cope with/reduce uncertainty
- Pressures of increasing global competition
- Perceived growth of particular industries
- Technological opportunities
- Shorter product life-cycles

There are noticeable similarities between these factors and those recognised in Chapter 1 as being important stimuli for the most recent wave of inter-firm collaboration in general (Dunn, 1992).

In order to assess the specific objectives of CVC as a means of coping with these pressures, respondents were given a list of sixteen possible motives which was compiled on the basis of motivations identified in several previous CVC studies. This list was dominated by 'strategic' considerations. While twelve of the sixteen listed objectives could be regarded as strategic, being made in vertically or horizontally related firms for largely technological, production and/or marketing purposes, the remaining four are concerned in turn with financial return on investment, educating the investing company about venture capital, social responsibility and publicity for the investing company. Table 3.1 indicates the primary and secondary motivations of the companies in this survey for making CVC investments ranked in order of importance. It is evident that the surveyed companies make CVC investments for a wide range of reasons, but by far the most significant is the identification of new markets, cited by nineteen firms (68 per cent) as a major objective. This supports Silver's (1993) suggestion that many large corporations have determined that a CVC operation is an effective vehicle for exposure to changes in the marketplace. Venture capital investment is used to identify and monitor particular target areas and in this sense offers a 'window on new commercial opportunities for technology' (Klein, 1987: 22). Such windows can help a corporation to understand emerging business areas that could potentially utilise existing corporate capabilities and provide synergistic growth opportunities (Sykes, 1993). In the case of British Gas, venture capital investments in North America provide an insight into the ways in which political and economic factors in that market are driving the creation of technological solutions (Corrigan, 1992). As Silver (1993: 61) observes 'corporations that operate in windowless offices cannot possibly see revolutions in their markets'.

Other important strategic motives for CVC investment are exposure to new technologies, the identification of new products to manufacture and the improvement of manufacturing processes. Also, ten companies invested specifically in order to establish further contractual relationships with investee firms including licensing deals and customer–supplier links. An important secondary objective is concerned with changing the corporate culture of the investing company, although this was not considered to be a primary motivation by any respondent.

Table 3.1 Ranked major corporate objectives for CVC investment

Objective	Primary objectives		Secondary objectives	
	Number of companies mentioning (n=28)	Rank	Number of companies mentioning (n=28)	Rank
Identification of new markets	19	1	4	8
Exposure to new technologies	12	2	3	11
Financial return on investment	10	3	12	1
Develop business relationships	10	3	7	3
Identification of new products	10	3	3	11
Improvement of manufacturing processes	9	6	4	8
Assess potential acquisition candidates	6	7	5	5
Learn about venture capital	5	8	4	8
Lower manufacturing costs	5	8	5	5
Social responsibility	5	8	1	14
Help suppliers/customers	3	11	5	5
Indirect benefits from enhanced small firm sector	2	12	7	3
Publicity for company	2	12	0	—
Assist spin-outs from company	2	12	1	14
Assure continued supply of materials/components	1	15	3	11
Change corporate culture	0	—	12	1

Source: survey

A further highly ranked major objective is financial return on investment (ROI). Moreover, even in twelve cases where the primary reasons for investing were strategically oriented, financial gain was an important secondary motive. The importance of ROI as a motive reflects the observation of several authors (e.g. Hegg, 1990; Mast, 1991) that if a CVC programme is not financially viable it is unlikely to survive long enough to generate strategic benefits.

The results displayed in Table 3.1 share many similarities with those in Silver's (1993) study in the USA which were outlined in Chapter 2. In Silver's study, the incubation of potential acquisition candidates was found to be the most common objective of companies making CVC investments, whereas it is ranked only seventh in this survey. However, exposure to possible new markets and the identification of new products were again ranked highly, further illustrating the overall strategic orientation of many CVC programmes regardless of geographic context. Other US studies (for example by Rind, 1981; Siegel *et al.*, 1988; Sykes, 1990; Block and MacMillan,

1993) have highlighted similar rankings of major corporate objectives of CVC investment.

Distinctions between direct and indirect CVC

The potentially different motives of companies making direct and indirect CVC investments were considered in Chapter 2. However, only one academic study (Sykes, 1990) has previously attempted to identify and analyse such differences. This differentiation is worthy of discussion since Winters and Murfin (1988: 210) have noted that 'before making an entree into venture capital, a corporation should first determine whether its participation is for financial reasons or strategic development objectives'. They go on to explain that 'a clear understanding of this difference is necessary before an appropriate strategy can be determined. A clouded view of this key objective can lead to an unfocused strategy and poor investment decisions'.

Of a sample of thirty-one companies in Sykes's (1990) study, twenty-five had made indirect investments and twenty-six had made direct investments (twenty had made both). He found the objectives of both CVC investment methods to be very similar with the identification of new opportunities and development of business relationships the two most important motives in both cases. Assessing potential acquisition candidates was also considered important for both indirect and direct investment. The only significant differences between the two were that learning how to do venture capital was found to be an objective of indirect CVC but not direct CVC, and direct CVC was identified as a means of changing corporate culture while indirect CVC was not. Objectives associated with financial gain and social responsibility were not mentioned in Sykes's study. In contrast, this survey identifies notable differences between the objectives of direct and indirect CVC. These differences are illustrated in Table 3.2 and Figure 3.2.

A diverse range of motivations exist for both direct and indirect CVC. In particular, the search for new technologies and new products, the establishment of further business relationships with investee firms and the chance to gain financially all appear to be important objectives for companies making either direct *or* indirect CVC investments. However, the survey results suggest that the objectives of companies undertaking indirect CVC are far more likely to be concerned with social responsibility and educating the investing company about venture capital than is the case with direct CVC investment.[1] Conversely, direct investment is much more likely to be motivated by the aim of targeting new market opportunities. Using Malecki's (1991) typology of generic motives outlined in Chapter 1, when indirect investments are motivated by strategic considerations, investors are likely to following a *window* strategy which provides them with a screening process for a wide range of technologies, products and markets. However,

Table 3.2 Ranked major corporate objectives for direct and indirect CVC investment

Objective	Direct CVC		Indirect CVC	
	No. of companies mentioning as a major objective (n=23)*	Rank	No. of companies mentioning as a major objective (n=12)*	Rank
Exposure to new technologies	9	2	6	1
Identify new products	7	4	5	3
Improve manufacturing processes	6	6	3	9
Lower manufacturing costs	4	7	2	10
Identify new markets	14	1	4	6
Assure continued supply of materials/components	1	12	0	—
Help suppliers/customers	3	8	0	—
Identify acquisition candidates	3	8	4	6
Develop business relationships	7	4	6	1
Learn about venture capital	1	12	5	3
Assist spin-outs	2	10	0	—
Financial return	9	2	4	6
Indirect benefits from enhanced small firm sector	1	12	1	12
Social responsibility	1	12	5	3
Develop an executive network	0	—	1	12
Publicity for company	1	12	2	10
Diversification	2	10	0	—
Need to become more entrepreneurial	1	12	0	—

Note: Includes seven companies that have made direct and indirect investments
Source: survey

direct investors are more likely to employ an *options* strategy allowing them to be more selective about the areas in which they participate.

The differing objectives of direct and indirect CVC are best exemplified by the seven companies in this survey that had made both direct *and* indirect investments. Three of these corporations explained that their direct and indirect investments were considered to be completely separate strategies driven by different motivations. Direct investments, which were described by the three respondents as 'true corporate venturing', were made largely for strategically-oriented reasons as they allowed more contact with investee companies and hence more chance of synergy. Indirect investments, in contrast, provided greater deal flow and were more conducive to educating a company about venture capital, providing the corporation with exposure to the venture capital business and the opportunity to form contacts with experienced venture capitalists. However, the lower

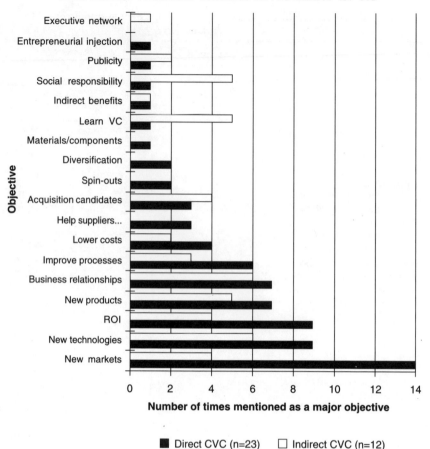

Figure 3.2 Major objectives of CVC: indirect and direct comparison
Source: survey

level of corporate resources committed to indirect CVC means that strategic returns can be expected to be less significant than with direct investment (MacDonald, 1991; Mast, 1991; Honeyman, 1992). Having developed an understanding of the venture capital process through indirect investment, and gaining the necessary experience, companies may then proceed to establish their own internally managed CVC programmes, as has been seen in the USA (Burstein and Hofmeister, 1985).

Of the sixteen companies that had made only direct CVC investments, twelve (75 per cent) explained that they used the direct rather than the indirect method as it offered more contact with and more control over investee firms. Seven of the sixteen companies specifically stated that direct investment was better suited to strategic objectives, and five commented on the benefits of a more focused investment portfolio. A quarter of the companies felt that a third party venture capitalist was unnecessary since their investments were largely strategically-oriented and therefore required a level of industry-specific knowledge that independent venture capitalists are unlikely to possess.

However, as was suggested in Chapter 2, the choice of CVC strategy is not entirely a function of corporate objectives. The availability of skills and resources are other important factors. Four of the five companies that had made only indirect CVC investments explained that they did not have the management skills or time for direct CVC, possibly implying that direct CVC would be the preferred strategy if the resources were available. In support of this, two of the seven companies that had made both direct *and* indirect investments had initially made direct investments before recognising that they lacked the required management skills and turned instead to externally managed investment. However, one further company that had made direct and indirect investments considered investing directly only if a specific investment did not fit within the focus of a particular externally managed fund. It was believed that the indirect method would provide the greatest chance of success due to the combination of the knowledge and experience of the professional venture capitalist and the financial strength, technical expertise and market knowledge of the investing corporation.

Complementarity with other strategies

Corporate venture capital investment is rarely considered to be an *alternative* to established corporate development activities, but instead is widely regarded as a *complement* to other corporate strategies (Bleicher and Paul, 1987; Klein, 1987; Hegg, 1990; Mast, 1991). Of the twenty-three companies in this survey that had made direct CVC investments, eighteen (78 per cent) considered their investments to complement other development and restructuring strategies of their company. Direct CVC was commonly regarded as a complement to other, more established corporate development strategies, namely in-house R&D, majority acquisition, and increasingly other forms of inter-firm relationship such as joint ventures, marketing agreements, and licensing. Four companies described direct CVC as an important part of the development of their core business, while three others considered it to be part of their diversification programme. Eight (67 per cent) of the twelve companies that had made indirect investments stated that these investments complemented other corporate development strategies or broader social responsibility programmes. While CVC investment, whether direct or indirect, is usually considered to be a complementary strategy when corporate objectives are either strategic or, to a lesser extent, related to social responsibility, it is regarded much more as a 'one-off' strategy when undertaken for financial or educational purposes.

Summary

In summary, the decision by a major corporation to become involved in venture capital investment can be the result of any one or more of numerous, diverse motivations. The majority of objectives are strategically oriented, and similar motives apply for both direct and indirect CVC investments. However, there are some important differences in emphasis which are worthy of note: companies undertaking direct investments are more likely to be concerned with the need to identify new markets, while indirect investments are more likely to be motivated by social responsibility aims and the desire to learn about venture capital. Therefore in its broadest sense CVC is more than a collaborative relationship designed purely for strategic purposes, as investments can also be motivated by social responsibility, educational and also financial aims.

COMPANIES THAT HAVE NOT MADE CVC INVESTMENTS: THE USE OF ALTERNATIVE STRATEGIES

Given the aim of this survey to understand the motivations of companies that have made CVC investments, there is a need to examine the degree of awareness and interest in CVC strategy that exists among corporate organisations that have *not* previously made such investments. An understanding of the reasons why such companies have not been involved in CVC and the factors which lead them to employ alternative strategies can provide clues both to the reasons why this strategy is underdeveloped in the UK and to the likely future levels of CVC investment.

The consideration of CVC strategy

Despite the nature of the sample selection process, almost two-thirds of the companies in this survey had not made any venture capital investments. In most cases this lack of involvement does not reflect a lack of opportunity since two-thirds of these companies had been approached by at least one venture capitalist regarding investment in the funds which they manage and, similarly, two-thirds had been contacted by entrepreneurs seeking direct minority equity finance for their firms. However, despite this exposure to investment opportunities, only 29 per cent of companies that had been approached had ever considered making indirect investments and only 44 per cent had considered making direct investments.

Companies that had considered making investments in externally managed funds had notably different motives for doing so than companies that had actually made indirect investments. Many of the companies that had only considered investing perceived indirect CVC to be a potentially useful vehicle for realising strategic advantages, while very few believed there to be any benefits associated with financial gain, social responsibility or learning about the venture capital process. This may reflect a lack of experience and understanding of the most appropriate investment strategies for particular objectives since non-strategic motivations have been identified as important considerations of companies that have been active in indirect CVC.

Companies that had considered making direct CVC investments also had largely strategic motives, most notably the desire to obtain windows on new technologies and new market opportunities, but also the need to establish further business relationships with small innovative companies. These objectives were therefore similar to those of companies active in direct CVC.

The use of alternative strategies

The eventual decision not to pursue strategic aims by investing in venture capital can be explained in most cases by the preference of corporations for alternative, and often more conventional, growth strategies. There are several reasons why a company may decide to use alternative strategies to pursue objectives which CVC itself has the potential to meet. Large corporations tend to require greater control over corporate operations than is offered by venture capital investment, even in its direct form. Indeed, Collins and Doorley (1991) considered strategic partnerships of any form to be appropriate only when a company either does not want control, cannot afford control, does not need it or is not allowed it. In addition, many companies lack the required management time and resources necessary for establishing and running a venture capital programme. Furthermore, many UK corporations do not believe that they can justify speculative investments to institutional shareholders, particularly at a time when a majority of corporations are concentrating on core business.

Most of the alternative growth and development strategies employed by companies involve integration and majority ownership. Two strategies were particularly common: acquisition and internal R&D. Almost 85 per cent of the companies used majority acquisition of both vertically and horizontally related firms for growth and development purposes rather than CVC, while 78 per cent considered the internal research and development of new ideas to be more appropriate. Almost half of the companies employed joint ventures, usually with other large firms but occasionally with universities or governmental organisations, and non-equity strategic alliances such as joint manufacturing and technology exchange agreements were used by 29 per cent of corporations.

The main objectives of these alternative strategies are very similar to the motives of companies for making CVC investments. In order of importance they are:

- Identification of new markets
- Identification of new products to manufacture
- Identification of potential acquisition candidates
- Opportunities to improve manufacturing processes
- Exposure to new technologies
- Development of mutually beneficial business relationships

These alternative strategies were considered more appropriate for meeting corporate objectives as they provided far more control than would be possible with relatively risky venture capital investments, and allowed access to technologies and products at a later stage once they had been developed to a greater extent. Indeed, Table 1.3 highlighted the higher levels of control associated with internal activities and acquisitions than with collaborative relationships, and in Chapter 2 it was hypothesised that many companies would prefer 100 per cent ownership to minority stakes for this reason. Similarly, Culpan (1993: 330) suggested that companies 'traditionally prefer a go-it-alone strategy as much as possible, thereby trying to internalise [ie: integrate through internal expansions or acquisitions] various business activities for their own gains'. This was confirmed by numerous survey respondents. One executive stated that 'if we are going to handle something we want control of it – we don't want a situation where we can't control quality of production and service'. Just over a quarter of the companies considered the strategies which they used to be more compatible with company culture and core business areas than would be possible in the case of venture capital investment, and executives from five foreign-owned corporations explained that strategic decisions were made by their foreign parents and as a result the UK subsidiaries had no influence in the decision whether or not to use CVC strategy.

CORPORATE INVESTMENT IN VENTURE CAPITAL: UK/US COMPARISONS

The findings of this survey therefore indicate that, for many UK-based companies, alternative corporate development strategies are preferred to CVC investment. This suggests that the low levels of UK CVC at least partly reflect a lack of motivation on the part of large corporations to make venture capital investments. The majority of corporate executives in this survey believed CVC activity, both indirect and direct, to be more widespread in the USA than in the UK. They identified several factors (Table 3.3 and Table 3.4) which help to justify this opinion and to indicate further why UK-based companies are more likely to use alternative strategies.

Executives consider the US business environment to be more entrepreneurial and more risk oriented than that in the UK and hence a greater number of large US corporations are willing to make speculative venture

Table 3.3 Views of survey respondents regarding the different levels of indirect CVC in the USA and the UK

Rank	Factors promoting CVC in USA	No.*	Rank	Factors impeding CVC in UK	No.*
1	More risk-oriented business environment in USA	19 (36)	1	Conservative/risk averse nature of UK companies	14 (26)
2	More investment opportunities/ entrepreneurial small firms	14 (26)	2	Conservative/risk averse nature of UK venture capital	4 (8)
2	More entrepreneurial business culture in USA	14 (26)	2	Less well established venture capital industry in UK	4 (8)
4	More established venture capital industry in USA	8 (15)	2	Control desire of UK companies	4 (8)
5	US companies have greater amounts of capital to invest	6 (11)	2	Decline of UK venture capital industry	4 (8)
5	US companies more inventive with investment strategies	6 (11)	2	Few investment opportunities/ entrepreneurial small firms	4 (8)
7	US companies better recognise the benefits of collaboration with small firms	4 (8)	7	UK venture capital associated with MBOs	3 (6)
8	Greater tax incentives in USA	3 (6)	7	UK companies are more short-termist	3 (6)
8	Greater number of large companies in USA	3 (6)	9	Well-developed alternative venture capital funding sources in UK	2 (4)
10	US companies are more long-termist	2 (4)	9	Poor performance of UK venture capital	2 (4)

Notes: * Number of companies that mentioned factor (respondents could mention more than one factor)
n=53 (number of companies expressing belief that levels of indirect CVC are greater in the USA)
Figures in parentheses are percentages
Source: survey

capital investments. This provides a major explanation for the higher levels of both indirect and direct CVC activity in the USA. Conversely, the UK business culture is seen to be plagued by conservatism, short-termism, a lack of entrepreneurial investment opportunities and a corporate desire for control. It was suggested in Chapter 2 that most UK companies do not make CVC investments because of their internal organisation and culture (Povey, 1986). This was supported by the Head of New Business Ventures

Table 3.4 Views of survey respondents regarding the different levels of direct CVC in the USA and UK

Rank	Factors promoting CVC in USA	No.*	Rank	Factors impeding CVC in UK	No.*
1	More entrepreneurial business culture in USA	22 (43)	1	Conservative/risk averse nature of UK venture capital	12 (24)
2	More risk-oriented business environment in USA	20 (39)	2	Few investment opportunities/ entrepreneurial small firms	4 (8)
3	More investment opportunities/ entrepreneurial small firms	12 (24)	2	UK companies are more short-termist	4 (8)
4	US companies better recognise the benefits of collaboration with small firms	7 (14)	4	UK companies do not perceive there to be any strategic benefit	3 (6)
5	US companies more inventive with investment strategies	6 (12)	4	Control desire of UK companies	3 (6)
6	US companies have greater amounts of capital to invest	5 (10)	6	UK companies are more cautious	2 (4)
6	Greater number of large companies in USA	5 (10)	6	Alternative sources of equity finance for small firms in UK	2 (4)
8	More established venture capital industry in USA	4 (8)	6	UK venture capital industry is too structured	2 (4)
9	US companies are more long-termist	3 (6)	6	City/shareholder pressure on UK companies	2 (4)
9	US companies quicker to appreciate potential of CVC	3 (6)	6	Decline of UK venture capital industry	2 (4)

Notes: * Number of companies that mentioned factor (respondents could mention more than one factor)
n=51 (number of companies expressing belief that levels of direct CVC are greater in the USA)
Figures in parentheses are percentages
Source: survey

at one UK utility company who explained that 'UK companies are not as adventurous as they might be. When it comes to venture capital they tend to think "why should we?" rather than "why shouldn't we?"' While US business is about aspiring to success it is also about not fearing failure (Bahrami and Evans, 1995). According to one Chief Executive 'there is no fear of failure in the USA and it is almost a mark of distinction to have tried but failed'. Failure is a part of the CVC process which must be tolerated (Littler and Sweeting, 1987a; Winters and Murfin, 1988). However, whereas failure is viewed in a positive light in the USA., there is a huge stigma attached to failure in the UK (Povey, 1986; Weyer, 1995), thus creating a business environment which restricts learning and prevents companies from undertaking speculative strategies which may offer high rewards.

However, as was suggested in Chapter 2, the underdeveloped nature of CVC in the UK in comparison with the USA may not only be a function of supply side factors. Botkin and Matthews (1992) highlighted a lack of demand for CVC funding in the UK, and referred to the shortage of growth firms in the small business sector. Indeed, the lack of investment opportunities was considered to be a significant problem in the UK by many survey respondents. The less well established venture capital industry in the UK and its relatively poor performance to date were also regarded as important factors by some executives. Potential corporate investors can be conceptualised as the 'primary customers' of the venture capitalist (Murray, 1994b) for whom fund managers must provide attractive investment opportunities and investment performance. Respondents highlighted the concentration of the UK industry on MBO investments and the lack of early stage, high technology funds as major explanations for the low levels of indirect CVC.

However, this argument implies that UK-based companies seek investment opportunities only within the UK. Contradicting this, Chapter 4 will show that many companies, and particularly those investing indirectly, also seek investments in foreign firms. Furthermore, the survey findings have already indicated that the lack of involvement of UK-based companies in CVC does *not* reflect a lack of investment opportunity since many large companies have been approached by fund managers and entrepreneurs regarding CVC financing. Although these findings do not provide any indication of the quality of this deal flow they do suggest that it is typically the UK company's desire for control, rather than a lack of CVC investment opportunities, that leads it to prefer alternative corporate development activities.

POTENTIAL FUTURE LEVELS OF CVC IN THE UK

Future involvement of surveyed corporations

The underdeveloped nature of UK CVC therefore largely reflects the lack of motivation on the part of large companies to invest in venture capital. A large majority of companies that have not made CVC investments consider that alternative growth and development strategies for the identification of new markets, products, processes, technologies and potential acquisition candidates offer more control and less risk and are therefore more appropriate for their needs. In-house corporate development strategies continue to be an important aspect of UK business culture, and any inter-firm relationships that are established tend to be large firm–large firm contractual agreements or joint ventures rather than minority equity investments in smaller firms which do not offer the required control.

Furthermore, several of the companies that have made CVC investments in the UK have now ceased venture capital operations. Six (50 per cent) of the twelve corporations in the survey sample that had invested in externally managed funds no longer make such investments and nine (39 per cent) of the twenty-three companies that had invested directly have abandoned their internally managed CVC operations. Several factors help to explain this trend, most notably disillusionment with the venture capital process resulting from poor previous experiences, and also pressures on companies to increasingly concentrate on core business activities. The withdrawal of companies from CVC will be considered in detail in Chapter 4.

However, the withdrawal of several companies from CVC has been partly offset by a number of new players who have only recently started to make venture capital investments. Of particular note are the recently privatised utility companies. Indeed, five of the eleven utility companies included in this survey had already made CVC investments (usually directly) almost entirely before 1998. Without doubt, the leading utility in this area is British Gas, whose externally managed dedicated fund *BG Ventures* was mentioned in Chapter 2. Furthermore, many companies plan to make CVC investments in the near future. Indeed, one-third of all the companies in the survey sample (n=72)[2] were planning to make venture capital investments in the following five years (Table 3.5)[3]. More than half (56 per cent) of the

Table 3.5 Plans for future CVC investment related to prior involvement in venture capital

Number of companies that . . .	. . . plan to make CVC investments in the next five years	. . . do not plan to make CVC investments in the next five years
. . . have previously made indirect CVC investments	2	3
. . . have previously made direct CVC investments	9	7
. . . have previously made both indirect and direct CVC investments	4	2
. . . have not previously made any CVC investments	8	37
Totals	23	49

Note: Based on data from seventy-two companies
Source: survey

companies that have previously made CVC investments plan to make further investments in future as do approximately one in five of the companies that have not made any CVC investments in the past. Again, the utility sector is likely to become increasingly significant. Seven of the eleven utility companies included in this survey planned to make CVC investments in the near future. Most have a preference for direct, strategically oriented investments that will help them to diversify, or more likely expand core business within the utility sectors. However, some companies are also considering investing for financial and social responsibility-related purposes.

Much of the CVC activity in the future appears likely to take the form of direct investment. Over two-thirds of the companies planning to undertake CVC in the future indicated a preference for direct rather than indirect investments (Table 3.6). This is primarily because direct investment has previously been the more common form of CVC, and companies are tending to use the investment strategy that they have used successfully in the past. However, three-quarters of the companies that had not previously made CVC investments also planned to make only direct investments. While this indicates the continuing importance of direct CVC relative to indirect investment, the particularly small number of companies planning to initially invest indirectly does imply a change of strategy among

Table 3.6 Form of future CVC investment among sample companies

Number of companies that . . .	. . . plan to make indirect CVC investments in the next five years	. . . plan to make direct CVC investments in the next five years	. . . plan to make indirect and direct CVC investments in the next five years
. . . have previously made indirect CVC investments	1	0	1
. . . have previously made direct CVC investments	0	9	0
. . . have previously made both indirect and direct CVC investments	2	1	1
. . . have not previously made any CVC investments	1	6	1
Totals	4	16	3

Note: Based on data from seventy-two companies
Source: survey

companies undertaking CVC. In the past, several companies have initially used indirect investment methods of CVC in order to learn about venture capital before switching to direct investments. It might be hypothesised that the abandonment of this 'learning curve' technique could reduce the likelihood of success among those companies planning to undertake CVC investment in the future.

The predominance of companies planning to make direct investments has three implications. First, it further reflects the desire for control exhibited by UK corporations who are not prepared to allow their investments to be managed by a third party. Second, it marks the continuing dominance of strategic motivations among the companies planning future CVC. Indeed more than half of these companies stated that their venture capital investments would be made to meet strategic objectives (Table 3.7), particularly the identification of windows on new technologies, products and markets, in the light of increasing global competition and rapid technological change. Third, it suggests that the majority of investee firms will be UK-based since 81 per cent of all companies that had received direct CVC finance in this survey were UK firms compared with only 45 per cent of indirect CVC investees (see Chapter 4).

Future levels of CVC investment: the views of survey respondents

Moving from a discussion of the strategies of individual corporations to a more extensive analysis of future trends, many executives expected to see a general increase in the number of CVC investments made by UK-based companies in the following five years. While one-third of all survey respondents predicted an increase in the extent of indirect CVC, over half believed that the levels of direct venture capital investment would rise (Figures 3.3 and 3.4). Many executives expected CVC levels to remain constant, with very few predicting decreasing levels of activity.

Most of the executives expecting to see an increase in the levels of CVC in the following five years believed that large, UK-based corporations

Table 3.7 Nature of the major motives of companies planning to make CVC investments by 1998

Nature of motives	Number of mentions as a major motive
Strategic	13
Financial	6
Social responsibility	4
Educational	1

Note: Based on data from twenty-three companies
Source: survey

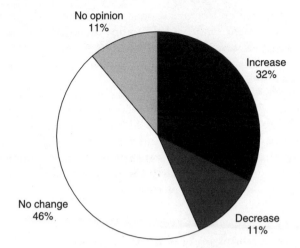

Figure 3.3 Views of survey respondents regarding future levels of indirect CVC among UK-based companies
Source: survey

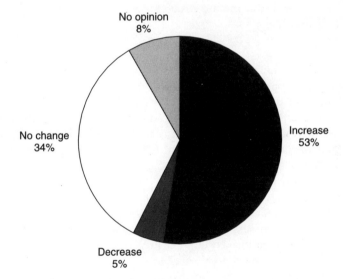

Figure 3.4 Views of survey respondents regarding future levels of direct CVC among UK-based companies
Source: survey

would begin to recognise the potential advantages of establishing mutually beneficial linkages of various forms, including venture capital investments, with small, innovative firms. This recognition would be driven by an over-riding necessity for corporations to become innovative and flexible on a

wide range of spatial and organisational scales in the light of rapid technological advancement and global competition. Several authors (e.g.
Anderson, 1993; Sykes, 1993; Stafford, 1994; Skjerstad, 1994) have
addressed this issue and the following quotes serve to reinforce the views
of the survey respondents:

> Cognizance of technology developments outside one's own R&D
> center is increasingly important. The in-house technical research group
> can at best be expected to create a small fraction of the total world's
> technology that may impact a corporation's business. Contacts with
> university and government research laboratories, as well as surveillance
> of start-up company activities is required.
>
> (Sykes, 1993: 5)

> The outlook for firms in the short term, irrespective of size, is that
> those internalising research will find it difficult to survive because of
> the rapid pace of technological change. In the long term there will be
> increasing levels of consolidation, with smaller specialised firms being
> integrated into larger corporate structures through collaborative, exter-
> nalised relationships.
>
> (Anderson, 1993: 1,832)

Approximately one-third of these executives added the caveat that most of
the growth would occur in research-based/technological industrial sectors,
reflecting the use of venture capital by corporations for largely strategic
purposes. In accordance with this, it was suggested that the levels of direct
CVC would increase to a larger extent than those of indirect CVC due to
the suitability of this form of investment for meeting strategic objectives. It
was not believed that companies would attempt to initially use indirect
investments to educate themselves about venture capital investment as has
previously been the case, although several respondents predicted that in
time many corporate venture capital managers will recognise that their
companies do not possess the necessary management skills for direct
CVC and will therefore turn to indirect investments.

Respondents expecting to see no change or even a decrease in future
levels of CVC underlined the shortage of initiatives from policy makers,
venture capitalists or any other intermediaries which attempt to attract large
companies to venture capital investment. Furthermore, several executives
felt that venture capital investment was simply not attractive enough for
most companies on account of its inherent riskiness and separation from
core business areas. Again control issues and external pressures to concentrate on core competencies were highlighted as reasons why a majority
of firms will continue to employ alternative strategies and abandon, or in
many cases not even consider, the venture capital option.

CONCLUSIONS

This chapter has provided detailed information regarding both the objectives of companies that have made CVC investments and also the alternative strategies of those that have not been involved with CVC. It has also provided important information regarding both the underdeveloped nature of CVC in the UK in comparison with the USA and the possible future levels of CVC in the UK.

Venture capital investment is an activity that has been undertaken by several UK-headquartered companies and overseas-owned subsidiaries in the UK. These companies tend to operate in the utilities, computers, electronics, engineering and oil and gas sectors of industry. Nevertheless, the number of corporations that have made CVC investments remains modest and very few have established deeply rooted programmes with the majority preferring to invest on an ad hoc basis.

The motivations of companies for making venture capital investments are largely strategic, supporting the findings of numerous researchers (e.g. Rind, 1981; Siegel *et al.*, 1988; Sykes, 1990; Mast, 1991; Block and MacMillan, 1993; Silver, 1993) in the USA, and show many similarities to the objectives of companies that are establishing other forms of collaborative inter-firm relationship. The main considerations of companies are related to the identification of new markets, new technologies, new products and new processes, as well as the opportunity to form further business relationships with both vertically and horizontally related investees. The use of collaboration *per se* to obtain *windows* or *options* on new areas of development was emphasised in Chapter 1 (Malecki, 1991). However, the objectives of companies for making CVC investments are not always strategically oriented. Supporting the comments of several writers (e.g. Winters and Murfin, 1988; Hegg, 1990; Honeyman, 1992), companies have been found to also invest for social responsibility and financial purposes, as well as to learn about the venture capital process.

Sykes's (1990) survey of US CVC found few differences between the motivations of companies for making direct and indirect CVC investments. However, this survey concludes that it is important to distinguish between the objectives of direct and indirect CVC. Direct, internally managed investments offer more contact with investee firms and more control. They are therefore made for largely strategic purposes, and particularly to target a small number of relevant technologies and/or markets. Conversely, indirect, externally managed investments provide greater deal flow and require less management time and resources and are therefore preferred by companies with social responsibility related objectives and companies seeking to learn about venture capital. Indirect investment may also be appropriate for companies motivated by particular strategic aims, such as the opportunity to gain windows on a wide range of new technologies.

Both direct and indirect CVC are sometimes used by companies seeking an attractive ROI, although this is often a secondary objective. In terms of the complementarity of CVC with other strategies, investments made for strategic or social responsibility-related purposes are usually considered to complement other corporate strategies. However, CVC is far less of a complementary strategy when objectives are financial or related to learning about venture capital.

The survey findings suggest that while CVC is far from non-existent in the UK, it does remain an underdeveloped strategy. The majority of corporations in the sample that have not undertaken CVC have been approached either by venture capitalists or entrepreneurs seeking equity finance. The lack of involvement of these companies in venture capital therefore does not reflect a lack of opportunities. However, many of them have not even considered the venture capital option. Because of a desire among UK corporations for control and a shortage of management time and resources, alternative development strategies such as acquisition and other internalised business development activities, which can be more easily justified to institutional shareholders, are still preferred. Supporting the comments of Botkin and Matthews (1992), there was a widespread belief among the surveyed executives that UK companies are more conservative, short-termist and risk averse than their US counterparts, which largely explains the differing levels of CVC investment in the two countries.

However, although the majority of companies have not made venture capital investments, and a number of companies that have made investments have since abandoned their venture capital operations, this has been partly offset by a number of 'new players' who have recently become involved in CVC and others who plan to do so in the future. In particular, the recently privatised utility companies seem likely to become increasingly involved. Most of the companies that were planning to make venture capital investments in the following five years have a preference for direct, strategically oriented investments, and it has been predicted that the importance of such investments will increase as the benefits of collaboration between large and small firms is recognised.

While this chapter has provided a detailed insight into the motivations behind CVC investments in the UK, it has not provided any details of either the investment process itself or of the experiences of investing companies. Given the main research aims and questions that this book addresses, there is a need to both determine the types of firms that raise CVC finance and to analyse in more detail the reasons why companies have withdrawn from CVC activity. The next chapter therefore investigates these issues using the same sample as has been employed in this chapter.

4

THE CVC INVESTMENT PROCESS
A strategy for bridging the equity gap?

INTRODUCTION

As a result of the neglect of CVC in the research literature, very little is known about either the investment process or the experiences of companies that have made these investments in the UK. These issues are important to this study for three reasons. First, an examination of the internal organisation and investee selection procedure used by investing companies will provide an insight into the corporate decision-making process and enhance our understanding of the dynamics and corporate objectives behind the CVC process. Second, identification of the performance of investments and constraints experienced by investors in the past may provide some further clues as to the underdeveloped nature of CVC in the UK. Third, and of particular significance, a consideration of the characteristics of CVC investments can help to determine which types of firms are most likely to benefit from this finance source. In the light of the second main aim of this book, namely to examine the role of CVC as a source of external equity finance for small firms and venture capitalists, the main focus of this chapter is on the role of CVC in the bridging of the equity gap.

The difficulties encountered by small firms, and specifically technology-based firms (TBFs), in raising capital for start-up and growth were considered in some detail in Chapter 2. These difficulties are particularly great in the UK, where, despite the rapid growth of the venture capital industry since the early 1980s, fund managers have consistently failed to back technology-based ventures in the early stages of their development (Murray, 1992b; 1995; Abbott and Hay, 1995). The reluctance of the venture capital industry to invest in such firms appears to be increasing, reflecting the preference of institutional investors for less risky later stage deals and MBOs/MBIs which tend to produce more consistent returns in shorter time periods (Abbott and Hay, 1995). Furthermore, venture capital providers are often unable to provide investee firms with appropriate value-added skills and resources (Murray, 1993; 1995).

The need for an alternative source of external equity finance for early stage TBFs has been emphasised by several authors and organisations (e.g. ACOST, 1990; Murray, 1991b; 1995; Duhamel *et al.*, 1994; Abbott and Hay, 1995). CVC has been recognised as such a source (e.g. by Ormerod and Burns, 1988; ACOST, 1990). Given the motivations of non-financial companies for making CVC investments (Chapter 3), and in particular the strategic orientation of many objectives, it can be hypothesised that early stage TBFs will be popular targets of corporate investors, who may also be able to provide entrepreneurs with essential industry-specific value-added assistance.

RESEARCH AIMS AND METHODOLOGY

Research aims

As stated, the main aim of this chapter is to examine the role of the corporate sector in closing the equity gap for small firms. The chapter therefore examines the characteristics of both indirect and direct CVC investments in order to identify the potential of both forms as alternative sources of hands-on finance for small firms, particularly early stage companies operating in technology-based sectors. An important prerequisite is an understanding of the differing organisational strategies and investee selection criteria used by companies making CVC investments. These will reflect the motives of investing companies identified in Chapter 3 and will influence the types of fund managers and investee firms sought in terms of their industry and technology focus and experience. Furthermore, the motives of investing companies will also help to dictate the degree of nurturing assistance provided to small firms and also the likelihood that further business relationships will be established. Given the underdeveloped nature of CVC in the UK (Chapter 3), particularly in comparison with the USA, this chapter also examines the extent to which companies' past experiences with CVC have resulted in their withdrawal from this activity.

The specific questions which this chapter addresses are therefore as follows:

- What organisational strategies are being used by investing companies and how do they reflect corporate motives?
- What are the corporate investors' investee and fund selection criteria?
- To what extent do CVC investments involve the nurturing of investee firms and the establishment of further business relationships?
- What are the characteristics of CVC investments?
- How well have CVC investments by UK-based corporations performed?
- Have there been any problems which have affected the performance of CVC investments?

Methodology

This chapter is based on the same survey of corporate executives outlined in Chapter 3. The nature of the research questions outlined above necessitated the identification of companies that had experience of making CVC investments. Therefore, those firms in the sample that had made CVC investments (a total of twenty-eight) were asked further sets of questions concerning both the nature and organisation of these investments, as well as their post-investment experiences.

ORGANISATIONAL STRATEGIES IN CVC INVESTMENT

Internal organisation of CVC investment

There is no unique way for a corporation to structure its venture capital investment programme as the objectives, needs, and capabilities of individual companies will dictate the precise organisation in each case (Winters and Murfin, 1988). Much depends on the degree of autonomy deemed necessary (Ginsberg and Hay, 1993) and the CVC approach (indirect or direct) chosen (Honeyman, 1992). As was noted in Chapter 2, the two main organisational alternatives are either to make investments via an in-house function or operating division, as is increasingly the case among US corporate venture capitalists (Mast, 1991), or to make them via a separate, fully or partially owned subsidiary. Furthermore, several authors (e.g. Winters and Murfin, 1988; Block and MacMillan, 1993) have recognised that direct, internally managed CVC investments can be made either by formally establishing a relatively large, separate pool of funds specifically earmarked for venture capital, or by funding deals on an ad hoc basis.

Figure 4.1 indicates that both indirect and direct CVC investments can be made via an in-house function *or* a separate subsidiary. In this survey, seven of the twelve companies that had made indirect CVC investments had invested via an in-house function (typically finance or corporate development), while the remaining five had invested via a subsidiary company (Table 4.1). However, only seven of the twenty-three corporations that had invested directly had established a separate subsidiary for this purpose. Moreover, while all four of the companies that had invested directly via an internally managed fund had established a separate subsidiary, only three of the nineteen companies making ad hoc investments used a subsidiary, preferring instead to invest via in-house functions or operating divisions. This suggests that in the case of direct CVC, subsidiaries are usually only established in order to manage formal funds and not ad hoc investments.

These patterns can be largely explained by the differing corporate objectives in each case. It was established in Chapter 3 that a diverse range of motivations exist for both direct and indirect CVC. In particular, the search

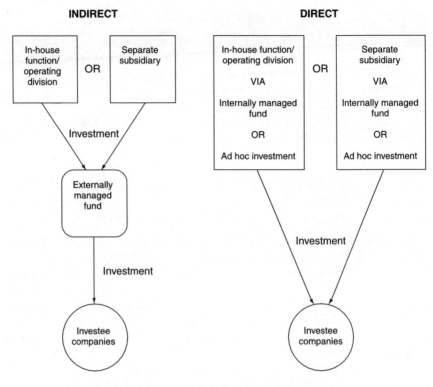

Figure 4.1 Internal organisation of CVC investment

for new technologies and new products, the establishment of further business relationships with investee firms and the chance to gain financially all appear to be important objectives for companies making either direct *or* indirect CVC investments. However, companies concerned with social responsibility and learning about venture capital were found to be more likely to undertake indirect CVC. Conversely, companies using CVC to gain access to specific new markets were more likely to undertake direct CVC.

The large majority of companies in this survey that had made ad hoc direct CVC investments had invested with strategically oriented motives. This form of investment tends to provide more opportunities for closer

Table 4.1 Internal organisation of CVC investment among survey sample

	No. of companies investing via in-house function/operating division	*No. of companies investing via subsidiary company*
Indirect CVC	7	5
Direct CVC	16	7

Source: survey

contact with investee firms and consequently clearer windows on new technologies and markets (Winters and Murfin, 1988). Several executives did not regard their company's ad hoc investments as 'true venture capital' since they were designed primarily for strategic and not financial gain and did not, therefore, warrant the establishment of a formal investment fund.

In contrast to the strategic orientation of most ad hoc investments, the objectives of most internally managed corporate venture capital funds are largely financial (Warren and Kempenich, 1984; Winters and Murfin, 1988). Indeed financial return on investment was considered to be a primary objective of three of the four internally managed funds in this survey, although only one of these, a subsidiary of a UK engineering company, was formed *purely* for financial gain. The other fund was established to make investments for social responsibility purposes. Making internally managed fund investments via a subsidiary company offers autonomy and the opportunity for financially oriented investments, which do not require close contact with the investing company, to be made via a separate organisational entity operating outside the constraints of the corporation (Pratt, 1994).

Investment approval process

In establishing a process for approving particular investments, a company has a choice of several options (Block and MacMillan, 1993). Approval from the company's main board may

- not be required at all
- be required but typically be a formality
- be required for deals above a designated size
- be required for all deals

In the case of indirect CVC, the results of this survey suggest that while one-third of companies require their main board to have final approval of all investments made in externally managed funds, a further third require no board involvement whatsoever. However, direct investments tend to involve more rigid approval structures. Six of the twenty-three companies to have made direct investments described the links between CVC manager and the company's main board as very close, and a further seven stated that the board has final approval of all investments. In only two cases did the company's main board have no influence over direct CVC investments. This relative lack of autonomy in direct investment may be largely due to the greater strategic orientation of direct investments, and particularly ad hoc investments where capital is contributed only on a deal-by-deal basis. Stand-alone venture capital fund subsidiaries, which are more often oriented to financial gain, tend to have more autonomy than departments making ad hoc investments. This also supports the findings of Siegel *et al.*

(1988) and Sykes (1990) who suggest that investing departments with greater autonomy (termed 'pilots') commonly regard financial return on investment to be a major objective of CVC, while departments with less autonomy (termed 'co-pilots') often attach greater importance to strategic benefits.

Indirect CVC: venture capital fund selection criteria

Indirect CVC requires a careful, systematic evaluation of externally managed venture capital funds (Collins and Doorley, 1991). Since industrial corporations make indirect venture capital investments for a wide range of reasons the identification of externally managed funds appropriate for individual corporate needs is imperative. Table 4.2 ranks the importance of various factors in evaluating the suitability of venture capital funds and their managers. Responses of survey participants were rated on a four point scale relating to the importance of each factor, and mean scores are provided.

Table 4.2 suggests two key factors to be of particular importance to the investing corporation in the selection of fund managers; first, venture

Table 4.2 Ranked importance of factors in selection of fund managers

Factor	Mean score	Per cent of respondents stating as 'essential'
Overall experience of venture capitalist	3.27	45
Venture capitalists' previous investment track record	2.82	9
Expertise of venture capitalist in particular stages of investment	2.82	0
Type of funds managed by venture capitalist (i.e. pooled, dedicated, etc.)	2.73	27
Hands-on investment philosophy of venture capitalist	2.45	27
Particular geographical focus of venture capital fund	2.36	18
Expertise of venture capitalist in particular sectors	2.18	18
Management fees	1.55	0
Previous links with venture capitalist	1.45	9
Venture capitalist with well-formulated exit strategies	1.27	9
Venture capital funds of particular life span	1.27	9
Venture capitalists that do not syndicate with other fund managers	1.18	0
Independent and not affiliated fund managers	1.09	0

Notes: Scale: 1, irrelevant; 2, desirable; 3, important; 4, essential
Based on data from eleven corporate investors
Source: survey

capitalist experience and previous track record; and second, investment focus and type of investment vehicle offered.[1] Both factors indicate the fund manager's expertise when seeking investment opportunities. The survey findings further suggest that companies with strategic objectives are more likely to invest in funds which have expertise in particular sectors and development stages and thus provide windows on specific areas of technological development. Conversely, companies investing for social responsibility and educational reasons are more often concerned with geographical investment focus on account of their desire to either learn about and/or provide finance for firms in particular countries and regions. Companies that invest to learn about venture capital tend not to set investment criteria themselves. However, companies seeking financial gain, and to a lesser extent strategic advantages, do tend to influence these criteria in terms of the stage of development, industrial sectors and geographical location of investees as well as investment sizes. Such an influence provides the corporation with an opportunity to manipulate fund investment philosophy in terms of the nature of the portfolio to its own advantage (Gabizon, 1985).

Direct CVC: deal flow

The responsibility for targeting potential investee companies in indirect CVC belongs to the external fund managers. However, in the case of direct investment the onus is on the corporation to recognise investment opportunities that suit its objectives. The survey findings indicate that companies actively seek investment opportunities. Potential investees are most commonly identified either through continual scanning for investment opportunities or via intermediaries. These include accountants, merchant banks and venture capitalists. Only four companies had been approached by small firms regarding equity financing. This is somewhat surprising given the finding in Chapter 3 that two-thirds of the forty-five companies that had not made CVC investments *had* been approached by entrepreneurs seeking direct CVC finance.

Co-investments with venture capitalists (parallel investments) are a potentially beneficial way of identifying investment opportunities and also accessing the investment expertise of the venture capitalist (Bailey, 1985). However, only nine of the twenty-three corporations in this survey that had invested directly had co-invested with independent venture capitalists. In two-thirds of these cases the venture capitalist was the lead investor. The relatively small number of companies making parallel investments may reflect a reluctance on the part of many venture capitalists to invest in such deals because of the possibilities of conflicting objectives with investing companies.

Large corporations may already have business relationships with small, vertically or horizontally related firms, and will take direct equity stakes in them once contractual relationships have been established in order to underpin the commercial relationship and participate in the investee company's successes (Collins and Doorley, 1991). In this survey eight of the twenty-three companies investing directly had linkages with investee firms prior to investment, including customer–supplier linkages as well as forms of contractual strategic alliance. A further three companies had identified business opportunities from inside their corporations and had decided to spin them out and take a minority equity stake. The finding that only a relatively small number of companies had made 'spin-off' investments may reflect the fact that few individuals are prepared to leave large UK companies in order to set up new ventures because of the tax incentives and stock option deals available in large companies (BVCA, 1995b; Weyer, 1995).

Direct CVC: investee company selection criteria

The survey indicates that the characteristics of a small firm's products and markets are the most significant factors in the investee selection process (Table 4.3). These findings support Roberts's (1991) comments that company characteristics are more significant than the entrepreneur and management team, but are in contrast to the findings of another US study which showed criteria related to the entrepreneur to take priority over product, market, or financial considerations (including investment size and exit possibilities) (Siegel *et al.*, 1988). However, the Siegel *et al.* study did confirm that entrepreneurial quality criteria are often sacrificed in order to achieve strategic fit with the corporation. The relative importance of factors associated with the nature of the small firm's business is in contrast

Table 4.3 Ranked importance of factors in selection of investee firms

Factor	Mean score	Per cent of respondents stating as 'essential'
Characteristics of product	2.78	32
Characteristics of market	2.78	27
Lead entrepreneur's experience	2.63	20
Country of origin of small firm	2.61	17
Management team's composition and experience	2.48	16
Geographical location of small firm in relation to investing company	2.43	13
Lead entrepreneur's personality	2.38	7
Financial considerations	2.13	9

Note: Scale: 1, irrelevant; 2, desirable; 3, important; 4, essential
Source: survey

to the findings of many research studies looking at the criteria typically used by independent venture capitalists when selecting investee firms. According to Murray (1995), these studies have indicated the dominance of factors related to the competencies and track record of the entrepreneurs in venture capitalists' investment criteria. Other notable findings from this survey of corporate investors include the greater significance attached to the lead entrepreneur's experience relative to the lead entrepreneur's personality, and also the low ranking of financial considerations. The strict evaluation procedure employed by companies making direct CVC investments is indicated by the fact that only one company in this survey had invested in more than 10 per cent of the potential investee firms that it had identified.

The importance that companies place on particular factors in the selection of investee firms is, of course, a function of corporate objectives. It was clear from the survey responses that, as would be expected, companies with strategic motives put greater emphasis on characteristics associated with products and markets since they typically invested in order to obtain windows on specific markets and technologies. Conversely, the few companies with social responsibility-related objectives are not as concerned with company characteristics and therefore rely more upon entrepreneur and management team criteria. Corporations with primarily financial objectives tend to evaluate investees in terms of entrepreneurial talent, financial, and product *and* market characteristics.

Indirect CVC: communication with fund managers and portfolio investees

The degree of communication between the twelve indirect corporate venture capitalists in this survey and the externally managed funds in which they had invested varied considerably. While some corporations contacted fund managers only on an annual basis, others spoke on most days, one communicating daily. However, the majority of companies contacted their fund managers monthly or a few times a year, usually for reports on investment progress and deal flow. The degree of communication with fund managers varied temporally. Contact is usually at a maximum soon after the initial corporate investment when venture capitalist and investing company become better acquainted with each other's objectives and philosophies and investment criteria are discussed in greater detail. The need for communication decreases as funds become fully invested and only intermittent progress reports are required, and will usually increase again only when the sale of investee firms is being negotiated.

The number of investing corporations that have subsequently become involved with any of the portfolio investees of the externally managed funds in which they have invested is minimal. None of the twelve corporations that have invested in externally managed funds provided hands-on or nurturing assistance to ventures, reflecting the limited number of companies investing indirectly for strategic purposes. This suggests that the amount of 'value-added' offered by companies investing this way is limited, despite the potential benefits of such nurturing outlined in Chapter 2. Furthermore, only three companies have formed further business relationships with investee firms. In all three cases contractual agreements such as customer and marketing agreements had been established. The purpose of these *strategic partnerships* was to enhance the chances of strategic gain through closer contact with new opportunities and greater chance of synergy. Companies that had not become involved with investee firms in any way did not have strategic objectives, and therefore such relationships were not required.

Direct CVC: communication with investee firms

The degree of communication between investor and investee companies is much higher in the case of direct CVC. Eighteen of the twenty-three direct corporate venture capitalists had taken a seat on the board of *all* investee firms, and a further four were represented on the boards of most of their investees. Aside from board meetings, communication with investees, usually on a weekly or monthly basis, enabled many of the investing companies to obtain progress reports and provide nurturing assistance to their smaller partners. Indeed, while nurturing was found to be non-existent in indirect CVC relationships, the survey findings suggest such value-added investment to be commonplace in the case of direct CVC. Sixteen of the twenty-three corporations that had made direct investments had provided nurturing assistance of some form for *all* of their investee companies, and a further three companies provided it for *some* of their investee firms, but not all of them.

The form of venture nurturing provided by companies can vary considerably. The most common forms in this survey (Table 4.4) are those concerned with helping investees with short-term problems, monitoring and evaluation. Most corporations tend to be more reluctant to heavily influence the operations of investee firms for fear of stifling their entrepreneurial nature and interfering more in the day-to-day operations of the small firm than the entrepreneurs find desirable.

Respondents justified their companies' nurturing approach to venture capital investment by emphasising the need to increase the level of involvement with investees in order to achieve objectives. Nurturing allows corporate investors to become better acquainted with the products and operations of investee ventures, and is particularly important when corporate objectives are strategically oriented. This therefore explains the propensity for direct CVC investments to involve nurturing. The process is

Table 4.4 Forms of nurturing provided by investing companies

Form of nurturing	Number of companies using this form of nurturing (n=19)*
Assistance with short-term problems	17
Monitoring operating performance	16
Monitoring financial performance	16
Serving as a sounding board to management team	14
Evaluation of product/market opportunities	13
Development of marketing plans	12
Motivating personnel	11
Development of business strategies	9
Providing contacts with customers	9
Help in obtaining finance from other sources	8
Providing contacts with suppliers	8
Replacement of members of the management team	6
Assistance with product manufacturing	5
Research and development of products	4

Note: * Respondents could mention more than one form of involvement
Source: survey

facilitated by the absence of a venture capitalist intermediary which can act as a buffer to corporate contact with investees.

Direct CVC investments are also more likely than indirect investments to lead to subsequent business relationships. This is again largely because of the strategic orientation and greater levels of contact with investee firms associated with this form of investment. Almost two-thirds of the companies that had made direct investments had formed such relationships compared with only one-quarter of the companies investing indirectly. These strategic partnerships included customer–supplier deals, licensing and research contract agreements as well as joint ventures. These findings confirm Mast's (1991) observation in the USA that direct CVC investments are increasingly being made to enable further business relationships to be established rather than to provide corporate investors access to potential acquisition candidates.

CHARACTERISTICS OF CVC INVESTMENTS

It is apparent that the motives of a company for undertaking CVC not only help to determine the form of investment and internal organisation used but also influence the types of fund managers and investee companies targeted and the level of contact sought. In the light of these findings, and given that the main aim of this chapter is to evaluate the potential contribution of corporate venture capital investment to providing finance for early stage and high technology firms, an examination is required of the characteristics of indirect and direct CVC investments made by the companies in this survey, and specifically the attributes of investee firms.

Indirect CVC

Characteristics of venture capital funds

The twelve companies in this survey that had made indirect, externally managed venture capital investments had invested in thirty-two funds managed by sixteen different fund managers. Only six (19 per cent) of the funds have been wound-up to date. A total of twenty-seven (84 per cent) of the thirty-two funds were closed funds, and in twenty-one cases the corporate investor had made just one investment in the fund. While in most cases investments were made in the form of a lump sum, one US-owned computer manufacturer provided the necessary funds only when an investee company had been identified by the fund managers. Four companies had each committed capital to a fund which had not made any investments at the time of interview.

Indirect corporate venture capital activity is not confined to national boundaries. While nineteen (59 per cent) of the funds in this survey were managed by UK-based fund managers, a further twelve (38 per cent) were US funds and one was Canadian (Figure 4.2).[2] Indigenous UK companies have invested in twice as many UK funds as foreign funds, but all of the

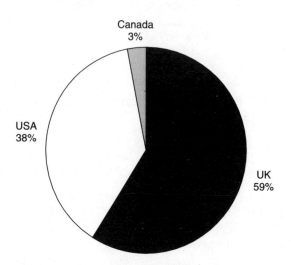

Figure 4.2 Country of origin of fund managers
Source: survey

foreign-owned subsidiaries have invested only in UK funds. This reflects the fact that foreign-owned subsidiaries typically make investments in the country in which they are based in order to gain knowledge of the venture capital investment opportunities within that country.

The first investment by a company in this survey in an externally managed venture capital fund was made in 1984, while the three most recent were made immediately prior to this survey which was undertaken in mid-1994 (Figure 4.3). The number of companies making indirect investments peaked in 1988, with six companies investing in that year. Since then, the trend has been rather erratic, fluctuating between a maximum of four investments in 1990 and a minimum of one in 1992. Signs of an increasing number of investments are evident in the figures for 1993 and 1994. (Note that the 1994 figure of three investments includes only the first six months of the year.)

More significant than the numbers of investments made are the amounts invested. Between 1984 and 1984 the corporations in this survey had invested a total of £58 million in externally managed venture capital funds.[3]

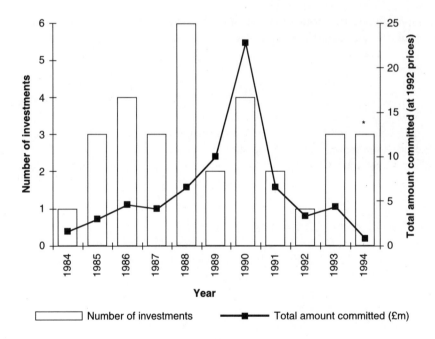

Figure 4.3 Dates of corporate investments in externally managed funds and amounts invested, 1984–94
Notes: * 1994 figure for first 6 months of year only
Amounts invested based on data from investments by 11 companies in 30 funds
Source: survey

The average amount invested by an individual corporate organisation was therefore £5.27 million and the mean investment in each fund was £1.93 million. However, these figures disguise a large range of investment sizes, the smallest investment being £25,000 and the largest £15 million. As might be expected, investments made for social responsibility purposes are usually significantly smaller than investments made for strategic reasons.

The amount invested by corporations in externally managed funds increased steadily between 1984 and 1989 (Figure 4.3). Peak investment occurred in 1990, slightly later than the number of investments, when the amount of finance invested almost equalled the total committed by the corporate sector in the previous six years. However, since this year of exceptional investment levels and high average corporate investment sizes,[4] there has been a marked decline in the amount invested with less than £1 million invested in the first six months of 1994.[5] The reasons for the decline in corporate contributions to externally managed funds will be discussed later in this chapter.

The temporal variations in indirect CVC investment identified in this survey parallel, but slightly lag, the figures for new capital commitments to independent UK venture capital funds from *all* sources, suggesting that corporate contributions fluctuate in a similar manner to those from institutional sources but with a time lag (Figure 4.4). The survey findings also show some correlation with the BVCA fund-raising figures shown in Chapter 2, in that these also indicated a steady increase in funds raised from large corporations during the late 1980s. However, there are two major discrepancies between the BVCA figures and the survey findings. First, while the BVCA figures show 1989 to be an initial peak fund-raising year (£62 million raised) with a significant *decline* in 1990 (£17 million raised), the survey findings indicate the *peak* to have been in 1990. This discrepancy partly reflects the fact that one-quarter of the total invested by survey firms during 1990 was invested in foreign funds rather than BVCA members. However, even when investments in foreign funds are excluded from the analysis, the survey findings still indicate 1990 to be a year of peak corporate investment. Moreover, almost three-quarters of the total amount invested in 1990 by the survey firms was invested by just one company in a dedicated fund. It is likely that this investment was excluded from the BVCA figures.

The second discrepancy concerns the survey finding that there has been a marked decline in the levels of indirect CVC investment since 1990. In contrast, the BVCA figures, particularly for 1994, indicate a significant increase in the amount raised by fund managers from corporations (£424 million in 1994) (BVCA, 1995a). There are two possible reasons for these differences; first, the survey figures refer to the first six months of 1994 only, and second, the large majority of funds raised by BVCA members from non-financial companies during 1994 came from foreign-based

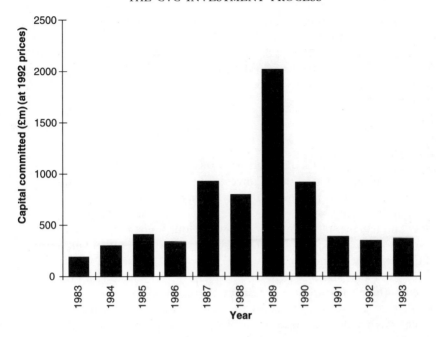

Figure 4.4 Capital commitments to UK independent venture capital funds
from all sources, 1984–93
Source: Adapted from Murray, 1994c

corporations that were not included in this survey.[6] Most of these corporations were US companies, indicating the international nature of indirect
CVC investment programmes discussed in Chapter 2 (Mast, 1991). The
BVCA figures therefore provide unjustified optimism concerning the
amount of indirect CVC finance invested by UK-based companies. However, given that investments by UK-based companies lag behind investments from other sources, and also that the total amount raised from all
sources increased significantly during 1994 (Chapter 2), it could be predicted that the amount raised from UK-based companies will increase in
the near future, despite the finding in Chapter 3 that few companies plan to
invest in this way.

The differences between pooled/multi-investor funds and client-based/
dedicated funds were discussed in Chapter 2. In this survey one-third of
investments (ten out of thirty-two) were in dedicated funds. The significance of this figure increases when it is noted that ten of the twenty-two
pooled fund investments were made by one company. If this company is
excluded, then investments in pooled funds only slightly exceeded investments in dedicated funds (twelve compared with ten). Whereas pooled
fund investments are typically made for educational or financial return

reasons, dedicated funds are used more often by companies with strategic or social responsibility objectives because they offer more contact with portfolio investees and avoid conflicting objectives with other investors. This supports the observation of Sykes (1990) and Mast (1991) that sole investor, client-based funds are more strategically effective for investing companies.

Characteristics of fund investments

The funds in which the companies in this survey had invested had themselves invested in a total of 432 investee firms.[7] This represents an average of 13.9 investments per fund. However, this mean figure is misleading since the number of investments made by individual funds varied considerably; one fund had made fifty investments while four funds were yet to invest for the first time. A majority of funds focus on the UK and USA in terms of the location of portfolio companies (Figure 4.5). Of the 432 investees, 194 were UK-based and 224 were US companies. The remaining fourteen were from continental Europe and Canada. Funds tend to invest in companies located in the same country as the fund managers. This reflects higher levels of deal flow from areas in closer proximity to the fund due to a distance decay effect (Florida and Kenney, 1988) and also the need for fund managers to be close to portfolio investees in order to facilitate contact and hands-on involvement. This therefore supports the earlier suggestion that

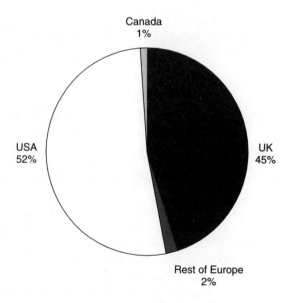

Figure 4.5 Country of origin of fund portfolio companies
Source: survey

120

foreign-owned subsidiaries invest in funds in the country in which they are based in order to evaluate the venture capital investment opportunities in that country. Also, many indigenous UK companies use indirect investments when investing abroad because they want a window on a broad range of international technologies, they frequently lack the knowledge and resources required to manage investments in foreign countries themselves, and they also often require less contact with investee firms.

The characteristics of the investments made by the funds in which corporates have invested are distinctive from those made by the venture capital industry as a whole. First, the size of investments is relatively small. The total amount invested by the thirty-one funds for which data were available was £343 million. Half of this total was invested in UK companies. The average investment size in all investees was £795,000, while the figure for UK investees only is slightly larger at £878,000. In comparison, 115 (out of 119) full members of the BVCA invested £1,231 million in 1,066 companies in the UK in 1993, representing an average of £1,155,000 (BVCA, 1994). However, the mean figures are again somewhat misleading because the survey data are skewed towards smaller investment sizes. Considering only investments made in UK-based companies, the median investment size in this survey was £0.33 million, and 60 per cent of investments were under £0.5 million. This provides some evidence that corporate investors are an important source of funding for venture capital funds specialising in making investments of less than £0.5 million.

Second, almost all (twenty-nine) of the thirty-two funds had a 'focused' investment strategy, in that they specifically targeted particular stages of development, levels of technology and industrial sectors. Again considering only UK investees, 84 per cent of investments have involved the provision of seed, start-up or other early stage finance (Figure 4.6). In contrast, only 14 per cent of the total financings made by members of the BVCA in 1994 were in these categories (BVCA, 1995b). Indeed, Mast (1991) noted that most corporations look only at focused funds today, and MacDonald (1991: 27) observed that 'a large corporation that invests in funds which have an investment strategy compatible with its own strategic interests can greatly increase its investment opportunities'. These findings therefore suggest that the corporate sector is a valuable source of finance for the diminishing number of venture capitalists specialising in making investments in early stage firms.

In addition to a focus on early stage firms, 80 per cent of investments in UK companies were in technology-based businesses (Figure 4.7). In 1993, only 21 per cent of all investments made by members of the BVCA were in high technology firms (BVCA, 1994), and most of these were later stage expansion, MBI or MBO deals (Cookson, 1994). Investments made by the funds in this survey concentrated on the utilities and computer sectors, closely followed by healthcare and pharmaceuticals, electronics

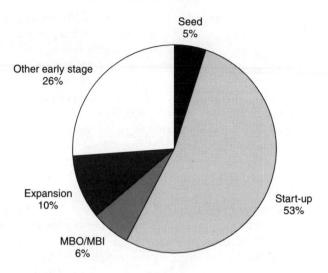

Figure 4.6 Stages of business development of investments by venture capital
funds in which corporates have invested (UK investees only)
Note: Based on data from 180 investee companies
Source: survey

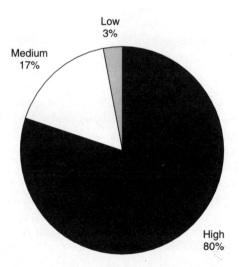

Figure 4.7 Technology focus of investments by venture capital funds
in which corporates have invested (UK investees only)
Note: Based on data from 172 investee companies
Source: survey

and biotechnology. Small firms operating in high technology sectors such as these tend to experience the greatest difficulties in raising equity finance due to their high-risk nature (Chapter 2). It is interesting to note that investments in non-UK (predominantly US) companies have been concentrated to an even greater extent in early-stage (96 per cent) and high technology (93 per cent) firms.

Given these findings it is reasonable to suggest that indirect CVC investment has a potentially valuable role to play in ensuring that venture capital funds specialising in investing in small early stage TBFs continue to survive. In this sense the corporate sector can help to guarantee the survival of *classic* venture capital investment in early stage companies (Bygrave and Timmons, 1992; Abbott and Hay, 1995). At a time when the fund-raising environment for all venture capitalists, and particularly those specialising in making investments in early stage TBFs, is causing considerable concern to the industry (Murray, 1992b; 1995; Murray and Lott, 1995), the identification of such an alternative funding source is of critical importance.

Direct CVC

Characteristics of direct investments

The twenty-two companies in this survey for which information is available (out of twenty-three companies) that had made direct, internally managed venture capital investments, invested in a total of two hundred and five firms. However, sixty of these investments had been made by one company which invested via an internally managed fund and, for the purposes of this survey, is referred to as 'Corporation X'. The three companies (out of four) for which information is available that had made direct investments via an internally managed venture capital fund had invested in a total of eighty-two companies (a mean of twenty-seven firms per fund, but a median of just eighteen). The nineteen corporations that had made ad hoc investments had a total of a hundred and fifteen investees (a mean of six per company, but a median of just two, with fifteen companies making four or less investments). In the cases of the majority (61 per cent) of the two hundred and five investees the investing company had only made one round of financing.

A majority of the investee companies were of UK origin (Figure 4.8), with UK companies accounting for 81 per cent (166) of all investees.[8] The dominance of direct CVC investments in UK-based companies contrasts with indirect CVC where 52 per cent of portfolio investees were based in the USA compared to only 45 per cent in the UK. Direct investments are usually made in UK firms because of the strategic motivations of companies making such investments. It was found earlier in this chapter that many

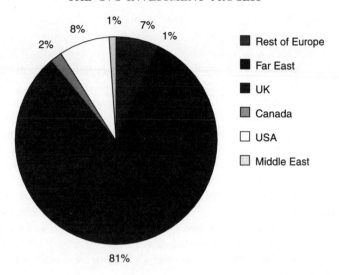

Figure 4.8 Country of origin of direct investee firms
Source: survey

direct corporate investors nurture their investees and establish further business relationships with them. Investors therefore seek investments within relatively close geographical proximity to increase the level of contact they have with investee firms. This is in contrast to indirect investors who often have non-strategic objectives, or are seeking a window on a broad range of foreign products and technologies and hence do not require close contact with investee firms.

All the internally managed CVC investments made by the companies in this survey were made in the period 1981 to 1994 inclusive, and at least one investment was made in every one of these years. The findings show an initial increase in the number of internally managed investments made in the second half of the 1980s (Figure 4.9). In 1989 the levels doubled those of the previous year, and a peak (thirty-eight investments/ten from Corporation X) was reached in 1990 (two years after the peak level for indirect investment). Since 1991, and particularly since 1992, the levels of direct CVC have declined, although the 1994 figure includes only investments made in the first six months of that year.

While the *number* of direct investments increased steadily to a peak in 1990/1991 before decreasing, the *amounts* invested each year form a less regular pattern (Figure 4.9). With the exception of 1981 when almost £6 million (approximately £11 million at 1992 prices) was invested (in only two investments), the amount invested prior to 1987 was minimal (total of £1.87 million – approximately £5 million at 1992 prices – from 1982 to 1986 inclusive). In contrast, in the late 1980s and early 1990s (until 1993)

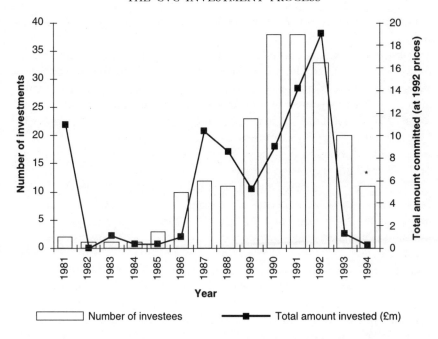

Figure 4.9 Dates of direct CVC investments and amounts invested, 1981–94
Notes: * 1994 figure for first 6 months of year only
Amounts invested based on data from investments by 16 companies in 118 investees
Source: survey

almost £60 million (nearly £70 million at 1992 prices) was invested with a peak of approximately £19 million being reached in 1992. Since 1992 the amount invested has declined considerably. The reasons for this most recent decline will be discussed later in this chapter.

A total of £68.7 million was invested by the sixteen (out of twenty-three) companies for which data were available in 118 investee firms, representing an average of £582,000 per investee. The total amount invested in UK firms (which accounted for 106 of the 118 investees) was £46.9 million with a mean investment size of £442,500. However, the mean investment size for non-UK investees was much larger at £1.82 million. As with indirect investments, these figures mask a broad range of investment sizes ranging from £30,000 (for the smallest social responsibility investments) to £7 million (for one strategically oriented investment). However, the median investment size for UK investees was just £80,000 and almost two-thirds of investments involved amounts of under £250,000. The few direct investments in non-UK-based companies were much larger, with a median size of £965,000. This clearly indicates that direct CVC is a source of finance with

125

the potential to help small UK firms which require funding in amounts less than £250,000.

Companies making direct CVC investments have typically invested in businesses seeking expansion finance. These accounted for almost three-quarters of investments in UK-based companies in this survey (Figure 4.10). This pattern is even more prominent than it initially appears since all direct CVC investments made in start-up firms in this survey were made by Corporation X. This is in contrast to indirect investments, 84 per cent of which were in either seed, start-up or other early stage firms, while only 10 per cent involved expansion finance.

The propensity for direct investments to involve the provision of expansion finance can be attributed to three main factors. First, many companies make direct CVC investments in firms which have a proven technology/product. The later stage orientation of direct investments is therefore consistent with the fact that the primary motive for this form of CVC is the identification of new *markets* and not necessarily new *technologies*. Also, strategic benefits are likely to be realised more quickly through investments in proven technologies. This will help to convince members of the investing company's board of the merits of direct investment (Collins and Doorley, 1991). Second, direct CVC investments are often made in companies with whom previous business relationships have been established. This supports Mast's (1991) comment that while companies are forming various kinds of relationships with small companies in their early stages, it is not until they become further established that the equity investment is made. The

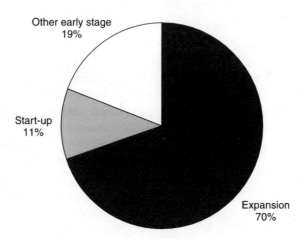

Figure 4.10 Stages of development of direct investee companies (UK only)
Note: Based on data from 161 investee companies
Source: survey

126

consequence is that corporations are increasingly investing directly in firms at the expansion and development stage. Third, the tendency for companies to invest directly in expansion stage firms may be the result of an inability on the part of corporations to identify investment opportunities soon enough to invest in early stage companies, as Roberts (1991) has suggested.

Direct CVC investments are also more likely than indirect CVC investments to be made in medium or low technology small firms (Figure 4.11). High technology companies accounted for only one-quarter of UK investees. While direct CVC investments were found to be common in the computer and information technology sectors (although the figures are somewhat misleading as forty-five of the fifty-one direct investments made in computer-related companies were made by just two corporations), investments were also abundant in the engineering, transport and service industries. This contrasts with indirect CVC where 80 per cent of UK investees operated in technology-based sectors, and is clearly related to the finding in Chapter 3 that many of the companies that make CVC invest- ments operate in low-technology industries. This also provides further confirmation that windows on new technologies are not the dominant objective of direct CVC investments. Access to new markets, business relationships and financial return are also important motives. Indeed, as was discussed in Chapter 2, investments in focused venture capital funds

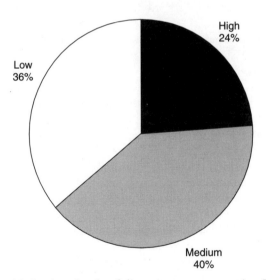

Figure 4.11 Technology levels of direct investee companies (UK only)
Note: Based on data from 161 investee companies
Source: survey

127

may be a more appropriate approach for corporations investing to obtain windows on new technologies. This is because such investments can potentially provide exposure to a much wider range of early stage technologies than is possible with direct CVC investments as a result of the relatively large number of deals screened by independent venture capitalists.

It is evident from these findings that while direct CVC can be a particularly valuable source of equity finance in amounts less than £250,000, it does not have the same potential as indirect CVC as a source of funding for early stage and technology-based companies. On the contrary, direct investees will frequently be established firms in medium or low technology industries seeking finance for expansion. Therefore, direct investment makes a positive, although currently modest, contribution towards closing the small business equity gap by providing funding in reasonably small amounts as well as value-added in the form of venture nurturing. Furthermore, direct CVC is much more likely than indirect CVC to involve investments in UK-based companies.

UK CVC: POST-INVESTMENT EXPERIENCES OF INVESTING COMPANIES

The survey findings therefore suggest that CVC investment has the potential to become a valuable source of finance for small firms. However, while this potential clearly exists, it was confirmed in Chapter 3 that CVC investment is underdeveloped in the UK, particularly in comparison with the USA, and therefore its contribution to closing the equity gap remains limited.

As was noted in Chapter 3, the underdeveloped nature of UK CVC has been exacerbated since the late 1980s as a number of corporations that have been involved in making investments have closed their venture capital operations. This trend is reflected in the decline in the number of companies making CVC investments in this survey (see Figures 4.3 and 4.9). Although more than half of the sample companies that have used CVC as a strategy continue to make venture capital investments, six (50 per cent) of the twelve corporations that have invested in externally managed venture capital funds no longer make such investments, and nine (39 per cent) of the twenty-three companies that have invested directly have stopped their internally managed CVC operations. Although this decline has been partly offset by a number of new companies that have only recently started making venture capital investments, the withdrawal of numerous companies from CVC requires an explanation. An important issue concerns the reasons why companies have stopped making CVC investments, and particularly whether their withdrawal from this activity is a result of disappointment with investment performance. The answers to these questions will provide further clues as to the underdeveloped nature of UK CVC.

CVC investment performance

Performance is not easily quantifiable, particularly when associated with strategic benefits, and awareness of potential inaccuracies caused by the subjectivity involved in rating one's own performance is vital (Siegel *et al.*, 1988). This survey required respondents to report perceived levels of performance of their CVC activities relative to their companies' objectives. While poor performance and dissatisfaction could clearly be the result of unrealistic objectives, the need remains to identify the importance of disillusionment with CVC strategy in determining why companies stop making investments.

Executives from all six of the companies that still make indirect CVC investments stated that their investments to date have performed at least satisfactorily. In contrast, the six corporations that no longer make indirect investments felt that their investments had performed badly. This is a clear indication that companies have stopped making externally managed CVC investments due to disappointment with the performance of their investments. Indeed, executives from five of the six companies that no longer make indirect investments explained that their companies had withdrawn from the activity because their investments had failed to meet objectives.

However, this distinction is less clear in the case of direct CVC. Of the fourteen companies that still make direct CVC investments, 86 per cent were satisfied with the performance of their investments while only 14 per cent had been disappointed. Of the nine companies that no longer make direct CVC investments, 67 per cent believed the performance of their investments to have been satisfactory or better, while 33 per cent felt that investment performance had been poor. These figures suggest that, at least in the case of direct CVC, the decision of many companies to no longer invest is often unrelated to the performance of their previous CVC investments. In support of this, executives from only three of the nine companies that no longer make direct investments attributed their companies' withdrawal from CVC to poor investment performance.

The perceived performance of CVC investment differs according to the parameters used to measure it. There is a need to distinguish between indirect and direct CVC since the performance of individual parameters may be different for each form of investment. Table 4.5 and Figure 4.12 indicate the perceived performance of indirect and direct investments. Responses are rated on a four point scale relating to the performance of various parameters for each company. Mean scores for each parameter are provided.

Companies making indirect CVC investments for non-strategic reasons believe their investments to have performed better than do companies investing with more strategically oriented objectives. Parameters associated with financial gain, social responsibility and learning about venture capital

Table 4.5 CVC performance ratings for individual parameters – indirect and direct CVC

Parameter	Indirect CVC*		Direct CVC**	
	Mean score	Rank	Mean score	Rank
Learn about venture capital	2.57	1	2.82	3
Obtain publicity	2.50	2	—	—
Social responsibility	2.13	3	2.60	7
Financial return on investment	2.00	4	2.14	13
Help suppliers/customers	2.00	4	2.63	5
Improvement of manufacturing processes	1.80	6	2.20	11
Assess potential acquisition candidates	1.80	6	2.33	9
Exposure to new technologies	1.67	8	2.15	12
Develop business relationships	1.67	8	2.83	2
Identification of new products	1.50	10	2.08	14
Lower manufacturing costs	1.40	11	2.25	10
Identification of new markets	1.40	11	2.35	8
Development of core business	1.40	11	2.62	6
Diversification vehicle	1.33	14	1.89	15
Assure continued supply of materials/ components	1.00	15	2.75	4
Change corporate culture	1.00	15	1.86	16
Assist spin-outs from company	1.00	15	3.67	1

Notes: Scale: 1, unsuccessful; 2, satisfactory; 3, highly successful; 4, outstanding
* Data from the twelve companies that had made indirect investments
** Data from the twenty-three companies that had made direct investments
Source: survey

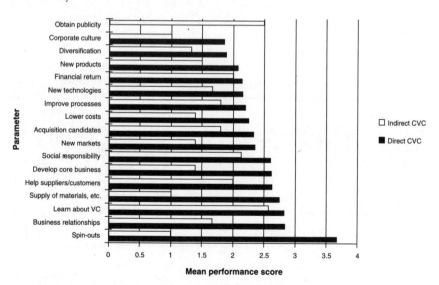

Figure 4.12 CVC performance: indirect and direct comparison

are ranked higher than strategic parameters. This further suggests that indirect CVC is a particularly appropriate investment method for companies with non-strategic objectives. Indeed, all six companies that are no longer involved with indirect CVC had previously made investments for strategic purposes.

Direct investments have performed better than indirect CVC across a wide range of parameters, with investments made for strategic, financial, social responsibility and educational purposes proving successful in many cases. Fourteen of the top sixteen parameters for direct CVC, ranked in terms of performance, were considered to be at least satisfactory by the survey respondents, compared with only the top five parameters in the case of indirect CVC. These high levels of success may explain the tendency for companies that have made direct investments to continue to do so and also further suggest that many companies that have withdrawn from direct CVC have done so for reasons unrelated to the performance of their prior investments. The highest ranked performance parameters for direct CVC were generally more strategically oriented than with indirect investment. By far the best performing parameter in this survey was the use of direct CVC as a means of spinning out ventures from within the corporation.[9] The high ranking of strategic parameters supports the observations of Siegel *et al.* (1988) who found exposure to new technologies, markets, products and acquisition candidates to be the best performing parameters of CVC.

Problems experienced by CVC investors

There are a number of potential problems that corporate venture capitalists might face which may hinder the progress and performance of their investments (Rind, 1981; Warren and Kempenich, 1984; Ormerod and Burns, 1988; Siegel *et al.*, 1988; Winters and Murfin, 1988; Sykes, 1990; Collins and Doorley, 1991; Block and MacMillan, 1993). These include a shortage of appropriately skilled corporate managers, lack of autonomy of investing departments and conflicts of interest between corporate executives, fund managers and entrepreneurs. However, respondents indicated that no such tensions were considered to be even slightly problematic for the companies in this survey. While individual respondents outlined the significance of particular obstacles, no constraints were problematic in aggregate form (Table 4.6).

For companies undertaking indirect CVC the most significant problems were inadequate deal flow, incompatible corporate and entrepreneurial cultures, conflicting objectives of corporate and venture capitalist, underestimation of the riskiness of venture capital by the investing company and a lack of clear mission of the company's investment programme. Most of the top seven ranked constraints for direct CVC, including lack of clear mission of investment programme, conflicting objectives of different parties and

Table 4.6 Rankings of obstacles to successful CVC performance – indirect and direct CVC

Obstacle/problem	Indirect CVC*		Direct CVC**	
	Mean score	Rank	Mean score	Rank
Inadequate deal flow	1.92	1	1.35	11
Incompatibility between corporate and entrepreneurial cultures	1.92	1	1.61	4
Conflicting objectives of corporate and venture capitalist	1.83	3	—	—
Underestimation of riskiness of venture capital by investing company	1.75	4	1.52	6
Lack of clear mission of company's investment programme	1.67	5	1.70	2
Lack of venture capital expertise in investing department	1.58	6	1.57	5
Inflexible corporate environment	1.50	7	1.52	6
Lack of communication with venture capital fund managers	1.50	7	—	—
Insufficient contact with investee companies	1.50	7	—	—
Not-Invented-Here Syndrome	1.42	10	1.43	8
Inadequate influence over investments made by venture capital fund	1.42	10	—	—
Short-term corporate philosophy	1.33	12	1.39	10
Legal problems	1.33	12	—	—
Poor state of UK venture capital industry	1.25	14	—	—
Lack of management time/resources	1.25	14	—	—
Lack of support from board level in investing company	1.17	16	1.22	14
Lack of experienced personnel in venture capital fund/s	1.17	16	—	—
Product compatibility problems	1.17	16	—	—
Lack of authority of investing department to make independent decisions	1.08	19	—	—
Lack of understanding of investees' strengths and weaknesses	—	—	1.83	1
Conflicting objectives of corporate and investees	—	—	1.70	2
Lack of independent venture capital investment expertise	—	—	1.43	8
Lack of communication with investee companies	—	—	1.26	12
Manufacturing difficulties	—	—	1.26	12

Notes: Scale: 1, insignificant; 2, slightly problematic; 3, significant; 4, highly problematic
* Data from the twelve companies that had made indirect investments
** Data from the twenty-three companies that had made direct investments
Source: survey

lack of venture capital expertise, are also ranked in the top seven problems for indirect CVC. However, inadequate deal flow, ranked first in the case of indirect CVC, is a much less significant constraint for direct CVC where it is ranked eleventh. This seems surprising given that one of the supposed advantages of investing in externally managed funds is a superior deal flow on account of the relatively large number of potential investees screened by independent fund managers.

These rankings largely support those of a survey of US corporations (Siegel *et al.*, 1988) that distinguished between obstacles originating from relations between the parent corporation and the CVC activity and obstacles related to the CVC activity itself. However, the US study – which did not differentiate between indirect and direct investments – did find a lack of authority of investing departments to make independent decisions to be a much more significant problem than is suggested in this survey.

Once companies have gained experience of the venture capital process, many of the obstacles encountered can be overcome. Indeed, Siegel *et al.* (1988: 243) stated that 'it is clear that the more experienced CVCs learn to ameliorate the impact of a number of obstacles that plague less experienced CVCs'. Two-thirds of executives from companies that had made CVC investments (indirect and/or direct) believed that a majority of the problems identified could be overcome. Approximately three-quarters of the companies that had invested directly, and experienced at least one constraint which they considered to be significant, still invested directly in venture capital. However, in the case of indirect CVC the more constraints encountered by companies the more likely they were to have withdrawn from CVC.

Summary

The survey findings indicate that for some corporations, and particularly those investing indirectly, poor investment performance has resulted in disillusionment with the CVC process and led to a withdrawal from CVC activity. While poor performance has sometimes been the result of particular problems encountered by investing companies, it has more often been related to an inappropriate choice of investment method and may often reflect unrealistic objectives. The results of this survey strongly suggest that while indirect CVC is usually more appropriate for realising financial and social responsibility goals, direct CVC is a more appropriate form of investment for corporations with strategic motivations.

However, despite the recognition of the importance of the performance factor in determining whether a company will continue its CVC operations, it must also be noted that many corporations that no longer make investments, and particularly those that have previously invested directly, nevertheless believe their investments to have performed well. Although the perceived success of direct investments may be the result of less rigorous performance criteria applied to ad hoc investments, it is notable that when constraints have been experienced they have often been successfully overcome and have therefore not been the cause of withdrawal from CVC activity. Rather than being disillusioned with direct CVC many corporations no longer make such investments because of a wider corporate decision to move towards concentrating on a more focused core business. Such restructuring has largely resulted from external pressures on companies to reduce investment in speculative areas and has curbed the need for strategic CVC investments and indeed strategic partnerships *per se* (Bakker *et al.*, 1994; Houlder, 1995). Withdrawal from direct CVC is relatively easy since many investment programmes are not deeply rooted.

CONCLUSIONS

The aim of this chapter has been to examine in detail the CVC investment process. The survey has built on our knowledge of the investing company's motivations for making CVC investments by outlining the internal organisation of CVC investment and the investee and fund selection processes used by corporate investors. Related to this, it has also identified the characteristics of CVC investments and the firms which typically receive this finance, thus providing an indication of the role of CVC in the closing of the equity gap. Finally, the post-investment experiences of investing companies have been examined, with particular emphasis placed on the role of these experiences in determining whether a company will continue to make CVC investments or withdraw from the activity.

It has been recognised that the two organisational alternatives for CVC are either to make investments via an in-house function or via a subsidiary company (Warren and Kempenich, 1984; Siegel *et al.*, 1988; Mast, 1991). This survey has found that the choice of strategy in this respect reflects the corporate objectives for investing. Companies investing indirectly invest via both in-house functions and subsidiaries. However, while companies investing directly via an internally managed fund usually establish a separate subsidiary for this purpose, ad hoc direct investors tend to invest via in-house functions. This distinction largely reflects the differing motives of these two sets of investors. Those investing via internally managed funds typically have financial motives and therefore do not require close contact with head office (Pratt, 1994), but those involved in ad hoc CVC tend to make fewer investments (i.e. not warranting the establishment of a subsidiary company) and often have strategic objectives, therefore requiring close communication with the investing company's main board.

The differing objectives of indirect and direct investors are also reflected in the selection of fund managers and investee firms. For indirect investors two factors are of major importance in the selection of fund managers;

first, the fund manager's experience and track record, and second, the fund's investment vehicle and focus. The latter factor is of particular importance in the case of companies with strategic motives. Companies investing directly identify potential investee firms through continual searching and via intermediaries. Some already have vertical or horizontal relationships with their investees. When selecting firms in which to invest, companies with strategic objectives place particular emphasis on the nature of the firm's business, and especially its products and markets. This largely reflects the typically strategic motives of these investors, supporting the comments of Roberts (1991). However, the relatively few companies that invest directly for social responsibility related purposes tend to be more concerned with entrepreneur and management team criteria.

Very few of the companies that have made indirect CVC investments provide nurturing assistance or establish further business relationships with investee firms. This largely reflects their non-strategic objectives. However, the degree of communication between investor and investee firms is understandably higher in the case of direct CVC because of the typically strategic motives of companies and the absence of a venture capitalist intermediary which can act as a buffer.

Therefore, the motives of investing companies have a strong influence on the form of CVC investments, the types of investee companies sought and the degree of contact that is required with these firms. Given that a wide range of corporate motives exist, CVC investments and the characteristics of investee firms are far from homogenous. This survey has found that CVC investments have been made in a number of small firms operating in technology-based and other industrial sectors at various stages of firm development. However, it is important to distinguish between direct and indirect CVC. Both indirect and direct forms of CVC can help provide finance in amounts of less than £500,000. Indeed, direct CVC investments often involve amounts of less than £250,000, an area of the equity finance spectrum that is particularly underdeveloped (Mason and Harrison, 1992; Murray, 1994b). In addition, a majority of indirect CVC investments are made in early stage TBFs, indicating the role of the corporate sector in aiding the growth of such companies while providing much needed finance for independent venture capital funds with an early stage high technology focus. However, direct CVC investments are far more likely to be made in later stage companies operating in medium or low technology sectors.

However, despite the potential of CVC as a source of equity finance for a broad range of small, unquoted firms, it was found in Chapter 3 that this form of investment remains underdeveloped in the UK. This partly reflects the withdrawal of several companies from CVC, and particularly indirect investment, since the late 1980s. This survey has provided an insight into the reasons for this withdrawal and has again emphasised distinctions between direct and indirect CVC. Companies that no longer make indirect

135

investments have typically been disappointed with the performance of their investments. This disappointment has sometimes been the result of specific post-investment operational problems, but largely reflects the failure of indirect CVC to meet the strategic objectives of some investors. However, companies that have withdrawn from direct CVC have typically done so as part of a move back to core business and not because of unfavourable post-investment experiences. These findings help to explain the observation in Chapter 3 that many of the companies that are considering making CVC investments for strategic purposes in the future are more likely to use internally managed techniques.

Chapters 3 and 4 have provided a detailed investigation of CVC from the perspective of the investing company. They have identified the motivations of companies that make CVC investments as well as the reasons why other companies prefer to use alternative strategies. They have examined the relationship between objectives and investment type, internal organisation, investee selection and investment characteristics and consequently aided our understanding of the role of particular forms of CVC in the bridging of the equity gap. Furthermore, these chapters have considered the reasons for the underdeveloped nature of CVC investment in the UK, particularly in comparison with the USA.

Chapters 5 and 6 of this book consider CVC from the perspective of the finance recipients, namely venture capital fund managers and small firms. These chapters are important for two reasons. First, in any study of inter-firm alliances designed to examine the dynamics and motivations behind a particular form of collaboration it is important to consider the relationship from both perspectives. Without such an approach, an understanding of the objectives, power relations and experiences of all parties is impossible, thus resulting in an incomplete picture of the nature of specific alliance forms. Second, a major aim of this study is to identify the importance of CVC as a source of finance for small firms, and particularly TBFs and the venture capital funds which specialise in investing in such firms. While Chapter 4 has provided an indication of this importance, it has been unable to view CVC from the recipient's perspective. This is clearly vital before an accurate assessment of the role of CVC can be made. Chapter 5 therefore considers indirect CVC from the venture capital fund manager's point of view, while Chapter 6 focuses on the experiences of technology-based firms that have raised CVC finance.

5

EXTERNALLY MANAGED CVC
The fund manager's perspective

INTRODUCTION

Indirect, externally managed CVC was defined in Chapter 2 as the process by which a non-financial company invests as a limited partner in an independent venture capital fund. This fund is managed by experienced venture capitalists and can be either 'multi-investor' or 'client-based' (Honeyman, 1992). The identification of non-financial companies as limited partners in venture capital funds is particularly significant given that fund managers are increasingly encountering problems in raising funds from institutional investors (e.g. insurance companies and pension funds). In Chapter 2, the pressures on fund managers to realise higher returns in shorter time periods were noted, along with the increasing ambivalence of institutions to investments in high risk early stage and technology-based deals. Despite record fund-raising figures for members of the BVCA in 1994 (BVCA, 1995a), the majority of these funds were raised by MBO/MBI specialists and not *classic* venture capitalists making early stage technology investments.

The findings outlined in Chapters 3 and 4 imply that, unlike other limited venture capital partners, non-financial companies *are* interested in investing in *classic* venture capital funds. This clearly reflects corporate objectives for making indirect venture capital investments, and specifically their desire to obtain a window on a wide range of early stage new technologies. Consequently, indirect CVC investment has been found (Chapter 4) to be a potentially valuable source of finance for small firms, and in particular TBFs that are in the early stages of their development (considered in more detail in Chapter 6). However, in order for the potential of the corporate sector as an alternative finance source for *classic* venture capital funds to be properly understood there is a need to examine the role of non-financial companies from the perspective of the fund manager.

137

RESEARCH AIMS AND METHODOLOGY

Research aims

This survey considers indirect CVC investment from the point of view of the venture capital fund manager. It aims to investigate further the sugges-tion that non-financial companies are an important alternative source of finance for venture capital funds, and in particular those which specialise in making investments in early stage technology-based firms. First, the char-acteristics of investments made by non-financial companies in venture capital funds are identified in order for the nature of the corporate inves-tor-fund manager relationship to be clarified. This includes an analysis of the fund managers' perceived motivations of corporate investors. Second, the investments made by the funds in which companies have invested are analysed so as to provide an indication of the funds' specialisms and specifically their role in financing early stage TBFs. Third, this survey examines the opinions of fund managers regarding the advantages and disadvantages of indirect CVC investment, not only for themselves, but also for investing companies and portfolio investees. This indicates the worth of indirect CVC investment from the point of view of the fund manager. Finally, fund managers' views on the extent of indirect CVC investment in the UK are considered, along with a discussion on the possible future levels of this activity.

This research therefore attempts to answer the following questions:

- How significant are corporate sources of finance for independent and affiliated venture capital funds in the UK?
- What are the characteristics of, and motivations behind, corporate investments?
- What are the characteristics of the investments of venture capital funds in which corporates have invested?
- What do venture capitalists perceive to be the advantages and disadvan-tages of corporate investment in venture capital funds?
- What are the possible future trends regarding corporate investment in venture capital funds in the UK?

Methodology

The empirical information reported in this chapter was derived from a survey of a sample of UK-based venture capital fund managers. The four major sources used for sample compilation were *Venture Capital Report: Guide to Venture Capital in the UK and Europe* (Cary, 1993), the *British Venture Capital Association Directory 1992/3* (BVCA, 1992), the *UK Venture Capital Journal* (1989 onwards), and the *European Venture Capital Journal* (1989 onwards). A two-stage selection process was used to identify venture

138

capital firms appropriate for the survey. In stage one, firms had to satisfy two criteria:

- *Independent or affiliated* To ensure that funds were raised from external sources, venture capital firms had to be 'independent' (i.e. their funds are raised from third parties), or 'affiliated' (they have a close affiliation with a larger group, often a merchant bank, but operate as autonomous associates, raising and managing funds subscribed by external investors). Venture capital firms classified as 'captive' (i.e. do not raise their own finance, but instead draw on the resources of a larger financial institution of which they are a part) were excluded from the survey as, by definition, non-financial companies would not have invested in these funds.
- *Non MBO/MBI specialist* It has been noted (Chapter 2) that since the late 1980s there has been an increase in the number of venture capital firms concentrating on investing in MBO and MBI deals (Abbott and Hay, 1995; Murray, 1993; 1995; Murray and Lott, 1995). It was found in Chapter 3 that non-financial companies rarely invest in the funds managed by these venture capitalists as they do not meet their objectives for investing. Therefore, such venture capital firms were considered to be inappropriate for this survey.

The research questions are largely concerned with the experiences of venture capitalists that have raised finance for their funds from corporate sources. As a result, the second stage of the selection process sought to identify venture capital firms which had, or at least were likely to have, raised finance from large companies. In addition, the views of the most experienced venture capitalists were considered to be of great importance. Therefore, the remaining venture capitalists had to satisfy one or more of the following three criteria based on information available in the source material or in industry literature and press reports.

- According to the source material, the business literature and/or the press, at least one of the funds managed by the venture capitalist has raised finance from non-financial companies.
- The venture capitalist is reported in any of the source publications to make investments in technology-based firms. This is important given both the finding in Chapter 4 that funds investing in TBFs are more likely to have raised finance from non-financial companies and also the aim of this survey to examine the significance and advantages of the corporate sector as a source of finance for funds which invest in early stage TBFs.
- The firm is well established and experienced in venture capital. In a survey of directors of UK venture capital organisations, Murray (1991a) outlined the importance of seeking the views of experienced fund managers in venture capital research.

These procedures resulted in the identification of forty-nine venture capitalists. Table 5.1 indicates the basis on which they were selected for the survey. All of these firms were contacted by introductory letter and follow-up telephone calls, with initial contact made with a company director, and thirty-nine agreed to participate in the survey (80 per cent response rate).

Either a face-to-face or a telephone interview was conducted with a fund manager from each of the thirty-nine participating venture capital firms. Face-to-face interviews were necessary for fund managers who had experience of corporate investors, while telephone interviews were more appropriate for venture capitalists who had not raised funds from non-financial companies reflecting the lower levels of information required and the consequent shorter interview duration. The advantages and potential problems of these methodological techniques were discussed in Chapter 2.

SIGNIFICANCE OF CORPORATE SOURCES OF FINANCE FOR UK-BASED VENTURE CAPITAL FUNDS

Over one-third (sixteen/41 per cent)[1] of the thirty-nine venture capitalists who participated in the survey had raised finance from the corporate sector. While this clearly tells us nothing about the absolute amounts raised nor the importance of this source relative to other finance sources, it does confirm that non-financial companies have been limited partners in a number of venture capital funds managed by UK-based fund managers.

Of those twenty-three venture capitalists that had not raised finance from corporate sources, approximately one-quarter had approached non-financial companies in search of funding but had been unsuccessful. The companies that had been approached had either disagreed with the concept of corporate venture capital altogether, believed that direct venture capital investment would be more appropriate for their objectives, or felt that it was economically a poor time for them to make any venture capital investments. Consequently they had chosen not to invest. The remaining

Table 5.1 Criteria for selection of fund managers

Criterion	Number of venture capitalists* (n=49)	Percentage
Reports of CVC involvement	26	53
High tech industry preference	27	55
Established and experienced venture capital firm	21	43

Notes: *Venture capitalists could satisfy more than one criterion
Number of venture capitalists satisfying all three criteria = 3 (6%)
Number of venture capitalists satisfying more than one criterion = 22 (45%)
Source: survey

seventeen venture capitalists that had not raised finance from corporate sources had chosen not to target corporates as they had felt that traditional sources of venture capital funding were more accessible and also more appropriate. Several did not believe that non-financial companies would invest even if they were approached, and therefore they had not tried. Others felt that their funds were not suitable for corporate investors, and recognised the potential exiting problems and conflicts of interest that could result.

CORPORATE INVESTMENT IN VENTURE CAPITAL FUNDS: SOME CHARACTERISTICS

The sixteen venture capitalists who indicated that they had been involved with indirect CVC managed a total of seventy-two funds, forty-four (61 per cent) of which had raised finance from corporate sources. On average each of the sixteen venture capital firms had raised finance for 2.8 of the funds which they managed from the corporate sector. Almost all of these funds were closed funds, and just less than half were fully invested. Several characteristics of the corporate investors and their investments can be examined in order to further our understanding of both the significance of non-financial companies as a funding source for venture capitalists and the nature of large firm-fund manager relationships.

Number of corporate investors

Based on information from forty of the forty-four funds that had raised corporate finance, corporates had made a total of eighty-four invesments.[2] The average number of corporate investors in each of the funds was therefore 2.1; however, over half had only one corporate investor, and 93 per cent of funds had three or less corporate investors. The largest number of investors in a single fund was fifteen (Table 5.2). The propensity for funds to have only a small number of non-financial companies as limited partners may reflect the fears of fund managers that too many corporate

Table 5.2 Number of corporate investors in venture capital funds

	Number of corporate investors per fund					
	1	*2*	*3*	*4*	*5–10*	*10+*
Number of funds	24	5	8	0	2	1
	(60%)	(13%)	(20%)		(5%)	(3%)

Note: Based on data for forty funds
Source: survey

investors could lead to conflicting objectives and hence unease among investors.

Corporate investment size

The proportion of total fund value accounted for by corporate investment varies considerably within this sample. Table 5.3 shows that sixteen of the funds in which corporates had invested – almost half the total – had not raised finance from any other source (i.e. dedicated/client-based funds). The relative significance of dedicated funds supports the findings outlined in Chapter 4 which showed almost half of the funds in which the sample of non-financial companies had invested to be client-based. While dedicated funds are clearly popular with corporate investors, only a small number of venture capitalists manage such funds. Indeed, only five venture capital firms in this survey managed client-based funds, and one of these firms explained that the corporate's involvement was primarily for reasons of social responsibility rather than for strategic benefit. Moreover, twelve of the sixteen dedicated funds were managed by just one venture capital firm (Advent International).[3]

Overall, corporate investors have been significant investors relative to other sources. The average fund size was £16.7 million, and the average total corporate investment in each fund was only just less than half that figure (£8.1 million). But here again, this figure is influenced by Advent International and its twelve dedicated funds. If Advent is omitted then the average fund size increases to £17.4 million, but the average corporate investment falls to £4.3 million.

Countries of origin of corporate investors

The majority of non-financial companies that have invested in the surveyed venture capital funds were not indigenous UK companies (Figure 5.1). Only one-third of the corporate investors which were identified by respondents were from the UK. The remaining two-thirds were of non-UK

Table 5.3 Corporate contributions to venture capital funds relative to fund size

	Percentage of total funds from corporate sources										
	1–9	10–19	20–29	30–39	40–49	50–59	60–69	70–79	80–89	90–99	100
Number of funds	4	2	4	3	1	2	1	0	1	1	16
	(11%)	(6%)	(11%)	(9%)	(3%)	(6%)	(3%)		(3%)	(3%)	(46%)

Note: Based on data for thirty-five funds
Source: survey

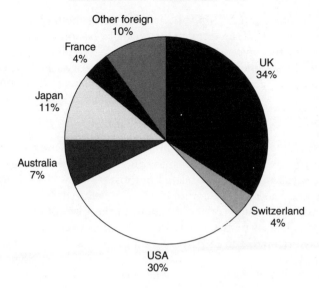

Figure 5.1 Countries of origin of named corporate investors
Source: survey

parentage, notably from the USA or Japan,[4] suggesting UK companies to be of only limited significance in providing finance for UK-based venture capital funds. This clearly confirms the suggestion made in Chapter 2 that most of the companies that have invested in UK venture capital funds are non-UK corporations.

Contacts with corporate organisations

The findings indicate that fund managers have to make the first move in attracting corporate funding. The overwhelming opinion among the respondents was that large corporate organisations have to be persuaded to invest and they will therefore rarely contact fund managers. Only 19 per cent of venture capitalists in this survey that had raised corporate finance indicated that corporates had approached them concerning the provision of finance for funds. The propensity for venture capitalists to contact potential corporate investors is supported by the finding in Chapter 3 that the majority of surveyed companies that had not made CVC investments had nevertheless been approached by fund managers regarding investment.

When negotiating funding, venture capitalists most commonly communicated with corporates at the board level. Indeed, fund managers believed that within most corporate organisations, venture capital investments were coordinated by top management at the executive committee level. New venture divisions and corporate development and finance officers also occasionally managed CVC operations, supporting the finding in Chapter 3 that some indirect CVC investments are made by in-house functions. In only two cases did the investing company employ a venture capital manager. While several respondents indicated the desirability of dealing with a venture capital manager specialised in the field, the opportunity to do so was a rarity.

Corporate motivations

According to the fund managers, non-financial companies make indirect CVC investments for three reasons: to benefit financially, strategically, or to invest for social responsibility-related purposes. Almost half of all venture capitalists that had received corporate finance believed that investing companies specifically sought financial benefit in the form of a high return on investment, while 31 per cent stated that the objectives of corporates were strategically oriented, and in particular concerned with obtaining windows on new technologies. One quarter of all respondents felt that individual corporates had both financial and strategic motivations. Corporate investors in 19 per cent of the venture capital firms were believed to be investing for reasons associated with social responsibility.

These findings suggest that the perceptions of fund managers are accurate since it was found in Chapter 3 that indirect CVC investments are typically financially or social responsibility-related, or motivated by the need to access new technologies. However, it was also found that many companies invest in order to learn about the venture capital process. This motivation appears not to have been recognised by fund managers.

Some venture capitalists felt that corporate objectives had changed over time, with several suggesting that financial motivations had become more significant as a result of dissatisfaction on the part of many corporates with the performance of strategically oriented indirect CVC investments. This supports the finding in Chapter 4 that several companies have now withdrawn from indirect CVC because of disappointing strategic returns. Alternatively, some large companies, having learnt about the venture capital process through indirect investment, may have turned to internally managed investment for meeting strategically oriented objectives, while investing indirectly for financial gain. Given that fewer companies are investing indirectly for strategic purposes, it follows that the small number of venture capitalists managing dedicated funds in the UK, which due to their very nature tend to be oriented towards strategic objectives, may reflect a lack of demand rather than a lack of supply.

Corporate involvement in funds

As was found in Chapter 4, the extent to which corporate investors become involved with the operations of the venture capital fund in which they have invested varies considerably. While half of the venture capitalists allowed substantial corporate involvement, usually in the form of a seat on the advisory committee or an influence in the assessment and monitoring of deals, almost as many permitted no corporate involvement at all. Not surprisingly, the degree of involvement tended to depend upon whether the managed funds were dedicated or pooled. As was suggested in Chapter 2, companies investing in dedicated funds experience far greater contact and closer communication with the venture capitalist managing the fund and enjoy more control over the investment process. In contrast, more than half of the investors in pooled funds were permitted no involvement with the funds, even if such involvement was desired.

Two-thirds of the venture capitalists set investment criteria themselves rather than allowing corporate investors to do so. Again, investors in dedicated funds tended to have a greater influence than those in pooled funds, although this influence was often limited to sectors of investment and investment size. It would seem that a further possible explanation for the lack of dedicated funds in the UK, and hence the lack of strategically oriented investment opportunities for large companies, is that venture capitalists are hesitant about allowing corporate investors too much influence over the investment process.

Corporate involvement with investee companies

A large proportion of the venture capital fund managers supported close contact between corporate investors and investee firms. Two-thirds of venture capitalists had permitted, and in some cases even encouraged, the establishment of investor–investee links in the belief that they would enable investing companies to gain access to windows on technology more easily, help establish contractual relationships between firms, and also provide other *value-added extras* to investments such as industry expertise. However, close contact with investee firms is usually desired only by companies investing for strategic purposes. Given that an increasing number of companies are investing for non-strategic reasons, largely as a result of their limited influence over fund investment decisions, it follows that the levels of contact are minimal, thus supporting the finding in Chapter 4 that the amount of value-added provided by companies investing indirectly is limited. Indeed, those fund managers that did not allow corporate investors contact with investee firms explained that the investing companies were not interested in strategic benefit and thus had no need to get closer to investees. Furthermore, some venture capitalists believed that too much direct contact and associated corporate pressure could harm the smaller firm.

145

CHARACTERISTICS OF VENTURE CAPITAL FUND INVESTMENTS

An investigation of the nature of the investments made by the forty-four funds in which corporates have invested can provide further evidence of the role of indirect CVC as an alternative funding source for small firms, and in particular early stage TBFs in the UK. The characteristics of fund investments are therefore examined under four headings.

Number and size of investments

In terms of number of investments made, great diversity existed within the sample. While the average number of investments made by each of the forty-four funds was 18.4, the figure ranged from zero to fifty. Average investment size per deal for these funds was £840,000, and half of the funds made typical investments of between £500,000 and £1 million (Figure 5.2). It was noted in Chapter 2 that the existence of an *equity gap* in the UK has been regularly debated (e.g. by Hall, 1989; Pratt, 1990; Mason and Harrison, 1992; 1995; Murray, 1993). The most frequently discussed aspect of the equity gap concerns the lack of provision of funds of less than £250,000 to new and small firms. It was recognised in Chapter 2 that the venture capitalist's reluctance to invest in small amounts reflects the un-economic nature of such investments given the high evaluation and monitoring costs associated with venture capital investment (Mason and

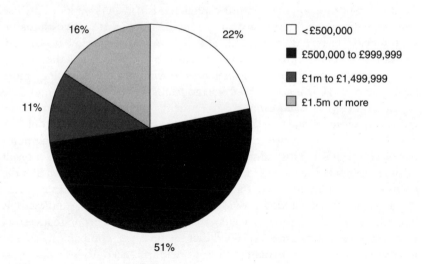

Figure 5.2 Investment sizes of funds that have raised finance from non-financial companies
Source: survey

Harrison, 1995). Although 22 per cent of the investments made by the funds in this survey were of less than £500,000, the findings still suggest that the role of funds in which corporates have invested in providing finance in tranches of less than £250,000 remains somewhat limited.

Investment type

A further aspect of the equity gap which is of particular significance to this survey, and indeed to the thesis as a whole, concerns the shortage of equity finance for early stage TBFs. It has been recognised (Chapter 2) that the number of venture capitalists specialising in making early stage technology-based investments has declined (Murray, 1992a; 1993; 1994b; 1995; Abbott and Hay, 1995; Murray and Lott, 1995) largely as a result of the preference of institutional investors for more cost efficient and safer later stage financings. However, the survey of companies that have made CVC investments outlined in Chapter 4 suggested that a large majority of indirect CVC investments are made via funds which specialise in investing in early stage TBFs as a result of the typical desire of investing companies to seek either strategic or financial gain from investments in such firms.

This survey supports the argument that non-financial companies are a valuable source of finance for venture capitalists with an early stage technology-based investment focus. A large majority (thirty-two/73 per cent) of the funds in this survey that had raised finance from corporates were described by the venture capitalists that manage them as *focused* rather than *general*, in that particular industrial sectors and stages of development were specifically targeted. In terms of industrial sector, the large majority of funds specialised in investing in technology-based sectors such as health-care, information technology, advanced materials, environmental products and services, and chemicals (Table 5.4). While this is not surprising given the nature of the sample selection process, it does support the findings of Chapter 4 by further indicating the significance of non-financial companies as a source of finance for funds with a technology focus. Moreover, the majority of funds specialised in making *early stage* investments. This is notable since it was recognised in Chapter 2 that a large proportion of the total number of venture capital investments that are made in TBFs involve MBO/MBI deals. Although most stages of investment, ranging from seed to MBO, were catered for by the forty-four funds in this sample, 65 per cent concentrated specifically on early stage investments (usually start-up and other early stage) (Figure 5.3). This is particularly significant since only 35 per cent of the funds managed by the twenty-three surveyed venture capitalists that had *not* raised finance from non-financial companies had an early stage investment focus. This therefore supports the suggestion that indirect CVC is an important source of finance for funds that specialise in making early stage technology-based investments.

147

Table 5.4 Sectors of investment of funds receiving corporate finance

Sector	No. of mentions	Sector	No. of mentions
Healthcare	11	Energy	1
Information technology	5	Industrial automation	1
Advanced materials	4	Food and drink	1
Environmental products and services	4	Defence	1
Chemicals	3	Leisure	1
Communications	2	Data sources	1
Computers	2	Electronics	1
Manufacturing	1		

Source: survey

Location of investees

A majority of the investments made by the venture capital funds in which corporates had invested were in UK companies. This supports the suggestion made in Chapter 4 that funds will tend to invest in firms located in the same country as the fund managers because of the greater deal flow from areas in close proximity to the fund (Florida and Kenney, 1988), and also the fund manager's need for close contact with investee firms. It also implies that UK-based TBFs are likely to benefit from indirect CVC

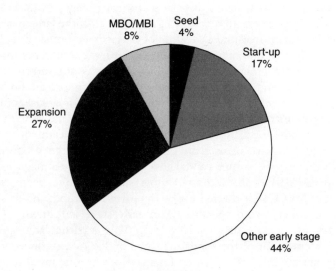

Figure 5.3 Investment stages of portfolio investees of funds that have raised finance from non-financial companies
Source: survey

investments made via UK-based funds. The findings show that fund investments that are made in UK firms are concentrated in the South East region. Indeed, Table 5.5 shows that for the funds for which data were available,[5] the spatial distribution of fund investments largely parallels the overall spatial distribution of venture capital investments in the UK. However, some differences are evident. First, indirect CVC investments are concentrated in the South of England to an even greater extent than is the case for venture capital investments in general (Martin, 1989; Mason and Harrison, 1991b; 1995). The greater concentration of indirect CVC investee firms in East Anglia is largely a result of the technology focus of the surveyed funds and the concentration of technology-based firms in Cambridge (Keeble, 1994) (see Chapter 6 for further discussion). Second, the Northern region has relatively more investments in the case of the survey sample which reflects the fact that one of the fifteen funds for which data were available had a regional investment focus and concentrated on investments in and around Newcastle. These findings imply that indirect CVC investment does not help to overcome the regional equity gap in the UK (as identified by Martin, 1989; Mason and Harrison, 1991b; 1995). It has been argued that a possible means of overcoming regional disparities is through the establishment of regional funds. The significant effect of the fund based in the North of England in this survey supports this suggestion.

Table 5.5 Spatial distribution of fund investments within the UK: comparison of survey funds and mean BVCA figures, 1989–94

Region	Percentage of investee firms	
	Surveyed funds*	BVCA members (mean figures for period 1989–1994)
South East	47.3	37.7
(Greater London)	(18.4)	(16.5)
(Rest of South East)	(28.9)	(21.2)
South West	2.0	5.7
East Anglia	8.0	4.0
West Midlands	7.0	8.5
East Midlands	3.3	6.3
Yorkshire and Humberside	3.9	7.7
North West	3.9	7.8
North	15.1	4.5
Scotland	10.0	12.2
Wales	0	3.7
Northern Ireland	0	2.0

Note: * Based on data from 15 funds and 152 investee firms
Sources: survey and BVCA, 1991; 1993; 1994; 1995a

The surveyed funds had also invested in companies in the USA as well as several continental European countries. As was noted in Chapter 4, the provision of indirect CVC finance for overseas companies is evidence of the global scanning process of multinational corporations. At a time of increasing global competition companies need to be aware of technological developments on a global scale and investment in innovative, foreign-based companies provides a way of keeping a watching brief on such developments. However, companies that do require windows on foreign technologies are more likely to invest in foreign venture capital funds because of the expertise of such funds in overseas markets (Chapter 4).

Fund performance

Any measure of the performance of a venture capital fund is relatively meaningless during the course of the fund's life. As a result, performance information is often cursory and subjective (Murray, 1994b). However, while it is clearly difficult to define, measure and compare the performance of different funds, a majority (60 per cent) of the venture capitalists in this survey believed that most of their funds which had raised finance from corporates were performing as well as other funds that had not received corporate money; indeed 19 per cent of respondents believed them to be performing better. Clearly, it cannot be implied from this that the presence of non-financial companies as limited partners in these funds has affected the funds' performance. However, it is possible to investigate the benefits, and indeed the problems, associated with corporate investors in venture capital funds. In order to do this there is a need to consider the advantages and disadvantages of this source from the fund manager's perspective. Such an analysis will further indicate whether non-financial companies are a valuable funding source for venture capital funds.

ADVANTAGES AND DISADVANTAGES
OF INDIRECT CVC

Corporate venture capital investment has been identified as one of a number of corporate development strategies that a large company may consider (Chapter 3). Clearly, the CVC option will be taken only if the non-financial company believes that the advantages of making venture capital investments outweigh the disadvantages relative to other strategies. Similarly, venture capital fund managers trade-off the advantages and disadvantages of raising finance from non-financial companies, and will not target corporate investors if they believe that their presence as limited partners will cause more problems than benefits for themselves and their portfolio investee firms. The sixteen fund managers identified in this survey as having raised corporate finance in the past identified several advantages

150

and disadvantages of indirect CVC for themselves, their investees and corporate investors. It is important to take these into account when considering the role of indirect CVC investment.

For the venture capital firm

Non-financial companies can be a highly beneficial source of finance for venture capital funds. Almost 90 per cent of the venture capitalists that had raised corporate finance stated that there were benefits to them of having corporate investors in their funds. Respondents recognised that large industrial companies can provide an alternative source of finance for venture capital funds at a time when the amount received from institutions is declining. Furthermore, many venture capitalists considered non-financial companies to be *value-added* investors, offering fund managers industry-specific knowledge and technical skills and advice, as well as providing an exit route for the venture capitalist in the form of a trade sale. Such value-added benefits help to distinguish the corporate sector from other, institutional investors. These findings support the comments of several authors (e.g. Bailey, 1985; Collins and Doorley, 1991; Murray, 1993) who have considered the benefits of corporate investors for fund managers.

However, as well as these advantages of indirect CVC for the fund manager, just over half of the surveyed venture capitalists drew attention to various disadvantages of this form of investment, most of which relate to the difficulty of understanding and managing the differing needs, motivations and levels of experience of corporate investors. For example, possible problems include the propensity for corporate investors to develop unrealistic expectations of their investments, and hence become very disillusioned with the venture capital process when the expected returns and strategic benefits do not materialise. As was found in Chapter 4, this disillusionment has led to the withdrawal of several companies from indirect CVC. Also, companies often become over-obsessed, consequently trying to place far too much pressure on investee firms and wanting to treat them as subsidiary companies. Fund managers may therefore have to act as a buffer to large companies. Corporate investors are often very short-termist, failing to recognise or understand the long-term nature of venture capital, and often problems arise due to the conflicting time scales and objectives of the venture capitalist and the corporate investors. This final observation has been reported numerous times in the corporate venture capital literature (e.g. by Hardymon *et al.*, 1983; Littler and Sweeting, 1987a).

For the corporate investor

Fund managers recognised several benefits for non-financial companies of investing in externally managed venture capital funds. Indeed, all but one of the venture capitalists in the survey believed there to be definite advantages to the corporate investor of investing in externally managed venture capital funds. According to respondents, investment in a fund allows the large company to benefit from the expert investment advice of the venture capitalist, a much larger deal flow and spread of investments than would be possible with even the most developed internally managed programme, as well as higher financial returns. According to three of the venture capitalists interviewed, corporates rarely understand venture capital well enough to succeed on their own. Lack of understanding of the nature of the venture capital process often leads the corporate to put too much pressure on the investee in direct deals, but by investing indirectly the venture capitalist acts as a buffer which protects the smaller company from direct and possibly damaging contact with the corporate investor. While many of these perceived benefits support the opinions of corporate executives highlighted in Chapter 3, it is again surprising that no fund managers recognised the possibility of corporate investors using the indirect CVC process to learn about venture capital before establishing their own internally managed operations.

There may also be several disadvantages of indirect CVC for the corporate investor, and indeed 81 per cent of the venture capitalists that had raised finance from corporate sources recognised areas of potential difficulty. Indirect investment in a venture capital fund may not allow companies with strategic motivations enough direct contact with investee firms, and hence make it difficult for them to establish close relationships. Particularly when investing in a pooled fund, a corporate may have very little say in the evaluation and selection of investments, and may find itself with stakes in companies totally unrelated to its business activities. However, it was recognised that these potential problems are only really relevant when the corporate objectives are strategic, and may be overcome with a more informed choice of investment method. As has been noted, dedicated funds, or indeed direct CVC investment, are more appropriate for investors seeking close contact with investee firms.

For the investee business

Benefits for investee firms of raising finance from a venture capital fund in which non-financial companies have invested (as opposed to a fund in which non-financial companies have not invested) were recognised by three-quarters of the surveyed fund managers. These benefits include the potential for obtaining *value-added extras* from the corporate investor such as industry-specific expertise, and also the possibility of forming strategic relationships with corporate investors. The presence of a corporate can also help to validate a small firm's products and thus enable it to compete successfully in the global marketplace. However, as has already been noted, the value-added benefits of corporate investors are usually realised only in cases where non-financial companies are investing with strategic motivations and desire closer contact and involvement with investee companies. It has been suggested that the number of companies investing indirectly for strategic purposes is decreasing. Nevertheless, any industry-specific knowledge made available to fund managers by investing corporations can indirectly benefit portfolio investee firms. The presence of the venture capital fund manager provides valuable financial expertise, as well as acting as a buffer to the corporate which, as mentioned earlier, can stifle the investee firm. This buffer is clearly not present when corporates invest directly in the equity of small companies.

Again, any advantages must be weighed against disadvantages. According to 44 per cent of fund managers, there can be problems for investee firms of receiving finance from funds in which non-financial companies have invested. Corporate impatience and the 'Big Brother' effect, whereby the presence of a corporate, even in this indirect form, may make other corporates suspicious and therefore unwilling to establish links themselves with the small firm, were issues mentioned by the survey respondents. In addition, corporate plans for acquisition and commercial confidentiality concerns, relating to Oakey's (1993) concept of *predatory networking* (i.e. the capturing or stifling of small firm ideas by corporate partners) (Chapter 1), were also seen as possible disadvantages for the investee company. Indeed, it was noted in Chapter 1 that much of the collaboration literature has drawn attention to the entrepreneur's distrust of large companies. While the venture capitalist buffer may reduce the likelihood of such corporate behaviour, the associated limited corporate exposure to investee companies may in turn inhibit the chances of small companies establishing further strategically beneficial relationships with their corporate investors.

CURRENT AND FUTURE LEVELS OF INDIRECT CVC

The survey of corporate executives (Chapters 3 and 4) provided confirmation of the underdeveloped nature of CVC investment in the UK. In Chapter 3, possible reasons for the relatively low levels of corporate involvement in venture capital in the UK in comparison with the USA were postulated, and the possible future levels of CVC investment in the UK were considered. It was found that while many corporate executives expect to see an increase in the levels of CVC, any increase is most likely to involve direct rather than indirect investment, reflecting the increasingly strategic motivations of corporate investors. This section considers the current and future levels of indirect CVC investment from the fund manager's perspective.

Corporate investment in venture capital funds:
UK/US comparisons

Although this survey has found a number of UK-based venture capitalists to have raised finance for their funds from the corporate sector,[6] and despite the recent increase in significance of corporate sources of finance for UK funds relative to their US counterparts (Chapter 2), the surveyed fund managers confirmed the commonly held belief that levels of indirect CVC in the UK are still considerably lower than in the USA. Almost all of the thirty-nine venture capitalists in this survey felt that in the UK, industrial corporations had been less willing to invest in venture capital funds than in the USA (Table 5.6). The limited involvement of UK-based companies in indirect CVC is exemplified by the fact that two-thirds of the corporate investors in this survey were non-UK companies (either based in foreign countries or UK-based subsidiaries of foreign-owned companies).

A number of reasons were postulated to explain the greater investment levels of non-financial companies in the USA. Many echo the comments of corporate executives outlined in Chapter 3. For example, US culture was commonly believed to be far more entrepreneurial and conducive to risk taking than is the case in the UK. In addition, the US venture capital industry is longer established than in the UK, dating back to 1946 with the formation of ARD (Bygrave and Timmons, 1992), while the UK industry has developed only since the late 1970s. As a result, US corporations are far more aware of the possibilities of becoming involved with equity investments. Numerous US venture capital firms have been established by former corporate managers, and several of the largest corporate players in the USA today were originally established during the 1950s, 1960s and 1970s with the help of venture capital backing (Bygrave and Timmons, 1992). Many such companies have since invested in venture capital funds themselves, with Apple, Lotus Development Corporation and Genentech providing good examples. The venture capitalists in this survey also felt that the greater propensity for US venture capital funds to invest in early stage technology-based deals helped to explain the increased tendency for corporates to invest in venture capital funds.

Table 5.6 Corporate willingness to invest in UK and US venture capital funds

'In the UK, corporates have been less willing to invest in venture capital funds than in the USA'	Number of respondents	Percentage
AGREE	35	90
DISAGREE	0	0
NO OPINION	4	10

Source: survey

Conversely, UK companies tend to be more inward looking, less adventurous, hesitant, untrusting, short-termist and extremely prone to the 'not invented here' syndrome. Such a corporate environment was recognised by Littler and Sweeting (1984) who described large mature companies as highly bureaucratised systems with extensive commitments to established business activities. According to Walker (1993) European business is essentially risk averse and frequently arrogant in its approach to small companies. Many UK corporations believe that they cannot justify risk to their shareholders, and are consequently more interested in outright acquisition or at least prefer direct CVC investments over which they have more control. This clearly corresponds with the findings from the corporate survey outlined in Chapters 3 and 4. Several venture capitalists believed that the performance of venture capital funds in the UK has not been as good as that of their US counterparts, and that this together with a more financially oriented investment philosophy and a lack of dedicated fund opportunities has left the industry unattractive to corporate investors.

Future involvement of surveyed fund managers

Many UK venture capitalists will not target the corporate sector for finance in the future. While only fifteen (38 per cent) of the thirty-nine venture capitalists in the survey stated that they would consider corporate sources of funding, twenty (51 per cent) said that they would not. The remaining four respondents were indecisive.

Venture capitalists that will target non-financial companies

The fund managers that indicated that they would target corporate investors for their funds in the future can be divided into those that had not previously raised finance from corporate sources and those that had. Approximately one-third of the venture capitalists that had not raised finance from non-financial companies previously stated that they would target corporate investors in the future (Table 5.7), largely because institutional funds had become less accessible, and also because corporates can be particularly beneficial investors and hence are well worth targeting. This not only further illustrates the need for alternative sources of venture capital funding in the UK, but also indicates that, for a number of venture capitalists that have not raised finance from corporates in the past, the perceived advantages of this source now outweigh the potential disadvantages. Half of the venture capitalists who had raised corporate finance for their funds in the past said that they would continue targeting this source in the future. They justified their decision by highlighting many of the specific advantages of corporate investment outlined earlier in this chapter.

Table 5.7 Indirect CVC: future involvement of surveyed fund managers

	*Venture capitalists that **will** target corporates in the future*	*Venture capitalists that **will not** target corporates in the future*	*Venture capitalists that **might** target corporates in the future*	*Total*
Venture capitalists that **have not** raised finance from corporates	7	13	3	23
Venture capitalists that **have** raised finance from corporates	8	7	1	16
Total	15	20	4	9

Source: survey

Most venture capitalists that planned to target corporates in the future stated that their most popular target group would be technology-based companies which sometimes includes overseas companies looking for windows on UK technology. This reflects the technology focus of many of the funds concerned. Other fund managers were interested in companies who want to invest for reasons of social responsibility. While 13 per cent of the venture capitalists planning to target corporates expressed a preference for medium-sized companies, a further 13 per cent said that they would target only the largest firms. The venture capitalists believed that their funds would be particularly attractive to corporate investors as they either specialised in early stage technology-based investment or had an impressive investment track record and/or experience of corporate investors. However, few respondents were prepared to tailor their funds specifically for corporate needs, despite the finding of this study that a clear understanding of such needs is vital.

Venture capitalists that will not target non-financial companies

The venture capital firms that indicated that they would not target non-financial companies in future can also be divided into those that had not previously raised finance from corporate sources and those that had. Just over half of the venture capital firms that had not received corporate finance stated that they would not look to corporates for funding in the future (Table 5.7). Of these firms many still believed other investment sources to be more accessible or more appropriate. Several others strongly believed that corporates would not invest in their funds if they were approached, and as a result they were not prepared to waste time targeting corporate organisations.

For the fund managers that had previously raised finance from corporates, experiences of indirect CVC have not been entirely favourable. Almost half (44 per cent) of these fund managers stated that they would not target them in the future (Table 5.7). Many had become disillusioned with links with non-financial companies and explained that raising finance from this source, as well as attempting to cater for the specific (often strategic) needs of corporate investors, was too time consuming. Thus, exposure to many of the potential disadvantages of indirect CVC has left many venture capitalists unwilling to try again and accept failure as part of the learning process. A small proportion of the venture capitalists that had raised corporate finance before but did not plan to target non-financial companies in future justified this by explaining that their investment strategy had changed and that corporates were therefore no longer suitable for their funds.

Expected trends to the year 2000

In the opinion of a majority (46 per cent) of the thirty-nine survey respondents, there is likely to be no change in the absolute levels of corporate finance committed to UK venture capital funds until at least the turn of the century, and just over one-quarter (26 per cent) expected the levels to fall in this time (Table 5.8). Although several fund managers did expect to see an increase in the relative importance of corporate finance as the total contribution from more traditional sources declines, venture capitalists suggested three main reasons why absolute levels of indirect CVC were likely to remain constant or decline. First, the UK venture capital industry will continue to fail to attract non-financial companies in any great numbers because of poor prospects of ROI and strategic benefit, as well as an increasing concentration on MBO and MBI deals (rather than early stage technology-related investments) which are of little interest to corporate investors. Discussing the future of the UK venture capital industry, Murray (1992b: 85) believed that the industry 'has to be able to demonstrate to

Table 5.8 Possible future levels of indirect CVC in the UK

Absolute increase/decrease in amount of corporate finance invested in venture capital funds in next five years	Number of respondents	Percentage
INCREASE	8	21
DECREASE	10	26
NO CHANGE	18	46
NO OPINION	3	8

Source: survey

157

institutional and other funders that it can furnish returns on capital that compensate adequately for the additional risks and illiquidity of investment in unquoted small and medium sized firms'. Second, a corporate environment which acts as a constraint to successful venture capital investment is both a cause and an effect of the very low levels of indirect CVC in the UK at present as there are few role models for corporates who consequently remain uneducated about the prospects of venture capital investment. Those companies that do get involved will do so through direct investments or via their pension funds. Third, initiatives from policy makers concerning the stimulation of indirect CVC in the UK are currently non-existent and there are no indications that this will change.

In contrast, only 21 per cent of venture capitalists believed that there will be an absolute increase in indirect CVC. First, they felt that UK companies would begin to recognise the potential benefits of venture capital investment at a time when the pressures on them to innovate are increasing. As Murray (1993: 25) notes, 'the imperative to maintain innovatory impetus by corporates in increasingly global, technology based industries will encourage large firms to take a long term view on such [CVC] experiments'. This belief is in line with the opinions of corporate executives themselves (Chapter 3), although they typically felt that such pressures were more likely to lead to an increase in the levels of *direct* rather than *indirect* investment. Second, a further decrease in finance from more traditional sources such as pension funds and insurance companies will make venture capitalists look towards the corporate sector in future.

Of the venture capitalists that stated that they were expecting to see a decrease in the amount of indirect CVC in the following five years, 80 per cent had received finance from non-financial companies for their funds in the past. Only a quarter of those respondents expecting an increase in the extent of the strategy had actually been involved with it before. This strongly reinforces the suggestion that venture capitalists' experiences with corporate investors have generally not been favourable in the UK, and as a result it is the venture capitalists who are less experienced in this area that are the more optimistic about the future levels of indirect CVC. Such an outlook may however be unrealistic.

CONCLUSIONS

The aim of this chapter has been to examine indirect CVC investment from the perspective of the venture capital fund manager. In particular, the survey sought to investigate in detail the fund manager–corporate investor relationship and to identify the significance of the corporate sector as an alternative source of finance for venture capital funds at a time when they are experiencing fund raising difficulties (Murray, 1991a; 1991b; 1994b; Abbott and Hay, 1995). This chapter has therefore provided an insight into the characteristics of indirect CVC investments, both in terms of corporate investments in externally managed funds and the subsequent investments made by these funds in portfolio investee firms. In the light of the experiences of fund managers, the benefits and problems of indirect CVC have been considered, along with the current and potential future levels of indirect CVC in the UK.

This survey has identified a number of UK-based venture capitalists that have raised finance for the funds which they manage from non-financial companies. Although the average number of corporate investors per fund is small, non-financial companies have still typically provided a significant proportion of the total fund value. However, many of the companies from which funds have been raised are not indigenous UK corporations, indicating the limited involvement of UK companies in the indirect CVC process.

Fund managers tend to have accurate perceptions of the motivations of non-financial companies for making indirect CVC investments. Financial, strategic and social responsibility-related objectives are all considered to be important. However, fund managers do not recognise the frequent desire of investing companies to simply learn about the venture capital process. Fund managers believe that the focus of many indirect CVC programmes has shifted from a strategic to a financial orientation. This reflects the failure of many previous investments to meet strategic objectives, and the increasing awareness of corporate executives that direct CVC investment is usually more appropriate for such goals. It also suggests that, despite the recognition of fund managers that many corporate investors have had strategically oriented motives in the past, they have failed to cater adequately for the specific needs of these companies. Indeed, in general only investors in dedicated funds have been allowed a say in fund investment decisions. Furthermore, many investors have either not been permitted close contact with investee firms or have not had the opportunity to ensure that funds invest in the types of firm that will be of strategic interest.

This survey has provided further evidence to suggest that non-financial companies can be a valuable alternative source of finance for venture capital funds investing in early stage TBFs. The majority of funds which have raised finance from corporate sources have an early stage technology focus which is in clear contrast to funds which have not raised finance from this source. What is more, most of the firms that have raised finance from these funds are UK-based firms, suggesting the role of indirect CVC in bridging this aspect of the equity gap in the UK. However, high regional variations in indirect CVC investment within the UK reflect the BVCA figures, with a high concentration of investee firms in the South of England. This therefore suggests that indirect CVC does not help to overcome the regional disparities in venture capital investment recognised by various authors (e.g. Martin, 1989; Mason and Harrison, 1995). The amounts invested in investee firms are relatively large, reflecting the high capital requirements of many TBFs in the early stages of their development (Baty, 1990; Standeven, 1993) (Chapter 2).

While the role of non-financial companies as indirect providers of finance for high risk firms is clearly evident, a major aim of this survey was to examine the advantages and disadvantages of indirect CVC in the light of the experiences of fund managers. Supporting the comments of Bailey (1985) and Collins and Doorley (1991), it has been found that corporate investors often provide fund managers with *value-added* benefits such as industry-specific knowledge, technical skills and advice as well as an exit route. These benefits indirectly benefit the investee firm, and in some cases corporate investors can nurture investee firms directly when close contact is permitted and desired. Investors themselves can benefit from the venture capitalist's expertise, a large deal flow and spread of investments.

However, fund managers have identified several problems associated with indirect CVC. For fund managers themselves, there can be notable difficulties in managing the specific needs of corporate investors. Non-financial companies often do not understand the venture capital process and therefore have unrealistic short-term expectations and want too much control over investee firms. Conflict between fund managers and investors is typical. For the investee business, hidden agendas on the part of the corporate can lead to conflict as can the 'Big Brother' effect. The buffer that is often created by the fund manager to protect investee firms from the unwanted attentions of corporate investors is itself a major cause of the disillusionment and frustration experienced by many corporate investors with strategic objectives.

The advantages and disadvantages of corporate investors in venture capital funds have to be weighed-up. The evidence suggests that the disadvantages are currently tilting the scales. Chapter 3 found that fewer UK-based companies are considering indirect CVC investment, and those companies that are investing in UK venture capital funds tend to be foreign corporations. Furthermore, this chapter has indicated that relatively few fund managers are interested in targeting non-financial companies for future funds. This reflects a venture capital community that is either unable to attract corporate finance, does not recognise the potential benefits of such investment or has been discouraged by poor previous experiences which have arguably been self-induced because of a failure to cater adequately for the needs of corporate investors.

It would therefore appear that absolute levels of indirect CVC in the UK will either remain constant in the next few years or will decrease. This is particularly disappointing since corporate investors appear to favour stages and sectors of investment which, due to their inherent riskiness, are hugely disadvantaged in the venture capital stakes.

This chapter has therefore involved a detailed examination of indirect CVC investment from the fund manager's perspective. In order fully to understand the nature of CVC relationships and the role of this form of investment in the financing of small firms there is a need finally to consider the CVC process and its benefits and problems from the point of view of the eventual finance recipients, namely the investee companies. Chapter 6 is therefore based on a survey of TBFs that have raised CVC finance in either its direct or indirect forms.

6

TECHNOLOGY-BASED FIRMS AND CVC

The investee company's perspective

INTRODUCTION

Technology-based firms (TBFs), defined as firms whose activities embrace a significant technology component as a major source of competitive advantage, are usually seen as an important source of product and process innovations, new employment creation and export sales growth (Rothwell, 1984; Slatter, 1992; Murray, 1993; 1994a; 1995). They therefore have an important role to play in the emergence of new technology-based sectors of industry (Rothwell and Dodgson, 1994) and in preserving and enhancing the economic competitiveness of established industries (Oakey, 1984; Rothwell, 1984; Slatter, 1992; Duhamel et al., 1994; Keeble, 1994; Segers, 1995). Indeed, Standeven (1993: 2) considered it to have become 'increasingly apparent that having a strong domestic technology sector is essential to the long-term health of an economy'.

It was recognised in Chapter 2 that for all new firms, finance is a critical factor for success (Roberts, 1991; Sargent and Young, 1991). It was also noted that the requirements of TBFs are distinctive because of the high costs associated with technological product and process development (Manigart and Struyf, 1995). However, a recurring theme throughout this thesis has been the difficulties encountered by small TBFs seeking to raise finance for start-up and growth. In addition to finance, young TBFs require appropriate value-added assistance in the form of technical and marketing related skills and advice. However, few investors possess the necessary knowledge and information (Murray, 1993; 1995; Abbott and Hay, 1995) at a time when TBFs are increasingly seeking value-added investors in order to compete (Roberts, 1991; Bygrave and Timmons, 1992; Deger, 1994; Onians, 1995).

Chapter 4 identified CVC as a valuable alternative source of finance for many firms of a range of sizes and from a broad range of industries. It was found that while indirect CVC investments typically focus on early stage TBFs (confirmed in Chapter 5), direct investments are more likely to be made in later stage companies operating in medium or low tech industries.

However, despite these distinctions, the findings suggest that a large number of the firms that raise CVC finance, in both its indirect *and* direct forms, can be defined as early stage technology-based firms. This reflects the objective of many companies investing indirectly and directly to obtain windows on *new technologies*. Furthermore, the findings outlined in Chapter 4 suggest that the typically strategically oriented motives of investing companies, and particularly those investing directly, can result in the investee firm benefiting from nurturing provided by the corporate investor.

While the findings so far therefore provide an indication of the importance of CVC in the funding of TBFs, and indeed the importance of TBFs for corporate investors, the role of CVC has not yet been considered from the TBF's perspective. Indeed, whereas the types of firms most likely to receive CVC finance have been identified (Chapter 4), it remains to be established how significant this source of finance is relative to other sources at particular stages of firm development, and what the experiences of investee firms have been. Such an analysis is vital if an accurate assessment of the role of CVC in the financing of early stage TBFs is to be made.

Furthermore, given that this book attempts to examine CVC as a form of collaborative relationship between large and small companies, it is vital to consider the motives of investee firms for seeking this form of alliance with large partners. It was noted in Chapter 1 that large companies and small TBFs have the potential to be able to benefit from complementary assets (Ahern, 1993a) and in particular the *material* advantages of the large company and the *behavioural* advantages of the small firm (Rothwell, 1993). The motives of corporate investors have been considered (Chapter 3), and as was noted in Chapter 1, there is a need to dedicate more attention to the interests and motives of small firms for establishing relationships with other firms (Belotti, 1995).

RESEARCH AIMS AND METHODOLOGY

Research aims

This chapter therefore examines the role of CVC in the overall context of TBF equity financing in the UK and identifies whether there are any specific benefits of this funding source for investee firms. The research focuses on the financial histories of TBFs that have raised CVC, and in particular the significance of CVC finance *relative* to other sources and the stages of firm development at which CVC has been raised. In addition, emphasis is placed on the decision to seek CVC finance and any benefits and problems associated with this form of investment. Particular attention is paid to the form that the relationship takes and the importance of the hands-on/nurturing role of non-financial investors.

This chapter therefore addresses the following questions:

163

- How significant has CVC been *relative* to other sources for the survey firms?
- At what stages of firm development has CVC been raised?
- Do TBFs actively seek CVC finance? If so, how do they seek it?
- What are the motivations of TBFs for seeking CVC finance? Do they foresee any advantages of CVC over other forms of external equity finance?
- What form does the CVC relationship take?
- Have any specific benefits and/or problems arisen for the investee firm from raising CVC?

Methodology

The research questions necessitated the identification of UK companies, ideally technology-based, that had raised direct and/or indirect CVC finance. A number of appropriate companies were identified through the surveys of corporate executives and venture capital fund managers discussed in earlier chapters, through reports in the business literature and press, and during discussions with experts in the venture capital and strategic alliance fields. A total of sixty-six firms were identified, all of which had raised direct and/or indirect CVC finance at some stage of their development. While it cannot be claimed that these firms are representative of the entire population of TBFs that have raised CVC finance, the sample identified was considered appropriate given the research questions and the exploratory nature of this survey. All firms were contacted by introductory letter and follow-up telephone calls. Initial contact was made with firms' Managing Directors. It was believed that these individuals would typically be knowledgeable about their firm's business histories, and indeed would often have been the companies' founders. Further, as was noted in Chapter 3, it was felt that if the letter requesting assistance was passed down from the Chief Executive or the Managing Director, the chances of a firm agreeing to participate in the survey would be higher. A total of forty-eight firms agreed to participate in the survey (73 per cent response rate).

Semi-structured questionnaires were used in telephone interviews with a director from each of the participating companies. The surveys of corporate executives and venture capital fund managers undertaken in this study indicated the greater willingness of company directors to participate in telephone surveys as opposed to face-to-face interviews. This largely reflects the longer duration of face-to-face interviews and the time constraints inherent in corporate interviews. Given the estimated shorter duration of interviews in this survey, telephone interviews were considered appropriate for all respondents in an attempt to maximise response rates.

GENERAL CHARACTERISTICS OF SAMPLE FIRMS

The survey sample consisted of companies that had, at least once previously, raised CVC finance directly and/or indirectly. Of the forty-eight participating firms, sixteen had received direct finance, twenty-five had received indirect finance and seven had received both forms. The majority of companies classified themselves as technology-based enterprises, operating in high technology industrial sectors. A total of eighteen of the twenty-three firms that had raised direct finance (direct investees) were technology-based, typically providing research, manufacturing and services in the medical, computing, acoustics and electronics industries (Figure 6.1). Similarly, the activities of almost all (thirty) of the thirty-two firms that had received indirect finance (indirect investees) included a significant technology component. One-quarter of these companies operated in the computing industry, while the medical, engineering, biotechnology and electronics sectors were also represented (Figure 6.2).

The age of the companies varied considerably, the oldest having been established in 1945 and the youngest in 1992. However, more than three-quarters of firms that had raised direct finance had been founded since 1984 (including six in 1990), with a similar proportion of firms that had raised indirect CVC established since 1982 (including five in both 1986 and 1987). The majority of firms considered themselves to be at the expansion, or sustained growth, stage of their development at the time of

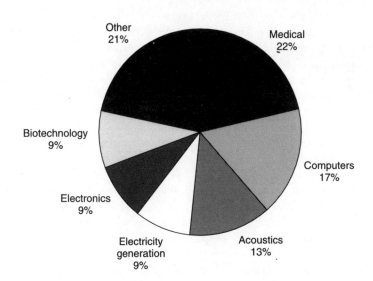

Figure 6.1 Industrial sectors of firms that have raised direct CVC finance
Note: based on data from twenty-three direct investees
Source: survey

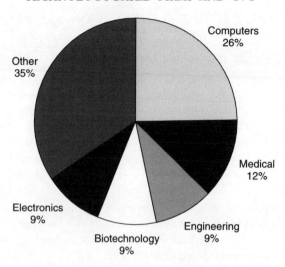

Figure 6.2 Industrial sectors of firms that have raised indirect CVC finance
Note: based on data from thirty-two indirect investees
Source: survey

interview. Just less than half of direct investees were expansion stage firms compared with just less than two-thirds of indirect investees. Remaining companies were either still early stage firms or were now mature companies.

Company size at the time of interview also varied significantly. The smallest firm employed just three people, while the largest had six hundred and fifty employees. The median number of employees of direct investees was sixty-five while the corresponding figure for indirect investees was fifty-eight. The size of the companies' boards ranged from one to ten directors, with the average number of board members for both direct and indirect investees being five. The majority of firms operated from just one site. However, as would be expected, those with offices or plants at more than one location tended to be the larger firms. Firms were dispersed throughout the UK (Figure 6.3), although a degree of concentration was evident in London, which has been recognised as having a higher than average population of TBFs (Keeble and Walker, 1994), and Cambridge, Leeds and Edinburgh, which have all experienced increases in high technology employment since the early 1980s (Keeble, 1994).

Non-financial corporations were still significant shareholders in the majority of surveyed firms. At the time of interview the largest single shareholdings in firms that had raised direct finance were owned by the direct CVC investor/s or by the companies' management. More than a half

Figure 6.3 Spatial distribution of TBF survey sample

of the largest shareholdings were accounted for by these two groups, with the remainder typically in the hands of the entrepreneurial team or venture capitalists. The largest shareholdings in firms that had raised indirect CVC were owned by venture capitalists (including those in which non-financial companies had invested). Just less than one-third of the largest shareholdings were owned by these fund managers while the firms' founders, management and, in some cases, the public accounted for the remainder.

THE ROLE OF CVC RELATIVE TO OTHER FINANCE SOURCES

In order to understand the role of CVC in the context of TBF financing, and particularly its importance as a source of funding for firms in the early stages of development, there is a need to examine the financial histories of companies. Although all survey firms were known to have raised CVC finance, the *relative* importance of this source compared to others for each firm was not known. Firms' financial histories highlight the significance of CVC *relative* to other sources of equity finance in terms of both the number of rounds and the amounts invested at each stage of a firm's development. To facilitate a clear understanding of the relative importance of both direct and indirect CVC investment compared with alternative finance sources, and to identify any differences which may exist between these two forms of CVC in terms of stages of investment, both are analysed and discussed separately.

Financial histories of firms that have raised direct CVC

During the various stages of their development, firms that had raised direct CVC had also typically raised external equity from other sources. Less than one-third had relied solely on finance from non-financial companies. As well as direct CVC finance, some firms also used venture capitalists (48 per cent of firms) and other financial institutions (17 per cent), the stock exchange (9 per cent) and business angels (4 per cent).

The twenty-three firms had raised a total of £285 million in equity finance from all external sources (ninety-two individual investors) in order to fund their start-up and growth. This represents an average of £12.4 million per investee and £3.1 million per individual investor. Table 6.1 illustrates that external equity was used at all stages including seed and MBO/MBI, but indicates its particular importance in the early stages of development after start-up,[1] as well as at the expansion stage. Financial institutions (including merchant banks and insurance companies) had provided the largest amount of finance (£125 million, or 44 per cent). However, the significance of this source is considerably reduced (to 3 per cent) when one particularly large investment is excluded from the analysis. Non-financial companies were the next most significant investors in terms of amount invested (£83.2 million or 29 per cent), followed by venture capital funds which invested £57.4 million (20 per cent). The median amount invested by each investor was high, although the figure varied considerably by source, ranging from £0.28 million for 'other' investors, which included trusts and universities, to £12 million for financial institutions. The median investments by individual venture capital funds and non-financial companies were also sizeable (£1.18 million and £1.5 million respectively).

168

Table 6.1 Amounts invested in direct investees by stage and source (£m)

Stage	Source of outside equity finance						Totals	Median amount invested per round
	Business angels	Venture capital funds	Financial institutions	Non-financial companies	Stock exchange	Other		
Seed	0	0	0	6.5	0	0	6.5	0.23
Start-up	0	7	0.8	9.3	0	0.6	17.7	1.53
Other early	0	40.8	120.6	48.4	0	2	211.8	1
Expansion	0.4	9	3.6	12.6	15	0.4	41	2.38
MBO/MBI	0	0.6	0	2.2	0	0	2.8	0.6
Other	0	0	0	4.2	1	0	5.2	2.6
Totals	0.4	57.4	125	83.2	16	3	285	
No. of investors	1	30	14	41	2	4	92	
Median amount invested per investor	0.4	1.18	12	1.5	8	0.28		

Note: Based on data from twenty-three direct investees
Source: survey

The external equity finance was raised over a total of fifty-six rounds (i.e. an average of 2.4 rounds per firm). More than two-thirds of firms had raised just one or two rounds, while a quarter had raised equity over four or more phases. The maximum number of rounds raised by any one company was six. The median amount invested by all sources per round was relatively low at the seed stage but rose considerably at other stages and was particularly high at start-up and expansion (see Table 6.1). Furthermore, Table 6.2 shows that when rounds are analysed by size and source, two-thirds of all rounds are found to be of between £0.5 million and £5 million in size. Indeed, almost half of the rounds were greater than £1 million.

The majority of rounds were raised by firms in their 'other early' stage of development (Table 6.3). It is also evident from Table 6.3 that the first round of outside equity financing most commonly occurred at the start-up stage although some firms had been able to raise finance prior to start-up (i.e. at the seed stage). This survey also finds that almost a half of firms raised their first round of external equity after start-up. Similarly, an analysis of the rounds invested at each stage by source of finance (Table 6.4) shows that the majority of rounds were invested at the other early stage of growth. Not surprisingly, this supports the finding that the amounts invested by each source were greatest at this stage. Again, non-financial companies and venture capital funds were the most significant investors in terms of number of rounds invested in survey firms.

The role of direct CVC

While it is important to remember that the survey firms were originally selected on account of them having raised CVC finance, the findings so far indicate that direct CVC has been of great importance to these firms *relative* to other sources. Despite the fact that most firms had raised external equity from other sources besides non-financial companies, when the one particularly large investment made by financial institutions is omitted from the analysis, non-financial companies have invested greater amounts and more rounds in the twenty-three survey firms than any other source. In addition, non-financial companies have invested in a range of sizes suggesting their suitability for a wide range of TBFs with different financial requirements.

Survey firms had raised direct CVC from a total of forty-one non-financial companies, representing an average of 1.8 per investee. The majority of firms (sixteen) had just one corporate investor, although four firms had each raised finance from four companies. Corporate investors were typically UK organisations (54 per cent), although several were of US or Japanese origin. They typically operated in the same or related industrial sectors as their investees, most notably pharmaceuticals, electronics and computing. This is not surprising given the expectation that many companies are investing in order to obtain windows on new technological developments within their

Table 6.2 Rounds invested in direct investees by size and source

Size of round (£)		Source of outside equity finance					
	Business angels	Venture capital funds	Financial institutions	Non-financial companies	Stock exchange	Other	Totals
<50,000	0	0	1	1	0	0	2
50,000–99,000	0	0	0	3	0	1	4
100,000–249,000	0	0	0	5	0	0	5
250,000–499,000	1	2	0	6	0	1	10
500,000–999,000	0	2	3	6	0	5	16
1m–5m	0	18	1	16	1	0	36
>5m	0	1	1	3	1	0	6
Totals	1	23	6	40	2	7	79

Note: Based on data from twenty-three direct investees
Source: survey

Table 6.3 Stage distribution of rounds: direct CVC

Stage	Round number						Totals	No. of investors
	1	2	3	4	5	6		
Seed	4	0	0	0	0	0	4	8
Start-up	8	0	0	0	0	0	8	18
Other early	4	10	6	4	3	0	27	60
Expansion	4	3	1	2	1	1	12	28
MBO/MBI	3	0	0	0	0	0	3	5
Other	0	2	0	0	0	0	2	5
Totals	23	15	7	6	4	1	56	

Note: Based on data from twenty-three direct investees
Source: survey

Table 6.4 Rounds invested in direct investees by stage and source

Stage	Source of outside equity finance						Totals
	Business angels	Venture capital funds	Financial institutions	Non-financial companies	Stock exchange	Other	
Seed	0	0	0	4	0	0	4
Start-up	0	4	1	5	0	2	12
Other early	0	13	3	17	0	4	37
Expansion	1	4	2	9	1	1	18
MBO/MBI	0	2	0	3	0	0	5
Other	0	0	0	2	1	0	3
Totals	1	23	6	40	2	7	79

Note: Based on data from twenty-three direct investees
Source: survey

own and closely related industries. While the overall importance of direct CVC for the survey firms in terms of *relative* amounts and number of rounds raised is clear, a more significant consideration given the aims of this particular survey concerns the stage distribution of direct CVC investment. In other words, at what stage of their development are TBFs raising most direct CVC and is this the first source of external equity used?

Most investee firms were in the early stages of their development when they initially raised direct CVC (Figure 6.4). Two-thirds of firms were at either the seed, start-up or other early stages of growth when they raised their first direct CVC finance. Moreover, from Table 6.5 it can be calculated that 77 per cent of the total direct CVC finance raised by the survey firms was raised at these stages and also that the majority of rounds were invested at the early stages of TBF development. Indeed, non-financial corporations accounted for the only source of seed funds raised by firms and over half of all start-up finance. Furthermore, 83 per cent of investees had raised direct CVC in their first round of external equity financing. Indeed, direct CVC was by far the most frequently used source of first round financing, with over twice as many firms raising funds from non-financial companies as from institutional venture capital funds. Almost three-quarters of the forty-one investing companies made their initial investments in the survey firms while these firms were in the early stages of development, often as lead investors attracting finance from other sources that may not otherwise have invested.

Several investees had raised follow-on finance for later stages of development from the same non-financial companies. Ten of the twenty-three firms had raised further finance from just less than half of the forty-one investing companies. Although this funding was required for further

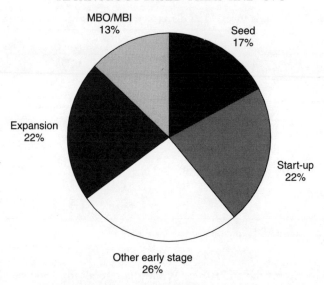

Figure 6.4 Stage of investee firms when direct CVC was initially raised
Note: Based on data from 23 direct investees
Source: survey

development, more than half of the follow-on rounds were raised by direct investees when they were still at the early stages of growth.

These findings provide considerable support for the hypothesis that many direct CVC investments are made in *early stage* TBFs. Although the findings presented in Chapter 4 suggest that many direct CVC investments are made in expansion stage companies, often in order to provide investors with windows on market opportunities, it appears that when investments are made in TBFs there is a much greater likelihood that the investees will only be in the early stages of their development. This enables the investors

Table 6.5 Summary of amounts and rounds invested by non-financial companies by stage

Stage	Amounts	Rounds
Seed	6.5	4
Start-up	9.3	5
Other early	48.4	17
Expansion	12.6	9
MBO/MBI	2.2	3
Other	4.2	2
Totals	83.2	40

Note: Based on data from twenty-three direct investees
Source: survey

174

to review technologies in their earliest stages (Taylor, 1989; Collins and Doorley, 1991)

Financial histories of firms that have raised indirect CVC

As was the case with direct investees, the thirty-two survey firms that had raised indirect CVC finance had also typically raised outside equity from other sources. In addition to raising finance from funds which had corporate investors as limited partners (termed 'indirect CVC funds' here), equity had also been received from other venture capital funds (44 per cent of survey firms), non-financial companies (22 per cent – i.e. in the cases of the seven firms which had raised both direct and indirect CVC), the stock exchange (19 per cent), other financial institutions (9 per cent) and private individuals (9 per cent). As with direct CVC, less than one-third of respondents had raised just CVC finance.

The firms had raised a total of £137.2 million from all equity sources during their development (based on data from twenty-eight indirect investees and eighty-six individual investors – average of £4.9 million per investee and £1.6 million per investor). This total amount is approximately half that raised by direct investees, although when the particularly large investment of £120 million received by one direct investee is excluded the figures become much more similar. From Table 6.6 it is seen that external equity was used at all stages of firm development, although it has been particularly important at the other early and expansion stages, and to a slightly lesser extent during the start-up phase. This again corresponds with the earlier findings for direct investees. Venture capital funds had invested by far the largest amount – £84.4 million (62 per cent). The next highest amount, invested by non-financial companies, was only just over one-quarter of that provided by venture capital funds (£22.4 million/16 per cent), although it is important to note that this finance was raised by just seven firms. As with direct CVC, the median amount invested by each investor varied considerably by source although all medians were reasonably high. The amounts ranged from £0.65 million for business angels to £7.75 million in the case of the stock exchange. The median investments for venture capital funds and non-financial companies were similar to those in the case of direct CVC, being £1 million and £1.9 million respectively. Again this indicates the significant amounts invested by individual funds and companies.

Equity finance from all sources was raised over eighty-one rounds representing an average of 2.5 rounds per investee firm. Just over one-third of the thirty-two investees had raised only one round of funding, while a quarter had received finance over four or more rounds. As with direct CVC investments, the median amount invested by all sources at each round was particularly high at the start-up and expansion stages. The

Table 6.6 Amounts invested in indirect investees by stage and source (£m)

| | Source of outside equity finance | | | | | | | |
Stage	Business angels	Venture capital funds	Financial institutions	Non-financial companies	Stock exchange	Other	Totals	Median amount invested per round
Seed	0	0.1	0	0.3	0	0	0.4	0.19
Start-up	0.8	18.4	0.6	7.2	1	0	28	1.5
Other early	0.5	39.9	0	8.5	0	3	51.9	1
Expansion	0	20	4.5	6.3	15	3	48.8	2.13
MBO/MBI	0	3.9	0	0.1	0	0	4	0.42
Other	0	2.1	2	0	0	0	4.1	2.03
Totals	1.3	84.4	7.1	22.4	16	6	137.2	
No. of Investors	2	63	5	12	2	2	86	
Median amount invested per investor	0.65	1	1.5	1.9	7.75	3		

Note: Based on data from twenty-eight indirect investees
Source: survey

smaller median amount invested at the other early stage reflects the smaller number of investors per round at this stage. Furthermore, 57 per cent of all rounds analysed by source were of between £1 million and £5 million (Table 6.7).

As with direct investees, the first round of outside equity was most frequently raised at the start-up stage (Table 6.8). However, only two firms had raised outside equity prior to start-up. Despite this, more than two-thirds of firms raised their first round of equity while they were in the early stages of development. Almost three-quarters of the total number of rounds were invested at the other early or expansion stages, and almost all follow-on rounds were raised at these stages. In terms of rounds invested at each stage by particular sources (Table 6.9), the other early stage was by far the most common phase of development for firms to raise rounds of external equity. Relatively high numbers of rounds were also evident at the expansion and start-up stages. At all stages, venture capital funds were the most significant investors in terms of number of rounds invested.

The role of indirect CVC

The *relative* importance of venture capital funds as a source of outside equity finance for the thirty-two TBFs in this sample compared to other sources is clear. However, it is necessary to gauge the significance of

Table 6.7: Rounds invested in indirect investees by size and source

| Size of round (£) | Source of outside equity finance | | | | | | Totals |
	Business angels	Venture capital funds	Financial institutions	Non-financial companies	Stock exchange	Other	
<50,000	0	1	0	0	0	0	1
50,000–99,000	0	3	1	1	0	0	5
100,000–249,000	0	5	0	1	0	0	6
250,000–499,000	1	6	0	4	0	0	11
500,000–999,000	2	11	1	1	0	0	15
1m–5m	0	37	3	8	1	2	51
>5m	0	0	0	0	1	0	1
Totals	3	63	5	15	2	2	*90*

Note: Based on data from twenty-eight indirect investees
Source: survey

177

Table 6.8 Stage distribution of rounds: indirect CVC

Stage	Round number						Totals	No. of Investors
	1	*2*	*3*	*4*	*5*	*6*		
Seed	2	0	0	0	0	0	2	2
Start-up	12	0	0	0	0	0	12	28
Other early	8	13	12	4	1	0	38	48
Expansion	5	6	1	5	3	1	21	42
MBO/MBI	4	0	0	0	0	1	5	11
Other	1	1	1	0	0	0	3	5
Totals	32	20	14	9	4	2	*81*	

Note: Based on data from thirty-two indirect investees
Source: survey

Table 6.9 Rounds invested in indirect investees by stage and source

Stage	Source of outside equity finance						Totals
	Business angels	*Venture capital funds*	*Financial institutions*	*Non-financial companies*	*Stock exchange*	*Other*	
Seed	0	1	0	1	0	0	2
Start-up	2	11	2	3	1	0	19
Other early	1	34	0	7	0	1	43
Expansion	1	14	2	3	4	3	27
MBO/MBI	0	5	0	1	0	0	6
Other	0	2	1	0	1	0	4
Totals	4	67	5	15	6	4	*101*

Note: Based on data from thirty-two indirect investees
Source: survey

indirect CVC funds in this context in terms of the proportion of the total amount invested that they account for and of the total number of rounds in which they participated. The thirty-two investee firms had raised external equity from a total of seventy venture capital funds (2.2 per investee), forty-four of which were indirect CVC funds (1.4 per investee). More than two-thirds of investees had raised finance from just one indirect CVC fund. All indirect CVC funds were managed by UK-based fund managers, supporting the findings in Chapters 4 and 5 that funds tend to invest in firms located in the same country as the fund managers both because of the decay of deal flow with distance from the fund and the need of fund managers for close contact with the investment portfolio. Also, the majority of funds were pooled/multi-investor funds in that they had been raised through finance from more than one source. Only eight of the forty-four funds were dedicated and had only one investor, which was by definition a non-financial company in each case. This again corresponds with earlier findings suggesting the number of corporate dedicated funds to be limited in the UK.

Indirect CVC funds have had a significant role to play in the financing of the survey firms *relative* to other venture capital funds. This would be expected given that almost two-thirds of the funds from which indirect investees have raised finance have been indirect CVC funds. These funds had invested a total of £53.6 million in twenty-eight of the thirty-two firms, representing a median of £0.84 million per fund (Table 6.10). Not surprisingly this accounts for almost two-thirds of the amount raised from all venture capital funds. Other venture capital funds had invested just £30.8 million (a median of £1 million per fund). Furthermore, indirect CVC fund investments were made over sixty-four rounds (Table 6.11), indicating that these funds participated in almost every round of venture capital fund financing. Other funds had participated in only approximately half of the rounds. However, as was the case with the analysis of direct investees, the more pertinent issue concerns the stage distribution of indirect CVC investment.

The majority of investee firms were early stage enterprises at the time that they first raised indirect CVC finance (Figure 6.5). As with direct CVC, more than two-thirds of indirect investees initially raised funds from this source while they were at the seed, start-up or other early stages of growth. Also, it can be seen from Table 6.10 that almost three-quarters of the total

Table 6.10 Amounts invested in indirect investees by stage and source (£m): comparison of indirect CVC funds and other funds

Stage	Source of outside equity finance		
	Indirect CVC funds	Other venture capital funds	Totals
Seed	0.1	0	0.1
Start-up	11.1	7.3	18.4
Other early	28.2	11.7	39.9
Expansion	10.8	9.2	20
MBO/MBI	2.3	1.6	3.9
Other	1.1	1	2.1
Totals	53.6	30.8	84.4
No. of investors	38	25	63
Median per investor	0.84	1	

Note: Based on data from twenty-eight indirect investees
Source: survey

Table 6.11 Rounds invested in indirect investees by stage and source: comparison of indirect CVC funds and other funds

	Source of outside equity finance		
Stage	*Indirect CVC funds*	*Other venture capital funds*	*Totals*
Seed	1	0	1
Start-up	11	5	16
Other early	33	19	52
Expansion	12	8	20
MBO/MBI	5	2	7
Other	2	1	3
Totals	64	35	*99*

Note: Based on data from thirty-two indirect investees
Source: survey

finance raised from indirect CVC funds was raised at these stages. Moreover, half of the total was raised during the other early stages alone. This marks a significant difference between the stage distribution of indirect CVC fund investments and investments made by other venture capital funds, since only one-third of the capital invested by other funds was invested in firms at the other early stage of growth. Indeed, less than

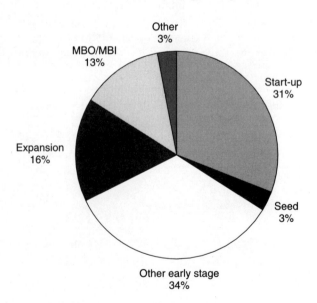

Figure 6.5 Stage of investee firms when indirect CVC was initially raised
Note: based on data from 32 indirect investees
Source: survey

180

two-thirds of the finance invested by these funds was invested in any of the early stages of development, providing further evidence to support the argument that venture capital funds in which non-financial corporations invest will be more likely than other funds to specialise in making investments in early stage TBFs. In addition, well over two-thirds of indirect CVC rounds were raised by the survey respondents when they were early stage ventures (Table 6.11). Over two-thirds of indirect CVC funds made their initial investments in the survey firms at these stages. In addition, 84 per cent of firms had raised indirect CVC as part of their first round of outside equity finance. These findings further illustrate the survey firms' use of indirect CVC early in their development.

Again in keeping with the findings for direct CVC, a number of investee firms had raised follow-on CVC finance. Several firms had raised follow-on funding from venture capital funds, including fifteen that had received second, third and occasionally more tranches from indirect CVC funds. The majority of investees that raised follow-on indirect CVC were no longer start-up enterprises but were typically still at other early stages of development, reflecting their need for substantial amounts of capital at the early stages of growth.

Plans to raise CVC finance in future

From this evidence, it is clear that CVC, in either its direct or indirect forms, has played an important role *relative* to other sources in the financing of the survey firms to date. Its function has been particularly noticeable at the early stages of development. In other words, this survey has confirmed the finding of the surveys of corporate executives and venture capital fund managers that CVC investment can help to provide funding for early stage TBFs and the venture capital funds that specialise in investing in these ventures. It will be recalled that it is these firms that, despite arguably the greatest need, experience the greatest difficulties in raising finance from more conventional sources largely due to their high-risk nature.

However, despite the important role that CVC has played in the development of the survey firms to date, only a relatively small number of them plan to raise CVC finance before 1998. This largely reflects the finding that only twenty-nine (60 per cent) of the forty-eight survey firms plan to seek external equity from any source during this period. Almost half of the firms that will seek equity will target sources of CVC finance. Ten firms will seek direct finance (seven of which have raised it before), one will seek indirect and two will seek both forms. However, the decision by many firms not to seek CVC highlights two important issues. First, entrepreneurs are increasingly doubtful of their chances of raising CVC finance. Indeed, a number of the respondents that stated that they would not target CVC sources had made several unsuccessful attempts to raise such finance in the *recent* past, despite having successfully raised CVC on previous occasions, and therefore did not believe that non-financial companies would want to invest again. This appears to support the general finding of this thesis that there has been a recent deterioration in the levels of CVC in the UK. Second, most respondents that will not seek CVC felt that other sources were more appropriate for their firms now that they had expanded. This suggests that corporate equity partners are perceived to be most useful during the early stages of a firm's development, and are therefore specifically sought by some firms at these stages. This usefulness not only may reflect the propensity for non-financial companies to invest in early stage firms but also may relate to other advantages of this source and specifically the value-added benefits that corporate investors have the potential to provide. The value-added factor will be explored in the remainder of this chapter.

THE SEARCH FOR CVC FINANCE

Investigation of the extent to which, and the reasons why, TBFs actively seek CVC finance can help to identify whether entrepreneurs expect there to be any advantages and value-added benefits associated with corporate investors. Botkin and Matthews (1992) emphasise the importance of carefully deciding which potential sources and investors to contact. Entrepreneurs rarely have the time or resources to approach a large number of possible investors and may experience difficulties in the selection process. It is therefore important in this survey to examine the extent to which TBF entrepreneurs make the first move in raising CVC finance, whether they consider that CVC can be substituted for other forms of equity finance, and whether indeed CVC has tangible and intangible advantages over these other forms. For firms that have specifically targeted CVC sources, an analysis of the mechanics behind investor selection can provide an indication of the efficiency of the CVC market. Again, in order to examine the differences between direct and indirect investment forms, both are considered separately.

Direct investees

The majority of firms that have raised direct CVC finance claimed that they had initially contacted potential corporate investors as opposed to being contacted themselves. Three-quarters of the direct investees in this survey approached companies in an attempt to sell them the CVC concept and outline the benefits to investors of investing in their companies. This suggests that firms use a similar 'knocking on doors' approach when seeking CVC finance as when seeking equity from venture capital funds (Bruno and Tyebjee, 1984; Sweeting, 1991b; Steier and Greenwood, 1995). Very few TBFs have been able to enjoy the luxury of being approached by a non-financial company that wants to take a minority equity stake in order to provide itself with a watching brief on technological developments. Indeed, only one of the twenty-three direct investees in this survey had initially been approached by *any* of its eventual corporate partners.

The need for entrepreneurs to approach potential corporate investors has already been suggested in Chapter 3. However, this is in contrast to the finding in Chapter 4 that the large majority of *investing* companies have to approach investee firms regarding CVC investment. This discrepancy could reflect the fact that both investor *and* investee companies consider themselves to have been active in instigating the formation of CVC relationships, even if they did not actually make the first move, and therefore both believe that they deserve credit. Alternatively, since Chapter 4 examined investments made in *all* types of investee firms, and not just TBFs, it is possible that the discrepancy reflects the fact that TBF entrepreneurs have been relatively more active in the search for finance as a result of the difficulties experienced by such firms in raising funds.

A further possible cause of the discrepancy outlined above is that in many of the cases where TBFs claimed that they had initially approached investors, the firms already had an established business relationship with the investing company prior to CVC negotiations. This suggests that the investor identification process is somewhat simplified for many firms, and does not involve a formal search for investors. Indeed, half of these firms had linkages including supplier and R&D collaboration agreements with their corporate investors. Equity investments may help to foster closer working relationships and more open flows of information, as well as allowing the investor to share in the increased valuation of the smaller partner that has resulted from collaboration (Collins and Doorley, 1991; Radtke and McKinney, 1991; Sykes, 1993). The possibility of equity investments arising from existing business relationships was mentioned in Chapter 4. Indeed, Hart *et al.* (1995) recognised the advantages for small firms seeking to attract resources of 'being known' by potential partners, and Grabher (1993: 15) noted that 'information on potential cooperating partners is determined by previous . . . relations and, in turn, influences the subsequent propensity to enter into additional relations'. It appears that the likelihood of this occurring is greater in the case of TBFs, possibly reflecting the high capital requirements of such firms and the large number of collaborative agreements between large and small firms in technology-based sectors (Chapter 1). Another four firms originated in some way with the investor. Two of these had been spin-outs from large companies that had then retained equity stakes for largely financial purposes, one was a joint venture between three multinational computer concerns, and one was a spin-off idea from a university. Those firms that did identify companies with whom they had no previous contact typically targeted organisations operating in their own industrial sectors via mail or telephone, or via intermediaries including accountants and venture capitalists.

Firms typically approached just one potential corporate investor, reflecting not only time and resource limitations but also the tendency for direct CVC investment to be considered as part of ongoing collaboration with a particular corporate organisation. However, larger-scale searches were evident; two firms contacted eight companies each and two more approached ten companies. One firm made forty speculative contacts. Most firms had serious negotiations with only one company, although the continuing interest of three or four potential CVC investors at the negotiation stage was not uncommon. Firms typically received offers of finance from all companies with whom they had serious negotiations. The final decision of which offer to accept reflected a range of factors (Table 6.12). The evaluation of individual corporate investment proposals and packages frequently took both financial and strategic factors into account, but with financial issues proving most influential.

Investee firms were particularly concerned with investment size, pricing and availability of follow-on rounds of funding. However, factors such as the industrial sectors of potential investees, the motives of companies and their hands-on investment philosophies were also often regarded as important factors, suggesting that investees were seeking more than just well-priced finance from the direct CVC deal.

Most direct investees had also sought external equity finance from

Table 6.12 Factors taken into account by direct investees when finally selecting corporate investors

	Number of mentions
Size of investment offered by investor	13
Industrial sector of investor	12
Percentage of equity sought by investor	10
Investing company's objectives	7
Willingness of investor to provide further rounds of finance	7
Investing company's previous CVC experience	6
Hands-on investment philosophy of investing company	5
Previous collaboration agreements with company	5
Types of shares wanted	3
Existence of contacts in company	3
Geographical location of company	2
Company was the only one to offer finance	2
Opportunities to establish further business relationships with company	1
Company was recommended	1
Seriousness of corporate executives about venture capital	1
Individual fund managers	1
Back seat role wanted by company	1

Note: Based on data from twenty direct investees
Source: survey

sources other than non-financial companies at some stage during their development. Indeed, in many cases CVC was seen as substitutional in that it was considered alongside other types of finance in the same round. Several investee company directors outlined the necessity of targeting a number of sources at the same time given the notorious difficulties of raising external equity. This supports the comment made earlier concerning the finding that many TBF entrepreneurs actively targeted CVC finance. In a number of cases direct CVC was the preferred choice of finance, but in many other cases it was not. Often, as has been seen, direct CVC was simply considered to be part of an ongoing collaborative agreement with the investing company while more substantial amounts were sought from venture capital funds. Indeed, 83 per cent of firms had not relied solely on direct CVC investment. Over three-quarters of firms had approached institutional venture capitalists at some time, just over half of which had been successful in raising finance from this source, and one-third had contacted other financial institutions. Only two firms had ever approached business angels.

Indirect investees

Indirect CVC is not seen as a separate form of equity finance from venture capital finance except in a small minority of cases. Consequently, very few TBFs in this survey specifically sought indirect CVC finance. Only eleven of the thirty-two indirect investees were even aware that the venture capital funds from which they had received finance were indirect CVC funds. Of these eleven firms, five indicated that their indirect corporate investors were UK companies, and four of these had received funding from BG Ventures (British Gas's dedicated fund). This suggests that those firms that are aware that they have raised indirect CVC finance are likely to have received it via a dedicated, rather than a pooled, fund. Their knowledge of corporate investors most likely reflects the greater levels of contact with these investors that have been possible via dedicated funds (Chapters 2 and 5).

Just as direct investees have had to make the first move in seeking finance from large companies, so the onus has also been on indirect investees to contact venture capitalists regarding equity finance. Only four firms in this survey had been approached first by venture capitalists.[2] In the great majority of cases venture capitalists were identified through personal contacts,[3] intermediaries and directories, and approached via these contacts and intermediaries or by mail. Several respondents explained that the identification process was not difficult given the relatively small number of venture capitalists prepared to invest in early stage technology-based firms. In contrast to direct CVC, very few indirect investees had established business relationships with investing non-financial companies prior to their indirect investments.[4] Only three firms had established previous relationships, these being research collaboration or supply deals. This lack of previous contact would be expected given that the majority of firms were unaware of their indirect corporate investors.

The search for venture capital funds is a complex time and resource consuming process. Since the vast majority of indirect investees did not benefit from the previously established contacts with potential investors that were enjoyed by direct investees, they often approached a larger number of potential investors. The average number of funds approached was ten, although approximately half of the firms contacted five or fewer venture capitalists. Despite the number of venture capitalists contacted, most firms had serious negotiations with only one or two fund managers. As with direct investment, firms tended to receive offers of finance from most of the venture capitalists with whom they had serious negotiations (including one firm which received ten offers).

The experience and expertise of the fund managers were by far the most significant factors in the investee firms' final choice of funds (Table 6.13). Of particular note is the importance placed on the fund managers' expertise in funding early stage TBFs. Previous contacts with fund managers, price/deal structure and the hands-on investment philosophy of the investors were also influential factors in some cases. In only one case was the presence of a corporate investor of importance in a firm's choice of fund, and even then it was considered to be only desirable and certainly not essential.

Indirect investees were not as likely as direct investees to have attempted

Table 6.13 Factors taken into account by indirect investees when finally selecting venture capital fund managers

	Number of mentions
Overall experience of the venture capitalist	15
Expertise of the venture capitalist in particular industrial sectors	15
Venture capitalist's previous investment track record	13
Expertise of venture capitalists in particular stages	12
Size of investment	6
Previous contacts with fund managers	6
Hands-on investment philosophy of fund managers	5
Price/deal structure	5
Venture capitalist was recommended	4
Individual fund managers	4
Fund managers approached us	3
Venture capitalist was only one to offer finance	3
Geographical location of venture capitalist	2
Type of funds managed by venture capitalist	1
Compatibility of venture capitalists (if more than one)	1

Note: Based on data from thirty-two indirect investees
Source: survey

to raise external equity finance from sources other than venture capital funds during the various stages of their development. Many indirect investees (38 per cent) had not considered the possibility of raising external equity finance from any other source, or at least considered their chances of raising finance from venture capitalists to be higher than from other sources. These firms had understandably approached the source which they believed was most likely to provide finance. Furthermore, many had sought venture capital finance for financial purposes as well as the hands-on advice of fund managers and were not concerned with any particular benefits that a corporate investor may be able to bring to the deal. Those firms that had sought equity finance from other sources typically targeted direct CVC and other financial institutions. Only four of the thirty-two firms had ever approached business angels.

THE PERCEIVED ADVANTAGES OF CVC FINANCING

Direct investees

When selecting sources of funding to target, TBFs foresaw a number of potential advantages to be gained from direct CVC finance when compared with other forms of external equity financing. Despite the fact that several investee company directors saw direct CVC as 'just another source of funding', the majority did anticipate certain potential benefits of direct corporate investors. The major advantages are related largely to the distinctions which must be made between the motives of non-financial companies that invest directly in TBFs and the motives of other venture capital providers. According to Collins and Doorley (1991), direct CVC investment is differentiated from the investments made by other venture capital sources as it does not aim solely at direct financial return. Indeed, it was emphasised in Chapter 3 that while financial viability is essential for CVC success, and therefore an important consideration for investors, the majority of corporate motivations for making direct CVC investments are strategically oriented.

Direct investees in this survey believed the major objectives of investing companies to include exposure to new technologies, the identification of new markets and new products, and the opportunity to establish further business relationships with investees (Table 6.14). A frequently cited secondary motive concerned the opportunity to improve manufacturing processes. These perceptions are clearly supported by findings from the survey of corporate executives (Chapter 3) in which non-financial companies were found to be making direct CVC investments largely for these reasons.[5] Furthermore, and again supported by earlier findings, almost all direct investees believed financial gain to be either a major or a minor motive of their corporate investors. It is important to note that the

Table 6.14 Respondents' perceived motives of companies making direct CVC investments

	Major motive	*Minor motive*
Financial return on investment	11	9
Exposure to new technologies	10	3
Access to new markets	9	8
Identification of new products	7	7
Establishment of further business relationships	7	7
Help suppliers and customers	4	2
Indirect benefits from assisting the small firm sector	4	0
Improvement of manufacturing processes	1	10
Assure supply of materials/components	1	4
Assist spin-outs from the company	1	0
Demonstration of presence in the market	1	0
In order to maintain market share	1	0
Diversification	1	0
Exploitation of joint idea	1	0
Spread risks	1	0
Lower manufacturing costs	0	3
Learn about venture capital	0	3
Assess acquisition candidates	0	1

Notes: Figures indicate number of mentions based on data from twenty-two direct investees
Source: survey

accuracy of the investee firms' perceptions of the motives of direct investors may have been enhanced by their often reasonably close relationships with investors prior to investment.

The perceived motives of investing companies led entrepreneurs to see the opportunity for benefiting more than just financially from direct CVC investment. Although respondents' reported pre-investment views may have been coloured by subsequent experience, many stated that they did foresee major strategic advantages and several minor financial advantages prior to receiving CVC finance (Table 6.15). Investee firms felt that corporate investors with largely strategic motives would want to have frequent contact with them and play a nurturing role. They therefore expected investors to provide numerous value-added benefits including technical and management expertise, assistance with short-term problems and access to their marketing and distribution networks. They also believed that their credibility in the marketplace would be enhanced significantly and that there would be opportunities to establish collaborative relationships with investing companies. Indeed, the relatively intangible benefit of being associated with a leading multinational company was the number one ranking advantage of direct CVC over other forms of equity financing, supporting Brokaw's (1994: 31) comment that 'beefy relationships with powerhouse companies distinguish the men from the boys in the high-tech world'.[6] In addition, many direct investees saw

Table 6.15 Factors considered by investee firms to be the main advantages of direct CVC over other forms of equity financing prior to receipt of finance

	Major advantage	*Minor advantage*
Credibility	11	6
Help with short-term problems	10	8
Access to corporate technical expertise	9	5
Opportunities to establish further business relationships	7	5
Access to corporate management expertise	6	10
Speed at which finance is obtained	5	5
Access to corporate marketing/distribution networks	5	3
Extra production/R&D support	3	7
Propensity for corporates to make investments in particular sectors	2	8
Opportunity to strengthen vertical relationships	2	0
Access to other finance sources	2	0
Pricing benefits	1	10
Patience of companies with regard to ROI	1	9
Access to corporate operational advice	1	0
Opportunities for synergy	1	0
Back seat hands-on role of corporate	1	0
Lower performance targets	0	10
Propensity for corporates to make investments of particular sizes	0	6
Propensity for corporates to make investments in particular stages	0	3
Access to possible exit routes	0	2
Access to more sophisticated financial control systems	0	2
Access to corporate office space	0	1

Notes: Figures indicate number of mentions based on data from twenty-two direct investees
Source: survey

several secondary advantages of direct CVC, many of which were more related to financial issues. In particular, respondents highlighted pricing benefits, lower (and more realistic) performance targets, and the relative patience of largely strategically-minded corporate investors as expected advantages, supporting the comments of Jenkins (1989) and MacDonald (1991).

Indirect investees

Prior to receiving indirect CVC investment, the TBFs in this survey did not anticipate the same advantages of this form of investment as in the case of recipients of direct CVC. Indeed, as was stated earlier, only eleven firms were actually aware that they had received indirect CVC finance and only one of these had taken the presence of a corporate investor into account when selecting venture capital funds. These firms typically believed corporate investors to be making indirect CVC investments in order to gain financially (Table 6.16). While many respondents believed that investing companies also had strategically oriented motivations for investing, with the exception of exposure to new technologies these were usually considered to be minor objectives. They attributed the relative unimportance of strategic objectives to the lower levels of contact between indirect investors and their investees. These assumptions are once more supported by the findings of the survey of corporate executives (Chapter 3) which indicated that indirect investors are more likely than direct investors to be motivated by social responsibility aims and the desire to learn about venture capital. Even when indirect corporate investors are motivated by strategic considerations, they are typically seeking windows on a broad range of new technologies and do not require as close contact with portfolio investee firms as is desired by direct CVC investors.

The perceptions among indirect investees of the motives of indirect investors can help to explain why the survey firms did not expect their corporate investors to provide the same levels of value-added that were anticipated with direct investment. These perceptions are a major reason why indirect investees do not foresee as many advantages of indirect CVC over other forms of external equity funding. Indeed, many of the direct investees in this survey explained that their decision to seek this form of finance rather than indirect finance reflected their suspicions that direct funding would offer far more value-added benefits.

Table 6.16 Respondents' perceived motives of companies making indirect CVC investments

	Major motive	Minor motive
Financial return on investment	8	3
Exposure to new technologies (broad range)	5	2
Identification of new products	2	5
Access to new markets	2	4
Improvement of manufacturing processes	1	5
Establishment of further business relationships	0	5
Learn about venture capital	0	3
Lower manufacturing costs	0	2
Social responsibility	0	2
Help suppliers and customers	0	1
Assess acquisition candidates	0	1
Indirect benefits from assisting the small firm sector	0	1

Notes: Figures indicate number of mentions based on data from eleven indirect investees
Source: survey

NATURE OF THE CVC RELATIONSHIP

Therefore, the majority of direct investee firms actively seek direct CVC investment for the value-added and financial benefits that they believe non-financial companies to be able to offer. In contrast, indirect investees do not usually actively seek indirect CVC finance and even when they are aware of indirect corporate investors they do not expect to benefit significantly from them. However, expectations will not necessarily be reflected in outcomes. Therefore, in order to identify the actual advantages and disadvantages of CVC, there is a need to explore the nature of the CVC relationship in terms of investment agreements and their favourability to investee firms, inter-firm power relations, communication between investors and investees and the hands-on role played by non-financial companies. It is also important to analyse in more detail the post-investment experience in terms of the benefits and problems faced by investee companies. Given the differing expectations of direct and indirect investees, the experiences of both groups will again be analysed separately.

Direct investees

Direct CVC investments were not typically accompanied by detailed investment agreements. There were rarely any formal rate of return, ratchet or exiting arrangements, although almost all investing companies had the option of at least one seat on the board of investee firms, supporting the findings outlined in Chapter 4. This lack of detailed agreements is because the investments were typically seen as strategic partnerships with corporate investors that were assumed to be more concerned with the strategic rather than the financial orientation of the deal. Investments were typically part of ongoing collaboration between the two companies, or were designed to initiate such collaboration. Indeed, some respondents indicated that a major feature of the investment agreement was the corporate expectation that investment would lead to further, long-term inter-firm business relationships. In some cases, where the non-financial company followed a lead venture capital investor, the corporate simply agreed to the terms and conditions of a previously drawn-up investment agreement.

The investment agreements were considered by respondents to be equally favourable to both investor and investee companies in almost all cases. Direct CVC agreements tend to be mutually beneficial for both partners, with pricing not creating the obstacles that are frequently associated with institutional venture capital investment. This supports the suggestion made in Chapter 2 that small firms that raise finance from corporate sources often receive more for their share capital because of the corporate investors' emphasis on strategic rather than financial factors (Bailey, 1985; Henricks, 1991). Only one investee company director felt that it had benefited more than the investing organisation, largely due to the favourable pricing arrangement, and only two believed that the agreement had benefited the investor to a greater extent by providing it with an undesirable level of control over the investee firm. Furthermore, the majority of direct investees did not experience any difficulties when negotiating investment agreements with investing companies. Only one-third of firms reported problems, these being associated with negotiating with companies with very different cultures or coordinating deals with more than one corporate investor.

Nevertheless, as Ohmae (1989: 151) has observed, 'equity investments almost always have an overtone of one company trying to control another with money'. That the large company often has control is to be expected given its greater level of resources (Taylor, 1987; 1995). Different levels of resources can bind companies into unequal alliances so that A has power over B to the extent that A can get B to do something that B would not otherwise do (Taylor, 1995). Indeed, various authors (e.g. Kotkin, 1989; Van Gils and Zwart, 1994) have recognised that in a strategic partnership it is usually the strategy of the large firm that determines the direction of the alliance. Two-thirds of direct investees in this survey believed that the investment agreements had given investors a certain level of power, usually through their board representation.[7] In some cases investors even had the option to completely reject board decisions. However, it is important to recognise that the potential power of corporate investors in direct CVC relationships is not necessarily undesirable. It has been argued that 'equals' do not always make the best partners (Skjerstad, 1994). Investors need to understand that while a guiding hand can be beneficial, in order to benefit from the entrepreneurial nature and flexibility of young TBFs they must be careful not to stifle them by attempting to take control. Indeed, only one-third of firms that stated that investing companies had the power to influence their operations believed that they had ever exercised this power to any extent and, as mentioned above, only two firms believed that corporate investors had taken excessive levels of control.

Most direct investees communicated with investing companies on a monthly basis for board meetings and progress reports. Firms that had contact with investors on a more frequent basis were typically those that had further collaborative arrangements with the investors. As was found in Chapter 4, very few firms communicated with investors less frequently than once a month, although one had only annual meetings. The regular contact between investor and investee firms reflects the hands-on nature of direct CVC investment. Of the twenty-three direct investees, twenty-one described the involvement of their corporate investors as hands-on. A company can be regarded as a hands-on investor if it has board representation, but investees were quick to note that investors typically offered more than would be expected of board members (Table 6.17). They often

Table 6.17 Degree of hands-on involvement of companies investing directly

Form of hands-on involvement	Number of investee firms receiving	Degree of usefulness rating*					
		5	4	3	2	1	Av.
Seat on investee's board	20 (95%)	6	7	6	1	0	3.9
Help with short-term problems	18 (86%)	4	7	6	1	0	3.8
Acting as a sounding board to investee management	12 (57%)	4	3	3	2	0	3.8
Help with development of business strategies	6 (29%)	2	2	2	0	0	4
Evaluation of products/markets	5 (24%)	2	1	2	0	0	4
Development of marketing plans	4 (19%)	1	2	1	0	0	4
Monitoring of financial performance	4 (19%)	0	2	2	0	0	3.5
Monitoring of operating performance	4 (19%)	0	1	3	0	0	3.3
Help with product R&D	3 (14%)	1	1	1	0	0	4
Product manufacturing assistance	2 (10%)	1	1	0	0	0	4.5
Replacement of members of the management team	1 (5%)	1	0	0	0	0	5
Providing contacts with suppliers	1 (5%)	0	1	0	0	0	4
Providing contacts with customers	1 (5%)	0	1	0	0	0	4
Help in obtaining finance from other sources	1 (5%)	0	0	1	0	0	3

Notes: * 5 = very productive/1 = very counter-productive
based on data from twenty-one respondents
Source: survey

provided help with short-term problems as well as acting as a sounding board to the TBFs' management. Some were also active in assisting with business strategies and evaluating product and market opportunities. In almost all cases, the hands-on involvement of corporate investors was considered to be productive.

Again supporting the findings of Chapter 4, for almost two-thirds of direct investees the receipt of direct CVC finance had not only provided a hands-on investment source but also led to further business relationships with investing companies or their subsidiaries. These took a variety of forms, but were most commonly research contracts or licensing deals instigated by either the investor, investee or both parties.

Indirect investees

The venture capital finance received by indirect investees was only slightly more likely than direct CVC to involve a detailed investment agreement. Although six of the thirty-two investees had rate of return and exiting agreements with their venture capitalists, the remainder did not. This is

TECHNOLOGY-BASED FIRMS AND CVC

perhaps surprising, given the financial aims of venture capitalists and their obligation to limited partners to provide a return on invested capital within a certain time. However, almost all lead venture capitalists did have board seats through which they could keep a close eye on investee progress. Only one deal involved any agreement to investigate possible synergies with the indirect corporate investors. Most indirect investees considered the investment agreements to be equally favourable to themselves, their venture capitalist investors, and the corporate investors (when firms were aware of them). Only three firms felt that the investment gave the venture capitalists too much control. Pricing was identified as the most difficult thing to negotiate with venture capitalists by a number of respondents, with the majority having to concede to the investor eventually after lengthy negotiations. This contrasts with direct CVC where pricing was found to cause very few problems. It is likely that this difference reflects the fact that indirect investments are, by definition, managed by independent fund managers who tend to place greater emphasis on the price of equity when negotiating a deal than corporate investors.

Through their board seats venture capital fund managers evidently have a certain amount of influence over the operations of their portfolio investees. However, as was found in Chapters 4 and 5, the involvement of indirect corporate investors in the development of these TBFs tends to be very limited. Five of the eleven firms that were aware of their indirect corporate investors never communicated with them and over half of the remaining firms met with representatives from indirect investors less frequently than once a month. No respondents considered indirect corporate investors to have the power to influence any aspect of the operations of their firms. This is not surprising given that large non-financial companies will have chosen the indirect investment route so that the independent fund managers can do the work for them.

As well as board representation, fund managers typically helped with short-term problem solving, monitoring and acting as a sounding board to management (Table 6.18). In all aspects their contribution was considered to be productive by most respondents. While almost all indirect investees considered the venture capital fund managers to be hands-on, only three indicated that corporate investors provided any hands-on assistance. When indirect corporate investors did play a hands-on role this tended to involve assistance with product R&D, product manufacturing and the development of marketing plans. Again the corporate contributions were productive. Four indirect investees had subsequently established further business relationships with investing corporations. As with direct CVC these were typically research contracts or licensing deals.

194

Table 6.18 Degree of hands-on involvement of venture capital fund managers investing in indirect investees

Form of hands-on involvement	Number of investee firms receiving		Degree of usefulness rating*					
			5	4	3	2	1	Av.
Seat on investee's board	29	(100%)	4	14	7	2	2	3.6
Help with short-term problems	14	(48%)	5	4	4	1	0	3.6
Acting as a sounding board to investee management	11	(38%)	4	7	0	0	0	4.4
Monitoring of financial performance	11	(38%)	2	6	3	0	0	3.9
Monitoring of operating performance	11	(38%)	1	6	4	0	0	3.7
Help with development of business strategies	9	(31%)	3	5	1	0	0	4.2
Development of marketing plans	8	(28%)	1	6	1	0	0	4
Evaluation of products/markets	6	(21%)	2	4	0	0	0	4.3
Help in obtaining finance from other sources	4	(14%)	2	1	0	1	0	4
Providing contacts with suppliers	2	(7%)	1	1	0	0	0	4.5
Providing contacts with customers	2	(7%)	1	1	0	0	0	4.5
Replacement of members of the management team	1	(3%)	0	1	0	0	0	4
Providing contacts with other organisations	1	(3%)	0	1	0	0	0	4

Notes: *5 = very productive/1 = very counter-productive
based on data from twenty-nine respondents
Source: survey

THE POST-INVESTMENT EXPERIENCE OF CVC

In the light of the findings concerning the nature of direct and indirect CVC relationships this section looks in more detail at the post-investment benefits and problems of CVC investment for the investee firm. This provides a final indication of the accuracy of investee firm expectations regarding the value-added and financial benefits of this form of investment, as well as identifying any unforeseen problems which may exist.

Benefits of CVC

Direct investees

As was anticipated by the TBFs prior to their receipt of finance, the benefits of direct CVC to the investee firm are more than just financial (Table 6.19). These benefits also confirm the advantages of this form of funding over more conventional sources of external equity finance that

Table 6.19 Benefits for investee firms that have arisen as a result of direct CVC finance (apart from the provision of finance)

	Number of mentions
Help with short-term problems	19
Access to corporate management expertise	16
Credibility	16
Access to corporate technical expertise	11
Pricing benefits	10
Lower performance targets	9
Access to corporate marketing/distribution networks	9
Extra production/R&D support	8
Opportunity to establish further business relationships	8
Access to more sophisticated financial control systems	1
Access to corporate office space	1
Access to possible exit routes	1
Synergy	1
Enhanced attractiveness to other investors	1
Stability	1
Access to corporate operational expertise	1
Strengthening of vertical relationships	1

Note: Based on data from twenty-three direct investees
Source: survey

were suggested in Chapter 2 and illustrated in Chapter 4. All direct investee firms in this survey had benefited from this investment in ways other than simply the receipt of finance. While firms did outline advantages associated with pricing and more realistic performance targets, they placed particular emphasis on the credibility which they had gained from their links with major multinational corporations, the help that they have obtained with short-term problems, their access to management and technical expertise, and also to the markets and distribution channels of investing companies. These benefits illustrate the importance of corporate investors in providing the TBF with operational, technical and marketing expertise and resources. As venture capital funds and private investors – the main sources of external equity finance – typically provide different types of value-added contribution, usually involving managerial and financial advice rather than technical assistance (MacMillan *et al.*, 1988; Landström, 1990; Harrison and Mason, 1992; Sadtler, 1993; Ehrlich *et al.*, 1994), these findings indicate the potential complementarity of direct CVC and other external equity sources for TBFs.

Indirect investees

The indirect investees that knew that they had received indirect CVC finance did not always feel that they had benefited specifically from their indirect corporate equity partners. Indeed, only five of the eleven firms felt that they had benefited in ways other than financially. This therefore supports the findings of Chapters 4 and 5 that indicated the limited levels of value-added provided by non-financial companies that invest indirectly. However, some investee firms recognised that indirect investment had led to the establishment of business relationships with investing corporations, while others identified the investors' help with short-term problems and assistance with production and R&D (Table 6.20). Although only a few firms felt that indirect CVC had been particularly beneficial, those that did emphasised the same advantages of this form of corporate investment as were outlined in the case of direct CVC, again suggesting that a corporate presence has the potential to be a useful complement to the expertise of the venture capitalist for TBFs.

Post-investment problems of CVC

Direct investees

Direct investees experienced very few post-investment problems, further illustrating the promising potential of direct CVC as a finance source. Almost half of the direct investees in this survey had experienced no post-investment problems at all, and most of the issues that were raised by respondents, including conflicting cultures, shortage of complementary capabilities and impatient corporate investors, were considered to be only minor (Table 6.21). The only problem that was considered to be of major significance to more than one company concerned the difficulties encountered obtaining further finance, not necessarily from the investing companies, but from other sources. These TBFs found that the presence of a large company left other potential investors wary of possible hidden

Table 6.20 Benefits for investee firms that have arisen as a result of indirect CVC finance (apart from the provision of finance)

	Number of mentions
Opportunity to establish further business relationships	4
Help with short-term problems	3
Access to corporate management expertise	2
Extra production/R&D support	2
Credibility	2
Pricing benefits	1
Lower performance targets	1
Access to corporate technical expertise	1
Access to corporate marketing/distribution networks	1

Note: Based on data from five indirect investees that had benefited from indirect CVC finance
Source: survey

197

Table 6.21 Post-investment problems experienced by companies that have raised direct CVC finance

	Major problem	Minor problem
Difficulties obtaining further finance	2	0
Conflicting corporate cultures	1	4
Conflicting objectives	1	2
Lack of support from investor	1	2
Exiting difficulties	1	1
Lack of experience of investor	1	1
Difficulties paying dividends	1	1
Slow corporate decision making	1	0
General conflicts with investor	1	0
Changing corporate strategies	1	0
Shortage of complementary capabilities	0	3
Lack of patience of corporate investor	0	3
Loss of firm's identity	0	2
Loss of control of company's operations	0	2
Unnecessary corporate interference	0	1
Investor takes more than it gives	0	1
The reorganisation required	0	1
Commercial trading conflicts	0	1
Lack of *unanimous* support from all corporate directors	0	1

Notes: Figures indicate number of mentions based on data from twelve direct investees that had experienced post-investment problems
Source: survey

agendas on the part of the corporate investor such as the desire to control and possibly acquire the investee firm.

The relatively problem-free nature of direct CVC relationships is surprising given the considerable attention paid to the potential problems of this form of investment in the literature. Various authors have highlighted the possible disadvantages of seeking non-financial companies as equity partners (e.g. Collins and Doorley, 1991; Roberts, 1991; Botkin and Matthews, 1992; Dunn, 1992; Ahern, 1993b; Dodgson, 1993; Oakey, 1993; Stewart, 1993; Garnsey and Wilkinson, 1994; Mamis, 1995). Investee firms may lose their independence, they may lose proprietary information to their partner without gaining sufficiently in return or they may become take-over targets (Roberts, 1991; Ahern, 1993b; Oakey, 1993). The investing company may interfere in the day-to-day running of the firm or may not offer the commitment necessary to overcome the inevitable conflicts of company cultures. Many of these issues were recognised in Chapter 1 as potentially problematic for all forms of large firm–small firm collaboration. An explanation for the findings of this survey may once again be related to the propensity for firms to have already formed business relationships with investing companies prior to their investments. The mutual understanding that develops between firms prior to equity investment (Hladik, 1988) can considerably reduce the extent of post investment difficulties.

Indirect investees

As with direct investment, indirect CVC posed very few post-investment problems for investee firms. Only three of the eleven firms that had knowingly received this form of CVC had experienced any difficulties, all of which had relatively greater contact with corporate investors than is usual (Table 6.22). One drew attention to the conflicting corporate cultures of investor and investee firms, another emphasised the constant need to reassure corporate investors and the third complained of a general lack of communication within the investing company. While the typical lack of contact between investor and investee firms in cases of indirect investment does not leave much room for significant post-investment difficulties, the favourable experiences of the majority of firms that were aware of their indirect investors do suggest the corporate sector to be a suitable alternative source of finance for venture capital funds that specialise in making investments in early stage TBFs.

CONCLUSIONS

The aim of this chapter has been to examine the role of CVC as a source of external equity finance for TBFs, and specifically to identify whether there are any benefits of CVC for investee firms. By focusing on the financial histories of a sample of TBFs, it has been possible to analyse both the significance of CVC relative to other sources as well as the stage distribution of CVC investments. Also, the motivations of small firms for entering into equity alliances with large corporate partners have been considered. Furthermore, the post-investment experiences of TBFs that have raised

Table 6.22 Post-investment problems experienced by companies that have raised indirect CVC finance

	Major problem	*Minor problem*
Conflicting corporate cultures	1	0
Constant need to reassure corporate investors	1	0
Lack of coordination in the investing corporate	1	0
Shortage of complementary capabilities	0	2
Short-termism in the investing corporate	0	1
Lack of support from investor	0	1

Notes: Figures indicate number of mentions based on data from three indirect investees that had experienced post-investment problems
Source: survey

CVC have enabled a more accurate assessment of the role of this source of finance to be made.

In the UK, TBFs of a range of ages and sizes and in a variety of locations have received sizeable tranches of CVC finance, either directly or indirectly, during the 1980s and early 1990s. The financial history of these firms indicates that for the majority of them this finance has represented a significant proportion of the total external equity raised from all sources and has been a particularly important part of their initial rounds of external equity funding, when they are typically still in the start-up or other early stages of development. This illustrates the importance and potential of CVC as an early stage source of funds for growth-oriented TBFs with large capital requirements. As suggested by numerous authors (including Winters and Murfin, 1988; Collins and Doorley, 1991; Roberts, 1991), and confirmed throughout this thesis, the concentration of investment in early stage technology-based ventures reflects the motives of corporate investors which are often strategically oriented, and specifically related to obtaining windows on *new* technologies, or are concerned with benefiting financially from the growth of such firms

Direct investees actively sought CVC finance from companies in their own industrial sectors. Firms typically approached just one potential investor at a time, and many had already formed business relationships with these companies. Consequently, investor identification was rarely problematic and investment negotiations were conducted through established contacts. The final selection of investors was influenced primarily by financial considerations concerning the nature of the deal, although strategic factors including the hands-on role of investors were often also influential.

In contrast, only a limited number of indirect investees have actively and knowingly sought indirect CVC finance. Most consider there to be no distinction between this and conventional venture capital funding. Furthermore, very few indirect investees are even aware that they have received indirect CVC finance. The identification and choice of venture capital fund managers is therefore not influenced by the presence of a corporate investor, since TBFs concentrate instead on the experience and financial expertise of the venture capitalist.

For direct investees the decision to specifically seek direct CVC finance largely reflects the belief that this form of investment has the potential to provide them with tangible and intangible value-added benefits. Non-financial companies are likely to be making direct venture capital investments in TBFs primarily in order to obtain windows on new technologies. Therefore, prospective investees supported the comments of Roberts (1980; 1991), Henricks (1991) and others and anticipated that they could benefit from the frequent contact and nurturing associated with this form of investment. Furthermore, as Bailey (1985) suggested, the preoccupation

200

of investors with strategic gains led TBFs to expect a more attractive pricing agreement than would be offered by a purely financially motivated investor. Again supporting much of the literature, firms also hoped that association with a large, multinational corporation would enhance their own credibility in the marketplace.

However, indirect CVC financing is not associated with the same level of advantages as direct investment. Although many indirect corporate investors were believed to be seeking windows on technologies, strategic motives were considered to be less important than with direct CVC, largely because of the lower levels of contact between investor and investee firms. As a result, indirect investees did not expect to receive the same value-added benefits from investing companies as with direct CVC. Instead, investees tend to be more concerned with the financial benefits of venture capital and the fund managers' expertise in these matters.

The expectations of TBFs, and indeed the comments of many commentators in the field, are borne out in the nature of CVC relationships. In the case of direct CVC, contact between investor and investee firms is relatively frequent and is often associated with the nurturing and further collaborative linkages between partners. Indeed, investors are usually hands-on, providing productive assistance with short-term problems and acting as a sounding board to investee management. They are also typically receptive to, or even instigate, the establishment of further business relationships. In contrast, indirect investors do not have the same levels of power or contact with their investees. Very few played a hands-on role or established any business relationships with TBFs.

The typically strategic motivations of direct investors and their close contact with investee firms are reflected in both the financial and, more significantly, the non-financial benefits of this form of investment for TBFs. Firms benefited from the patience and understanding of corporate investors and the relatively high valuation of their equity. Moreover, TBFs gained credibility in the marketplace, access to management and technical expertise, and marketing and distribution channels. These non-financial value-added aspects of direct CVC suggest the complementarity of this form of investment and other, more conventional, forms which offer the benefits of more financially oriented advice and management expertise. Conversely, indirect investees did not benefit as often from the value-added offered by corporate investors. This was largely a consequence of the lack of contact and control of indirect corporate investors over the deal. However, on the few occasions when investees did experience value-added, it took the form of technically oriented advice and credibility, as was the case with direct investment. Neither direct nor indirect CVC investment created significant post-investment problems for investee firms despite the considerable attention that has been paid to this issue in the academic and management literature (e.g. by Collins and Doorley, 1991; Roberts, 1991; Botkin and Matthews, 1992).

There is an ongoing need for alternative sources of equity finance for growth-oriented TBFs and entrepreneurial companies in general. This need is particularly great in the UK. This survey has indicated that CVC provides attractively priced, early stage external equity finance in appropriate amounts for TBFs. In addition, the unique value-added benefits made available to investee firms through CVC, particularly in its direct form, make it a particularly important finance source. Through CVC, small firms benefit from a more sympathetic, realistic and understanding finance source, while large companies can gain both financially and strategically. These findings suggest that the encouragement of collaboration between large and small companies, particularly in technology-related areas, is vital for helping to maintain the competitive advantage not only of the partners but also of the national economy. CVC is a way of watering the seeds of industry and helping to rebuild an indigenous design and manufacturing base.

Corporate venture capital investment has now been considered from the perspectives of corporate executives that have been involved in making investments, venture capital fund managers that have raised funds from non-financial companies and directors of small TBFs that have received CVC finance. The research outlined in this book has enabled a detailed analysis of, not only the levels and nature of CVC activity in the UK, but also the motives and experiences of participating organisations. Chapter 7 draws together the research findings into an overall summary before discussing CVC in the light of the main study aims, namely to examine CVC in both the context of inter-firm collaboration theory and as a possible solution to the ongoing problem of the equity gap. The chapter also considers the practical implications of the study findings before highlighting avenues for further research.

7

CONCLUSIONS

The purpose of this concluding chapter is to summarise the main findings of this book and to discuss their implications for academics, practitioners and policy makers. First, the major research findings are identified. They are then discussed in the light of the main research aims which concern the role of CVC both in terms of inter-firm collaboration and as a source of external equity finance for small firms. Suggestions are then made regarding the ways in which corporate executives, venture capitalists, entrepreneurs and policy makers can encourage the development of CVC. Finally, questions arising from this study are used to propose an agenda for further research.

CORPORATE VENTURE CAPITAL: SUMMARY OF MAIN FINDINGS

The main research questions to be addressed by this book were outlined in Chapter 2. They concerned the extent of CVC in the UK, the objectives of this particular business strategy, the nature and forms which it can take and the post-investment experiences of participating organisations. The study has provided information relating to all of these issues and each shall be considered in turn.

Scale of CVC in the UK

The research indicates that the levels of CVC remain modest in the UK in comparison with the USA. However, the number of organisations that either have been, or still are, involved in some form of CVC activity in the UK has been found to be greater than is often believed to be the case. It was suggested in Chapter 2 that the accuracy of past estimates of the extent of CVC in the UK was in doubt. The low-key approach of many companies was put forward as a possible explanation for why many cases of CVC investment failed to be recognised. It will be recalled that ACOST

(1990) considered there to be a complete absence of CVC in the UK. This thesis has clearly indicated the inaccuracy of this statement.

Chapter 3 found CVC investment to be an activity that has been undertaken by a number of UK-headquartered companies and overseas-owned subsidiaries in the UK in recent years. These companies typically operate in the utilities, computers, electronics, engineering and oil and gas sectors of industry. Chapter 5 indicated that a large number of UK-based venture capital fund managers have raised finance for their funds from non-financial companies, albeit that a significant proportion of these companies were of non-UK parentage. Finally, all three surveys identified a considerable number of small, innovative UK companies that have received CVC finance, either directly or indirectly, knowingly or unknowingly, at some stage of their development. In view of these findings, research on the topic of CVC investment is clearly overdue.

Organisation of UK CVC

Corporate venture capital investment in the UK has taken a number of different forms. Chapter 3 suggested the most commonly used form to be direct, internally managed investment, although Chapters 5 and 6 have also emphasised the significance of indirect investment. Companies have invested directly via captive funds and also indirectly via pooled or dedicated funds. However, the majority have preferred to invest on an ad hoc basis, often in a small number of firms with whom they have already established contractual business relationships. This provides support for the hypothesis formulated in Chapter 2 which suggested that the tendency for companies to invest in an 'informal', one-off manner had led to an underestimation of the levels of CVC activity in the UK.

In terms of the internal organisation of CVC investment, the two main alternatives are (i) to make investments via an in-house function or operating division, or (ii) to invest via a separate subsidiary company (Mast, 1991; Honeyman, 1992; Block and MacMillan, 1993). This study has found that companies investing indirectly tend to use both of these organisational strategies. In contrast, companies investing directly, and particularly those making ad hoc investments, rarely invest via subsidiary companies since their investments tend to require more rigid investment approval processes and hence closer contact with the company's main board.

The underdeveloped nature of UK CVC

While this study finds that CVC is far from non-existent in the UK, it does confirm that it remains an underdeveloped corporate strategy in comparison with the USA. As was suggested in Chapter 2, this reflects both a reluctance of large companies to experiment with the venture capital option, and indeed with collaboration *per se*, as well as the withdrawal of numerous companies from the venture capital arena since the late 1980s. Both of these factors will be considered in turn.

The reluctance of UK-based companies to make venture capital investments does not reflect a lack of opportunities – although these may not be quality opportunities – since a majority of the corporations considered in Chapters 2 and 4 that have not undertaken CVC have been approached either by venture capitalists or entrepreneurs seeking equity finance. However, despite these approaches, many large companies have not even considered the venture capital option. Because of a desire among UK corporations for maximum possible control over their business activities, and also a shortage of information, time and management skills, alternative development strategies such as acquisition and other internalised business development options, which can be more easily justified to institutional shareholders, are still preferred.

Several of the companies that have previously made venture capital investments have now withdrawn from this activity. Two main factors help to explain this withdrawal. First, some companies have been disillusioned by poor previous investment experiences. This has been particularly marked in the case of indirect CVC with several executives expressing disappointment with the performance of their companies' externally managed investments and consequently pulling out of venture capital. Second, some companies have disbanded their CVC operations as part of a return to concentration on core business areas. This has been particularly evident where companies have previously invested directly.

The withdrawal of several companies from CVC has been partly compensated for by a number of 'new players' who have only recently become involved in CVC and others who plan to do so in the future. The most noteworthy new players are the privatised utility companies, supporting the comments of Dunn (1992) and Scottish Enterprise (1993) who noted the propensity for newly privatised companies to invest in venture capital. The utility sector seems likely to become increasingly significant in the CVC arena as more companies attempt to counteract the risks associated with greater regulation of their prices.

However, while the modest number of companies planning to make CVC investments is reasonably encouraging, this research has indicated that many entrepreneurs and venture capitalists have lost faith in the corporate sector as a potential funding source. Only a relatively small number of the TBFs identified in Chapter 6 plan to raise CVC finance before 1998. While this is partly a result of the decision by many of these firms not to seek external equity finance from *any* source during this period, it also reflects the fact that entrepreneurs are increasingly doubtful of their chances of raising CVC finance. Indeed, several firms that have attempted to raise CVC recently have been unsuccessful. Similarly, a number of independent fund managers have become disillusioned with corporate investors largely because catering for their specific needs is often too time consuming. Consequently, many fund managers will not attempt to raise finance from this source in the future.

It therefore seems unlikely that there will be anything but a modest increase in CVC investment in the UK in the near future. However, while few entrepreneurs and fund managers anticipate increases in the levels of this activity, many corporate executives do expect to see increasing levels of CVC, and particularly direct investment in research-based sectors. They predict that corporate managers will recognise the benefits of links with small firms and the importance of flexible organisational strategies as the economy moves further out of recession. Indeed, an economic upswing will significantly increase the likelihood of CVC investment becoming an important strategy, and BVCA figures (BVCA, 1995a) indicating the increasing significance of CVC relative to other sources (albeit that this largely reflects investment from foreign companies) suggest that such an upswing may already be underway.

Why large companies make CVC investments

It was suggested in Chapter 2 that the corporate motivations for making CVC investments were diverse and often confused by authors (Winters and Murfin, 1988). The findings of this study clearly illustrate this diversity and help to overcome some of the confusion surrounding this issue.

The motivations of corporations for making venture capital investments are largely strategic. This supports the findings of several authors in the USA (e.g. Rind, 1981; Collins and Doorley, 1991; Mast, 1991; Block and MacMillan, 1993). The identification of new markets, new technologies, new products and new processes, as well as the opportunity to form further business relationships with both vertically and horizontally related investees are the main considerations. However, companies also invest for financial or social responsibility-related purposes, as well as to learn about the venture capital process.

It is clear that the optimal structure of a CVC programme is company specific. However, there are, as was suggested in Chapter 2, notable distinctions between the motivations of companies making direct and indirect investments, and these distinctions form a clear pattern. Prior to investment, companies believe direct, internally managed investments to offer a high level of both contact with investee firms and control over the CVC relationship. Such investments are therefore made for largely strategic reasons, and particularly to gain access to possible new markets. Indirect, externally managed investments are believed to provide greater deal flow and access to an external fund manager's expertise and experience, and to require less management time and resources. They are therefore thought to be especially appropriate for companies with social responsibility-related objectives and companies seeking to learn about venture capital. Companies motivated by particular strategic aims, such as the opportunity to gain windows on a wide range of new technologies, may also prefer the indirect investment method. Both direct and indirect CVC investments are made for financial purposes, although this is often a secondary objective. When corporate motivations are strategically or social responsibility oriented they are usually considered to complement other corporate growth strategies such as acquisition and organic growth. However, when objectives are financial or related to learning about venture capital, the degree of complementarity between CVC and other development strategies is much lower.

Why small TBFs seek CVC finance

The decision of the TBF manager to seek CVC finance is a reflection of both financial and strategic motivations. Financially, both direct and indirect CVC are seen as other possible sources of funds by most entrepreneurs. Furthermore, companies that seek direct CVC investment correctly perceive the objectives of most corporate investors to be strategically oriented and therefore, supporting the comments of Bailey (1985), anticipate a more attractive pricing agreement than would be offered by a purely financially motivated investor.

In terms of strategic objectives, this research has uncovered marked differences between the motivations of firms seeking direct and indirect CVC finance. Prior to investment, TBFs typically believe that direct CVC has the potential to provide them with both tangible and intangible value-added benefits in addition to finance. Because these firms expect non-financial companies to be making direct CVC investments in TBFs primarily in order to obtain access to new technologies, they believe that they will be able to benefit from the frequent contact and nurturing offered by investing companies as they attempt to establish close relationships. TBFs also hope that association with a large, multinational company will enhance their own credibility in the marketplace.

However, indirect CVC is not associated with the same level of perceived strategic advantages as direct investment. Many entrepreneurs are unaware of who is funding venture capital funds. Not surprisingly therefore, few firms are even aware that they have received indirect CVC finance and therefore clearly do not anticipate strategic advantages. However, even firms that are aware of their indirect corporate investors did not expect to benefit strategically from these investors prior to investment. These firms correctly believed strategic motives to be less important for companies investing indirectly, largely because of the lower levels of contact between investor and investee firms. As a result, TBFs do not expect to

207

receive the same value-added benefits from investing companies as with direct CVC.

Why independent fund managers target corporate investors

The survey findings outlined in Chapter 5 concerning the reasons why venture capitalists seek to raise finance from the corporate sector serve to confirm the comments of many authors (e.g. Bailey, 1985; Collins and Doorley, 1991; Murray, 1993). The majority of fund managers sought to raise funds from non-financial companies because they considered the corporate sector to be a valuable alternative source of funds in the current difficult fund raising climate. As was indicated in Chapter 5, the sample of venture capital fund managers excluded those *merchant capitalists* (Bygrave and Timmons, 1992) which specialise in MBO/MBI deals, but concentrated specifically on more *classic* venture capital funds whose investments focus on early stage, often high technology deals. The difficulties which such classic funds are experiencing in raising finance from institutional investors were outlined in Chapter 2. The surveyed fund managers typically believed that the corporate sector would be particularly interested in investing in early stage TBFs (and hence their funds which have experience in such areas) either because of their desire to gain a window on technologies, or because of the attraction of the possibility of considerable financial gain.

In addition to being a potentially valuable source of funds, venture capitalists believed that large companies could bring industry-specific advice to deals. The combination of the fund manager's investment skills and the corporate investor's industry knowledge and technical know-how was considered to be potentially beneficial for the portfolio investee. Furthermore, fund managers foresaw the usefulness of corporate investors as a potential exit route for their investments. Such an investor may buy out the venture capitalist's stake in an investee firm as part of a trade sale if it considers the small firm and its products to be of strategic relevance to its own business. Also, it is anticipated that the presence of a corporate investor may help to enhance the credibility of an investee firm, thus leaving it more attractive for later stage investors.

The CVC investment process

The differing objectives of companies involved in direct and indirect CVC are strongly reflected in the nature of the investment process in each case. This process can be considered in terms of both the selection of investee firms and fund managers, and the selection of investing companies.

CONCLUSIONS

The investee/fund selection process

The research has clearly indicated the search process and selection criteria employed by large corporations looking to invest directly or indirectly in venture capital. Companies investing directly identify investee firms through continual searching and via intermediaries. Some already have business relationships with their investees such as customer, supplier or contract links. The importance that corporations place on particular factors in the selection of investee firms is largely a function of objectives. Companies with strategic motives tend to place greater emphasis on characteristics associated with products and markets while the few companies with social responsibility related objectives are more concerned with entrepreneur and management team criteria.

For non-financial companies interested in making indirect investments, two key factors are of particular importance in the selection of fund managers; first, the venture capitalist's experience and previous track record, and second, the investment focus and type of investment vehicle offered. However, fund evaluation is again strongly related to corporate objectives. Companies with strategic motivations are typically more interested in the focus of funds on particular sectors and development stages, and companies with non-strategic objectives are more concerned with investment track record.

The investor selection process

The methods and criteria used by fund managers and entrepreneurs in the search and selection of corporate investors were also considered in this research. In the case of indirect CVC, the initial onus is usually on the fund managers to attract corporate investors to their funds. Venture capitalists therefore typically approach a large number of companies at the executive board level. Very few corporations were found to have a venture capital manager with whom to correspond. Fund managers tended to approach large, well-known companies regardless of industry sector, and only a small minority coordinated the focus of their funds with the type of company approached (e.g. contacting corporates in technology-based sectors if the fund specialised in investing in TBFs).

As has been noted, some small firms seeking CVC finance approached potential corporate investors and fund managers. However, the research has identified significant differences in the extent to which young TBFs actively seek direct and indirect CVC. Direct investees sought finance from companies in their own industrial sectors. Firms typically approached just one potential investor at a time, and many had already formed business relationships with these companies. Consequently, investor identification was rarely problematic and investment negotiations were conducted

209

through established contacts. The final selection of investors was influenced primarily by financial considerations concerning the nature of the deal, although strategic factors including the hands-on role of investors were often also influential.

In contrast, only a limited number of indirect investees have actively sought indirect CVC finance. Most consider there to be no distinction between this and conventional venture capital funding, and indeed it has already been noted that many firms are not even aware that they have received indirect CVC finance. The identification and choice of venture capital fund managers is therefore not usually influenced by the presence of a corporate investor, since TBFs concentrate instead on the experience and financial expertise of the venture capitalist.

Characteristics of CVC investment

As with the nature of the CVC investment process, the differing motives of companies involved in direct and indirect CVC affect the characteristics of investments in each case. The differences between these two forms of investment can be considered under four subheadings.

Investee characteristics

This research has identified a diverse range of firms that have raised CVC finance since the early 1980s. CVC has been used to fund companies at a range of different stages of development in many different industries. Firms that have raised indirect CVC are more likely than those that have raised direct CVC to be in the early stages of development and to operate in technology-based industrial sectors. It follows that the funds in which non-financial companies are investing tend to specialise in making investments in early stage TBFs. Corporations that invest directly are mainly providing expansion and development finance to established firms which have proven products and technologies. Also, direct investments are more likely to be made in low or medium technology firms. This is because although the opportunity to obtain access to new *technological* developments is an important objective of direct corporate investors, this research has found that a more common objective of direct CVC is the identification of new *markets*.

Despite the distinctions outlined above, a significant number of the firms that receive CVC finance, indirectly or directly, are technology-based firms (TBFs). Indeed, the findings show that TBFs of a range of ages and sizes have raised CVC finance during the 1980s and 1990s. While many of these firms have also raised external equity finance from a number of other sources, both direct and indirect CVC finance have accounted for a significant proportion of the total external equity raised. Furthermore, CVC has been a particularly important part of the survey firms' initial rounds of external equity funding when they are typically still in the start-up or other early stages of development.

The majority of the firms identified in this research as having raised CVC finance were of UK origin. While these firms tend to be geographically dispersed within the UK to some extent, there is a marked concentration of indirect investee firms in the South of England, and TBFs that have raised CVC are often located in areas with a recognised concentration of such firms (e.g. Cambridge and Edinburgh). However, some CVC investments have been made by UK-based companies in non-UK firms. Again, there are important distinctions between direct and indirect CVC. Firms that had raised direct CVC were more likely to be UK companies than those which had raised indirect CVC. This reflects the typically strategically oriented nature of many direct investments and the consequent desire for investor and investee companies to be within close geographical proximity. In contrast, many companies investing abroad to keep a watching brief on developments in other countries use indirect CVC. These firms often lack the knowledge and resources required to manage foreign investments themselves and also usually require less contact with investee firms.

Investment size

The size of individual corporate investments, both direct and indirect, is small compared to that of independent venture capital funds. The typical investment size for both forms of investment, and particularly direct CVC, was found to be less than £$\frac{1}{3}$ million, suggesting that CVC can be a useful source of finance in tranches of less than £$\frac{1}{2}$ million. However, CVC investment is not limited to this size category. Technology-based firms often require much larger amounts of funding because of the capital-intensive nature of their operations. As a result, and as Chapter 6 indicates, non-financial companies that invest in TBFs are prepared to invest much larger amounts, sometimes over several rounds.

Level of involvement of corporate investors with investee firms

The extent to which investing companies become involved with investee firms varies considerably. In the case of indirect CVC, the degree of involvement is minimal, despite the approval of many fund managers, but does reflect the nature of the fund; investors in dedicated funds typically have more strategically oriented motivations and hence closer involvement and contact with investee firms than is the case with pooled funds. However, even in dedicated funds the amount of value-added offered by investing companies to investees is limited. The level of involvement was found to be much higher in the case of direct CVC, with many investors playing a hands-on role and taking seats on the board of investee

211

companies largely as a result of their typically strategic objectives. Direct CVC relationships also frequently provided opportunities for investing companies to nurture their investees and establish further business links with them.

Level of involvement of corporate investors with fund managers

The extent to which indirect corporate investors become involved in the operations of the independent funds in which they had invested also varies from case to case, as well as temporally. Some investors took a board seat giving them a say in the investee evaluation process, and some received periodical progress reports. However, other companies were permitted no involvement at all with fund managers. The research indicates that level of involvement is related to fund age and type. Fund age is important since contact between corporate investors and fund managers is usually at a maximum soon after initial corporate investment, but decreases as funds become fully invested. In terms of fund type, by definition, the managers of dedicated funds tend to allow corporate investors to set investment criteria, evaluate potential investees and develop links with portfolio firms. In contrast, the corporate investor in a pooled fund is not often allowed an influence over the investment process since it is only one of a number of limited partners and the fund manager must avoid conflicts with other institutional investors. It is also important to note that corporate investors in pooled funds may not wish to influence the investment process since it is likely that one of the reasons for investing indirectly was to ensure that the independent venture capitalist managed the process for them.

Post-investment experiences

As well as identifying the expectations and motivations of companies that become involved in the venture capital process, this study has examined the extent to which these expectations have been accurate by considering investment performance. The experiences of investors, investees and fund managers are considered in turn.

Investing companies

The majority of companies that have made CVC investments have been satisfied with their performance. However, the need to distinguish between direct and indirect investments is again apparent. Most direct CVC investors expressed satisfaction with their investments across a wide range of parameters. The highest ranking parameters were generally strategically oriented, including the use of CVC for spinning-out firms from within the company, developing further strategic business relationships and strengthening vertical relationships. Many direct investments made for financial, social responsibility and educational purposes were also considered to have performed at least satisfactorily. However, as has already been noted, the proportion of indirect investors that were satisfied with their investments' performance was much lower. Dissatisfaction with the performance of indirect investments largely reflects the inappropriate objectives of investing companies. Those indirect investors whose investments had performed well typically had non-strategic motivations, while those who had withdrawn from CVC as a result of poor performance had strategic objectives. This clearly supports the suggestion that this form of investment is more appropriate for non-strategic objectives.

The research findings indicate that companies making CVC investments, whether directly or indirectly, experience very few problems related to the investment process. Most of the tensions that have been identified, including lack of clear mission and conflicting objectives, apply equally to direct and indirect CVC. It appears that these issues are related to inexperience in the venture capital process and are often overcome in time.

Investee companies

In terms of benefits of CVC for the investee firm, the expectations of TBF directors, and indeed the comments of many commentators in the field, have been largely borne out in post-investment experiences. In the case of direct CVC, contact between investor and investee firms is relatively frequent. Investors are usually hands-on, providing productive assistance with short-term problems and acting as a sounding board to investee management. They are also typically receptive to, or even instigate, the establishment of further business relationships. In contrast, indirect investors do not have the same levels of power or contact with their investees. Very few played a hands-on role or established any business relationships with TBFs.

The typically strategic motivations of direct investors and their close contact with investee firms are reflected in both the financial and, more significantly, the non-financial benefits of this form of investment for TBFs. Firms benefited from the patience and understanding of corporate investors and the relatively high valuation of their equity. Moreover, TBFs gained credibility in the marketplace, access to management and technical expertise, and marketing and distribution channels. Conversely, indirect investees did not benefit as often from the value-added offered by corporate investors. This was largely a consequence of the lack of contact and control of indirect corporate investors over the deal. However, on the few occasions when investees did experience value-added, it took the form of technically oriented advice and credibility, as was the case with direct investment. Neither direct nor indirect CVC investment created significant

213

post-investment problems for investee firms despite the considerable attention that has been paid to this issue in the academic and management literature (e.g. by Collins and Doorley, 1991; Roberts, 1991; Botkin and Matthews, 1992).

Independent fund managers

As they had anticipated, many venture capital fund managers benefited, not only from the funds obtained from indirect corporate investors, but also from the industry-specific advice and skills which large companies can offer the venture capitalist. Fund managers typically felt that they had benefited specifically from the technical knowledge of their corporate investors and the help that this provides when evaluating potential investee firms. However, raising funds from large companies has also caused problems for many independent venture capitalists. For example, numerous fund managers have found companies that make indirect CVC investments to have unrealistic objectives, want too much control and be short-termist. As has been noted, many venture capitalists regard catering for the specific needs of corporates to be too time consuming. Also, companies investing in pooled funds sometimes have strategic motivations other than to obtain broad windows on new technological developments. It has been emphasised that this form of investment is more appropriate for meeting non-strategic goals, and dedicated funds, or indeed direct CVC, are more suitable for companies with strategic motives. Poor choice of investment strategy for particular objectives has led to disillusionment and unrest among corporate investors, and hence conflict with fund managers.

CVC AND INTER-FIRM COLLABORATION THEORY

As was noted in Chapter 1 of this book, corporate venture capital investment is a form of inter-firm relationship between a large and a small company (Klein, 1987; Chesnais, 1988; Ormerod and Burns, 1988; Hull and Slowinski, 1990; Collins and Doorley, 1991; Henricks, 1991; MacDonald, 1991; Manardo, 1991; Radtke and McKinney, 1991; Hagedoorn, 1993a). However, given the great diversity of alliance forms and the motives leading to their formation, there is a need to identify the specific characteristics of individual alliance types, including the CVC relationship, in order to proceed towards a more informative classification of inter-firm collaboration. Chapter 1 considered various theories which attempt to explain alliance formation (Table 1.1). These included both conventional alliance theories (transaction-cost theory, strategic behaviour theory, resource dependence theory) as well as macro-scale considerations within the modern business environment. The findings of this study (and particularly those outlined in Chapters 3 and 6) serve to indicate the appropriateness of these theories in explaining the formation of the CVC relationship. Chapter 1 also considered the spatial scale of inter-firm collaboration and in particular the debate concerning the relative importance of local industrial districts and the global economy. The research findings stimulate discussion as to the position of CVC within this debate.

CVC, collaboration and strategic alliances

As was noted in Chapter 1, companies of all sizes have been confronted by numerous interrelated macro-level pressures since the mid-1980s. These include increasing competitive intensity and globalisation, shorter product life-cycles and rapidly changing technologies (Lewis, 1990; Lorange and Roos, 1992; Van Gils and Zwart, 1994). Companies have responded in various ways to these pressures, one of which has involved the use of collaborative relationships with other firms and organisations, particularly in technology-based industries. These relationships can offer reduced costs and risks, economies of scale and scope, access to markets and technologies, the opportunity to pool resources and vertical quasi integration. Through collaboration companies therefore seek either flexibility, market power (supporting strategic behaviour theory), efficiency (supporting transaction cost theory) or competencies (supporting resource dependence theory), or any combination of these factors in pursuit of a strategy appropriate for their business market position. Large firm–small firm collaboration has the potential to be particularly beneficial given the complementary strengths of large and small companies (Niederkofler, 1991; Botkin and Matthews, 1992; Ahern, 1993a). It has been hypothesised (e.g. by Hull and Slowinski, 1990) that large companies that collaborate with small firms are principally interested in technology, while small firms are more concerned with financing and marketing.

This book provides evidence to suggest that the motivations for the formation of CVC relationships correspond to a large extent with those for collaboration *per se*, and therefore imply the relevance of alliance formation theories to CVC. In Chapter 3 the main macro-level considerations of companies for making CVC investments were identified. They included the need to cope with uncertainty, increasing global competition, technological opportunities and shorter product life-cycles. These correspond with the macro-scale factors responsible for initiating the recent trend towards inter-firm collaboration.

From the large firm perspective, the majority of CVC investments have been made for strategic purposes. Using Malecki's (1991) terminology for collaboration in general, companies making CVC investments have typically adopted either a *window* strategy, designed to identify and monitor a wide range of new technologies, products and markets, or an *options* strategy, in order to designate a small number of market or technical areas in which to participate. Companies have also invested in order to strengthen vertical relationships or indeed to form further business relationships with investee firms. The generic motives of investors have been both offensive and defensive, and all of the potential advantages of large firm–small firm collaboration for large companies identified in Table 1.5 have been found to be important considerations of companies making CVC investments. The emphasis which these companies place on enhancing their flexibility and market power and hence improving their competitive positions within a turbulent economic environment suggests the relevance of strategic behaviour theory in this context. CVC investment could also be considered as a means by which investing corporations gain access to the intangible, behavioural resources of the small firm, including its flexibility, thus supporting the views of resource dependence theorists who argue that companies collaborate in order to develop competencies. However, firms do not typically employ CVC strategy specifically as a means of reducing transaction costs and gaining efficiency. This suggests Williamson's (1975) theory of transaction costs to be a less important explanatory tool for this form of collaboration at least, and indicates the relative importance of a company's *environment* and *social context* in the collaboration decision (Grabher, 1993).

For the small investee company, the main consideration when seeking CVC finance is the need for tangible and intangible resources in order to commercialise its products and compete in an increasingly competitive marketplace. Small firms often lack finance, marketing expertise, manufacturing know-how, management capabilities and credibility (Hisrich, 1986; Dickson et al, 1990; Larson, 1990; Lawton Smith *et al.*, 1991; Botkin and Matthews, 1992). A CVC relationship with a large established corporation can provide all of these. Indeed, as was the case for large companies, all of the advantages of collaboration for the small firm shown in Table 5.1 are relevant in the case of CVC. As has been noted, the needs of TBFs are particularly great, and just as a concentration of large firm–small firm alliances has been recognised in technology-based sectors, so this thesis has identified the focus of many CVC programmes on TBFs. The motivations of small firms clearly suggests the relevance of resource dependence theory as a model for the objectives of investee firms in CVC. According to Pfeffer and Salancik (1978), this school of thought proposes that firms depend on other organisations within their environment to acquire resources which are vital for their survival and success.

However, the motives for CVC are far more complex than has been implied in the previous two paragraphs. As is the case with collaboration in general, CVC relationships are formed for a broad range of purposes, particularly from the investor's perspective, and can involve horizontally or vertically related firms. While most investments are strategically oriented, companies also have financial, social responsibility and education related objectives. It has already been emphasised that clear distinctions exist

216

between the objectives of direct and indirect CVC investments. Direct investments tend to be more strategically oriented on the part of the investing company and are largely part of an *options* strategy whereby individual products and technologies are targeted. Largely as a result, direct investments provide the investee firm with the opportunity to benefit strategically from value-added nurturing. As was suggested in Chapter 2, such relationships clearly warrant the title *strategic* alliance. However, many indirect investments are not motivated by strategic gain at all, and although some companies do invest indirectly in order to gain a window on a broad range of technologies, most consider this form of investment to be more appropriate for non-strategic purposes. Both a cause and a consequence of the non-strategic objectives of many indirect investors is the very limited contact between investor and investee. Indeed, it has been found that many investee firms are not even aware of their corporate investors. Clearly, CVC in this form does not constitute a *strategic* alliance, and it is also debatable whether it can even be considered to be a *collaborative relationship* in any sense given the lack of contact between firms.

The conceptualisation of CVC within the context of inter-firm collaboration is therefore somewhat complex. In many cases CVC investments can be considered to be forms of strategic collaboration between large and small firms. However, the identification of these relationships is often further confused by the existence of another collaborative relationship between investor and investee companies. CVC investments, particularly in their direct form, can either precede further contractual collaborative relationships between firms or follow them (see Table 1.4 for a list of large firm–small firm alliance types). It is often difficult to discern between the characteristics of the CVC investments and those of the other collaborative relationship. Some authors (e.g. Radtke and McKinney, 1991; Teece, 1992; Silver, 1993) argue that the emphasis of a CVC investment is not on the business relationship between investor and investee firms at all, but purely on financial issues. In this sense, a CVC investment is never a form of strategic collaboration on its own but has to be accompanied by a contractual business relationship. However, the findings of this study have clearly illustrated that while CVC investments are often only part of more complex strategic alliances, they also frequently warrant consideration as strategic alliances in their own right when the objectives of investor and/ or investee firms are strategically oriented and they therefore typically involve close cooperation and nurturing.

The spatial scale of CVC investment

A further issue of relevance to this debate concerns the spatial patterns of CVC investment and their relationship to the spatial dimension of alliance formation in general. It was recognised in Chapter 1 that while it is clear that the various forms of collaboration have an influential role to play in the spatial organisation of industries (Anderson, 1993; Curran and Blackburn, 1994), what is not clear is the spatial scale involved, and in particular the relative importance of local, national and international economies.

It is argued here that the findings of this study of CVC provide support of a kind for both agglomeration/industrial district theories (as championed by Brusco, 1982; Piore and Sabel, 1984; Sabel, 1989; Storper and Scott, 1990; Vatne, 1995 among others), and also the globalisation thesis (Ohmae, 1985; Cooke and Wells, 1991; Gordon, 1991; Anderson, 1993; Clark, 1993; Curran and Blackburn, 1994; Malecki, 1995). Direct CVC investments made by UK-based corporations are far more likely to be made in UK companies than in foreign firms. While it is accepted that the UK in its entirety cannot be regarded as an industrial *district* – although Gertler (1992) and Amin and Thrift (1993) have considered the size (in terms of areal extent) to which the industrial district concept can be extended – the reasons for the spatial pattern of direct CVC do provide support for the arguments behind industrial district theory and the concept of 'milieu'. According to this theory, spatial proximity and cultural identity can facilitate information exchange in inter-firm relationships (Camagni, 1991; Amin and Thrift, 1992; Gertler, 1992; Bahrami and Evans, 1995; Vatne, 1995). It has been seen that the main objectives of direct CVC investors are strategically oriented, requiring close contact and hands-on communication between companies, and it is argued that the tendency for such investments to be made in UK firms reflects the need for geographical proximity. It is, however, unlikely that the suggestion (by Storper, 1995) that agglomeration is a means of reducing transaction costs has relevance in the case of direct CVC since companies do not appear to consider such costs when forming CVC relationships.

In contrast, indirect CVC investments are much less confined to national boundaries. This reflects the different objectives of companies investing indirectly and the relative unimportance of spatial proximity for both investor and investee firms. This study has shown that UK venture capital funds raise much of their corporate finance from overseas companies, and also UK-based corporations sometimes invest in foreign venture capital funds.[1] As has been noted, large companies often use indirect CVC when investing abroad in order to obtain an international window on a wide range of new developments. They often have neither an in-depth knowledge of foreign markets nor the resources to manage foreign investments. They also typically do not require close contact with investee firms. All these factors combine to make indirect investment the most appropriate option for these companies. Indirect CVC investment therefore tends to support the argument that some forms of inter-firm collaboration (assuming that indirect CVC can be considered to be one) do not require close geographical proximity and indeed benefit from the geographically dispersed nature of firms.

Levels of CVC relative to alternative strategies

This book has therefore succeeded in providing an insight into the dynamics, motivations and spatial organisation behind one form of large firm–small firm collaboration. The need to better understand the complementarity of large and small firms was highlighted in Chapter 1, and this study has gone some way to addressing this need. However, despite the advantages of CVC for all participating organisations, it has been noted that CVC remains an underdeveloped strategy. It was suggested in Chapter 1 that the levels of collaboration are limited in the UK largely as a result of the British legacy of firms dealing with each other at arm's length. The findings of this study suggest that this legacy continues to play a significant role in inhibiting the levels of CVC in the UK, with arm's length transactions and internal business development continuing to be the preferred strategies of the majority of companies.

The use of these more *traditional* mechanisms reflects both the desire of UK corporations for control and also their fear of failure. It does not appear to be related to attempts to reduce transaction costs. Neither does it appear to be strongly correlated with a lack of CVC investment opportunities nor problems experienced by companies that have been involved in the CVC process. Chapters 1 and 2 emphasised the potential problems associated with large firm–small firm collaboration, and in particular CVC. However, this study has found the problems experienced by corporate investors to be minimal and far from insurmountable. The decision of some companies to withdraw from CVC has largely reflected a move back to core business rather than disillusionment with the CVC process. What is more, very few investee firms regarded any aspect of the CVC process to be particularly problematic. These findings therefore suggest that the low levels of this form of large firm–small firm collaboration in the UK tend to reflect a reluctance on the part of large companies to invest rather than post-investment problems which cannot be overcome. This in turn implies that the CVC process is a viable, relatively problem-free strategy which many companies are not prepared to attempt or consider.

CVC AND THE 'EQUITY GAP'

Chapter 2 identified the shortage of external equity finance available to early stage, technology-based ventures and also the venture capital funds which specialise in investing in such firms. While this shortage is evident on a world-wide scale, it is particularly severe in the UK, largely reflecting the poor performance of small TBFs since the mid-1980s and the preference of investors for lower risk investments, as well as issues related to UK investment culture such as short-termism and the fear of failure (Weyer, 1995). CVC has been proposed as a potentially valuable alternative source of funds for small firms, and specifically TBFs in the early stages of growth (e.g. by ACOST, 1990; Roberts, 1991; Rind, 1994). This book has provided substantial evidence to support this proposal by identifying the financial and value-added benefits available to firms that raise CVC finance.

In terms of the financial benefits of CVC, it can be concluded from Chapters 4, 5 and 6 of this book that both direct and indirect CVC have provided a number of small entrepreneurial UK ventures with much needed finance at various stages of their development. There is a need to distinguish between the investment focus of companies investing directly and those investing indirectly. Direct investments are more likely than indirect investments to be made in expansion stage companies operating in medium or low technology industries, while companies investing indirectly are more likely to be concerned with investing in early stage, technology-based firms and therefore concentrate on investing in funds which have a specialisation in these areas. However, despite these distinctions, both forms of investment can be considered to be important sources of finance for early stage TBFs. Chapter 6 identified the importance of CVC finance for investee firms *relative* to other sources, and found companies to be providing finance in appropriate amounts during the early stages of firm development when it is most needed.

As well as the provision of finance, CVC investment has provided important value-added benefits for the investee firm. Again, there are important distinctions to be made between direct and indirect forms of investment. As a result of the typically strategically oriented motivations of companies investing directly, many seek closer contact with investee firms and, as part of this contact, nurture investees by providing technical and marketing expertise and advice. The complementary assets of large companies and small TBFs have already been discussed, and in return for a closer window on new technologies and the behavioural advantages of TBFs, corporate investors have allowed these firms access to their material resources. Given that the value-added advice provided by independent venture capitalists is typically financially oriented, it is proposed that a combination of direct corporate and independent venture capitalist investors can be particularly beneficial for the small firm. Companies investing indirectly do not usually enjoy close contact with investee firms and therefore cannot provide the same level of nurturing that is evident for direct investment. However, independent venture capital fund managers can benefit from the industry-specific advice which the corporate investor can offer when investing indirectly.

PRACTICAL IMPLICATIONS

In addition to informing an academic audience of the role of CVC in inter-firm collaboration and the closing of the equity gap, the research findings also have implications for practitioners and policy makers. While this research has concentrated on CVC within the UK context, many of the findings and their implications have relevance for CVC activity wherever it may be undertaken. Suggestions for corporate executives, venture capital fund managers, entrepreneurs and policy makers will be considered.

Implications for corporate executives.

Investing in venture capital can provide large companies with the opportunity to meet a broad range of objectives. These can be strategically or financially oriented, related to social responsibility or learning about the venture capital process. The findings suggest that CVC has particular potential in research-based industries where access to new technologies is a vital component in maintaining a large company's competitive advantage. As Collins and Doorley (1991) noted, by participating in the venture capital process, large companies can gain up to two years' advance warning of new technological opportunities. However, the findings indicate that CVC, and particularly direct investment, also has application in sectors other than those defined as high technology. CVC strategy is also appropriate for investments in expansion stage companies and can be used to establish or complement horizontal or vertical inter-firm relationships in many, often medium or low technology, industries.

CVC is a highly flexible investment tool and there is no unique way for a corporation to participate (Winters and Murfin, 1988). The optimal structure of a CVC programme is company-specific, depending on an individual corporation's objectives, resources and constraints. In order to increase its chances of success, each individual corporation should carefully evaluate these factors and, seeking experienced advice from venture capitalists concerning time scales and risks, should decide upon a strategy best suited to its particular circumstances. Clear, realistic objectives, an understanding of the most appropriate strategies to meet these objectives, and careful evaluation of investees and fund managers are all vital if investments are to be successful. As Block and MacMillan (1993: 363) note, 'the firm must know the success factors required in the venture capital business and either make sure it can supply them or stay out of the business'.

The research has suggested that indirect, externally managed CVC is more appropriate for investing in early stage, high technology firms and where the motives are related to social responsibility and/or learning about the venture capital process. If funds are dedicated they offer more opportunities for focus, control and hence strategic gain in the form of windows on early stage technologies. Indirect CVC may be the most appropriate form of CVC for companies that are investing for the first time since it provides an opportunity for corporate executives to learn about the venture capital process before embarking on their own internally managed programmes. Direct, internally managed investments allow more contact and control than indirect CVC and therefore suit strategic objectives associated with accessing new markets, products and processes in more established firms. However, direct investments can also provide investing companies with valuable access to new technological developments, but are more appropriate when a focus on a small range of technologies is required. Both indirect and direct CVC can provide significant financial returns, although this clearly depends on the quality of investee firms.

Implications for independent venture capitalists

Venture capitalists which raise independent finance can do much to encourage corporate investment in their funds and hence create an additional, and potentially very beneficial source of capital at a time when independent venture capital groups that do not focus on MBO/MBI financing are experiencing fund-raising difficulties (Anslow, 1994). Furthermore, venture capital fund managers can help to promote direct CVC by investing in parallel deals alongside industrial corporations.

In order to attract companies to invest in venture capital funds, there is a requirement for fund managers to understand the needs and motivations of individual corporate organisations and offer investment opportunities to meet these needs. Corporations investing with strategically oriented or social responsibility-related motives will often favour funds which focus on investments in particular sectors and target early stage high technology investees. Specifically in the case of social responsibility investments, companies may also prefer funds with a particular geographical focus. Companies seeking focused investments may require dedicated fund investment opportunities. Alternatively, companies investing for educational or financial reasons may prefer pooled funds with portfolios covering a wider range of industrial sectors, levels of technology and stages of business development. Of particular importance is the need for venture capitalists to market their funds more aggressively to non-financial companies in order to enhance awareness of investment opportunities among the corporate sector. Improved communications between venture capitalists and large companies will help to nurture trust and understanding and encourage mutually beneficial information networks.

The study findings suggest that the majority of future CVC investments will be internally managed. There is therefore a role for venture capital managers to seek corporate investors with which to co-invest. In doing so the venture capitalist will have access to the industrial and technical exper-

222

tise of the corporation, which will in turn benefit from the investment experience of the venture capitalist. By receiving external equity finance directly from both non-financial companies and institutional venture capitalists the investee will be able to benefit from the industry specific technical expertise of the corporate as well as the investment experience of the venture capitalist. Companies that invest directly will often have strategic motives for doing so and consequently will require greater control and contact with investee firms than would typically be the case when investing via an externally managed fund.

Implications for entrepreneurs

Corporate venture capital investment can provide entrepreneurs with a valuable source of finance as well as possible additional non-financial benefits. Just as an increasing number of corporate executives are recognising the value of collaborative inter-firm relationships with small firms, so entrepreneurs need to understand the potential advantages for their companies of linkages with large corporations. Given that many investing companies make CVC investments in an attempt to gain windows on new technologies, the potential benefits of this form of investment are particularly great for small TBFs. Indeed, corporate investors can become very important assets for TBFs, both financially and strategically, as they provide tangible and intangible value-added resources which can play an invaluable role in TBF growth.

Small firm directors seeking CVC for their companies must decide upon their motives and the degree of contact required with corporate investors. These considerations should affect the form of CVC investment sought. Entrepreneurs with the primary objective of seeking finance for their companies tend to require only limited contact with investors and should therefore approach independent venture capital funds which have raised finance from corporate sources. Although these funds are often difficult to identify, the corporate partners can provide investee firms with industry specific and technical knowledge which venture capitalists alone do not often possess. At the same time venture capitalists can act as 'buffers' to investing corporations in cases where only limited contact is desired.

If the entrepreneur's motivations are more strategically oriented, then contact should be made directly with corporations operating in the same industry as the small firm (or a related sector) or with venture capitalists managing focused or even dedicated funds for corporations. It has been noted that the newly privatised utility companies are particularly interested in venture capital investment, suggesting that for small firms in the electricity, water, gas and telecommunications industries CVC may be a particularly viable option. Direct CVC links offer greater opportunities to form

223

further collaborative business relationships with corporations and benefit from corporate knowledge and resources.

Implications for policy makers

This study suggests a dual role for policy makers as both facilitators and educators in encouraging the CVC process. To address the former first, it is suggested that a major governmental role concerns the provision of tax incentives to companies prepared to make venture capital investments. Tax breaks are an important method for initially stimulating interest in an activity that many corporate executives are possibly not currently considering. They have recently been used to encourage private individuals to invest in small unquoted firms (e.g. via the new Venture Capital Trusts) and policy makers should consider offering large companies similar incentives. One small firm director suggested 100 per cent first year allowances for companies investing in firms with turnovers of less than £4 million. This proposal supports the comments of Abbott and Hay (1995: 342) who suggested that

> the implementation of . . . taxation measures proceed with all haste. If that happens [all parties] involved in [TBF] formation and growth will receive the clearest possible signal that *now* is the time to start the long process of 'realizing our potential' . . . in science, engineering and technology.

In addition to tax incentives, policy makers should investigate the feasibility of establishing some form of 'Guaranteed Funding Potential Scheme' operated by consultants, venture capitalists and other experts which could provide would-be investors with advice and information concerning potential investees. Linked to this is the concept of a government-funded 'marriage bureau' service to act as a match-maker for investor and investee companies, or the promotion of existing business angel marriage bureaux to non-financial companies as well as private investors.

In their role as educators, there is a need for policy makers to stimulate science and technology within UK education and business (Chesnais, 1988) and to encourage the transferral of technology from universities to industry via small companies. The technology transfer process can be encouraged by reducing the levels of bureaucracy that exist in UK business and promoting collaborative relationships between large and small companies, including CVC. Policy makers should underline the need for, advantages of, and guidelines for success in inter-firm strategic partnerships via seminars and reports to business leaders. Government should place particular emphasis on the importance of publicising successful examples of alliances and specifically CVC role models both in the UK and overseas.

AN AGENDA FOR FURTHER RESEARCH

This book marks the first comprehensive study of corporate venture capital investment in the UK, and one of the first to be undertaken anywhere. Previous academic and practical research in the fields of collaboration and small firm financing has largely neglected this topic. The shortage of information available on the subject of CVC has hampered progression of our understanding of the role of CVC within the context of inter-firm collaboration. Mariti and Smiley (1983: 450) recognised that 'the field of study of co-operative agreements between firms seems a very promising one'. However, they went on to suggest that 'the great variety of forms co-operative agreements can take may . . . have discouraged research'. It is argued here that the field of study of collaboration is still a very promising one, and that while the level of research on this topic has increased significantly since the mid-1980s, the broad range of alliance types has resulted in many general studies of collaboration but very few which have considered individual forms of collaboration, such as CVC, and their characteristics. The low levels of research into CVC have also restricted our knowledge of the actual and potential role of this strategy as a source of equity finance for small firms. While this book has gone some way to furthering our knowledge of CVC, its very nature as a pioneering and exploratory study means that one of the results has been the identification of a number of issues which would benefit from further study, possibly using different research approaches. Indeed, as Fried and Hisrich (1988: 26) note, 'venture capital research is a wide open field with room for a variety of research approaches'.

The motivations of companies for making CVC investments have been discussed in some detail, and the most appropriate strategies for particular objectives are now understood to a far greater extent. However, the debate concerning the compatibility of financial and strategic objectives is still not fully resolved. Siegel et al. (1988: 246) commented on the need for further study 'in order to determine how corporate venture capitalists successfully integrate financial and strategic considerations, and which benefits are most likely to be achieved'. While this study has gone some way to improving our knowledge in this area, there is a need for further research, possibly of a more qualitative nature. Also from the investor's point of view, there is a need to further consider the role of CVC alongside other strategies. CVC is not a replacement for other corporate development strategies in all circumstances (Hegg, 1990), but when it is more appropriate than other options, and how and when it best complements other options, are important issues for further research.

A related issue concerns the investing company's attitude towards risk. The concept of risk reduction through combining a portfolio of ventures with different risk/return profiles has been considered in the financial theory and management studies literatures (Murray, 1995). It has been recognised that an increasing number of venture capitalists are turning to safer later stage investments made via larger funds in order to reduce risk. However, while corporate investors, at least in the UK, have been identified as being risk *averse*, they do show a preference for ad hoc direct investments in only a small number of (typically *high* risk) ventures. As has been seen, this clearly reflects the strategic motives of many investors and their desire to establish close links with investee firms. However, what is not clear is the investing company's techniques for risk evaluation and reduction (if indeed such techniques exist). Further research, relating CVC investment to financial theory, is therefore required.

This book has provided an indication of the partner selection process and the general nature of the CVC relationship. It has examined the degree of contact between companies and the benefits and problems which arise from this contact. However, there remains a need for further research to analyse in greater detail the collaborative CVC interface. It has been tentatively suggested that not all forms of CVC should be described as *collaborative*, but research is required to investigate this proposal further; to what extent do the participants in the CVC process consider it to be a collaborative process? How do they define collaboration? A related issue concerns the power relations between firms. This study has identified to some extent the levels of control investing companies enjoy over investee firms. However, the nature of these power relations and their effects on firm performance are not adequately understood; what level of control should investors have over investee firms in order to maximise the chances of a successful relationship?

From the investee firm perspective there is a need for longitudinal research to further investigate the long-term effects of venture nurturing, and in particular the extent to which it helps to improve firm performance. Indeed, the requirement for more in-depth empirical studies of the ways in which the value-added provided by *all* forms of venture capital investor facilitates or inhibits the growth and development of small firms has been emphasised in the literature (e.g. by MacMillan *et al.*, 1988; Timmons and Sapienza, 1992; Ehrlich *et al.*, 1994). As Murray (1995: 26) observes, 'the extent to which . . . advice from the investor actually adds to the value of the supported enterprise still remains a matter of debate'. This research is seen as particularly important although there are obvious difficulties involved in isolating the effect of the value-added variable on firm performance. There is also a need to better understand the circumstances in which nurturing is, and perhaps more importantly, is not desirable.

Another issue which has been considered worthy of further study in the context of venture capital financing as a whole (e.g. by Fried and Hisrich, 1988), and certainly warrants attention from the CVC perspective, is that of investment harvest (exit). Still very little is known about the eventual outcomes of CVC investments despite the understandable interest of both investor and investee firms and venture capitalists in this issue. Several questions require attention, for example; how long after initial investment does exit occur, is there a relationship between performance and method of exit, are corporate investors looking to acquire investee firms or form further strategic relationships with them?

A further, broader issue concerns the need for research into collaboration *per se*, at a time of increasing company flexibility and extension of core competencies (Hagedoorn, 1995). Research into other individual forms of collaboration would enable a more detailed classification of collaboration and a greater understanding of the motivations and most appropriate circumstances for individual strategies. This book has attempted to provide an initial investigation into the nature of CVC strategy and the extent to which it relates to the general theories of alliance formation. There remains a requirement for similar research into other forms of collaboration. For example, research examining the various forms and objectives of informal collaboration between large and small companies would not only indicate the use of such linkages in particular business environments but also suggest ways in which CVC and informal collaboration are, or could be, compatible. It is suggested that failure of collaborative relationships, including CVC, is often the result of a lack of understanding of the most appropriate strategy for particular circumstances, and there is a need for research to inform both academics and practitioners in order to enhance the chances of success.

Indeed, further attention must be paid to the ways in which participating companies can improve their chances of success in CVC and overcome disillusionment and failure. While this study has found many CVC relationships to be successful and has been able to provide some indications of best practices for corporate investors, research is still required that can help establish more detailed guidelines concerning issues such as the selection of firms with whom to collaborate through CVC rather than compete with, and the monitoring of investments once made. According to Teece (1992: 1), 'the challenge to policy analysts and to managers is to find the right balance of competition and cooperation, and the appropriate institutional structures within which competition and cooperation ought to take place'.

If we are to see the development of CVC strategy in the UK the emphasis must be on encouragement and this book has provided implications for practitioners and policy makers. However, there is still a need for further research to examine the value of encouragement of CVC activity. The full ramifications of policy measures to stimulate the levels of CVC are unknown and require attention. What level of regulation is most desirable in the long term, and to what extent should or can policy makers alter the ingrained conservative corporate culture that is evident in many large UK companies? These proposals support the comments of Timmons and

Sapienza (1992) who highlighted the need for research into the effectiveness of policy issues within the venture capital arena in general. Assuming that policy makers do have an important role to play, questions arise concerning the viability and most appropriate implementation of match-making services, guaranteed funding potential schemes and other ways of encouraging companies to make investments. The failure of the NEDO/ BASE Corporate Venturing Centre and Register was noted in Chapter 2. Was this a result of poor implementation or more fundamental problems concerning the concept of encouraging CVC investment?

Therefore, ample opportunities exist for further research to contribute both to the development of theories concerned with CVC and inter-firm collaboration, and to the accumulation of knowledge of relevance to practitioners and policy makers. There is scope for the corporate investor, the investee firm or the venture capital intermediary to be the unit of analysis. However, as Timmons and Sapienza (1992: 404) suggested, research opportunities in the venture capital field 'will be realised only if researchers seek methods and issues which bring them in close contact with the industry in the pursuit of an intellectual collision with the real world'. As in any field of academic study, meaningful research and an enhancement of knowledge will result only from close contact with research subjects.

> Ignorance of the realities and nuances of an industry and an unwillingness to engage in 'an intellectual collision' can lead to voluminous but meaningless research.
>
> (Timmons and Sapienza, 1992: 433)

NOTES

2 CORPORATE VENTURING AND CORPORATE VENTURE CAPITAL

1 'Closed' funds have a set value and a fixed life. They are distinct from 'open' funds which do not have a set value or duration.
2 Investments by corporate pension funds are also for financial reasons but are not defined as corporate venture capital (Winters and Murfin, 1988).
3 The successive growth stages of the firm are the pre-start-up or seed stage, the start-up stage, the initial growth or 'other early' stage and the sustained growth or expansion stage. While this is not the only classification used, it is that employed by most authors (e.g. Roberts, 1991; Standeven, 1993; Mason and Harrison, 1994; Murray, 1995; Murray and Lott, 1995) as well as by the BVCA, and is therefore deemed suitable for this study.
4 Information obtained from personal communication with Maurice Anslow of Venture Economics.
5 Information obtained from personal communication with Akio Nishizawa of Keiwa College, Japan.

3 CORPORATE VENTURE CAPITAL INVESTMENT IN THE UNITED KINGDOM

1 This is particularly the case for foreign-owned companies who have little experience of UK markets. In this survey, three of the four foreign-owned subsidiaries that had made indirect investments had invested primarily to learn about UK venture capital.
2 Data unavailable for one company.
3 Survey undertaken in 1994.

4 THE CVC INVESTMENT PROCESS

1 Only one executive regarded venture capitalist's track record to be an *essential* factor, and none regarded the expertise of the venture capitalist in particular stages of investment as essential.
2 Nine of the investments made in US funds were made by one company.
3 Figures apply to the investments in thirty of the thirty-two funds.
4 Average corporate investment size in 1990 was approximately £6 million, while

229

in 1988, the year of peak number of investments, it was approximately £1 million (figures at 1992 prices).

5 Although three investments were made during the first six months of 1994, their combined value is less than £1 million, indicating that only relatively small amounts have been invested.

6 Information obtained from personal communication with Charlotte Morrison of the BVCA, who explained that during the first eight months of 1994, the amount raised from foreign corporations was ten times that raised by UK-based companies.

7 Data available for thirty-one of the thirty-two funds.

8 Corporation X was responsible for sixty of the 166 UK investees identified in this survey.

9 However, it must be noted that only two companies made direct investments for this purpose (see Table 3.1).

5 EXTERNALLY MANAGED CVC

1 It will be noted that although the source material, the business literature and/or the press identified twenty-six of the forty-nine contacted venture capitalists as having raised finance from corporate sources (see Table 5.1), only sixteen of the participating thirty-nine venture capitalists had raised corporate finance. This suggests that either all ten non-respondents had raised finance from corporates or that these sources were inaccurate.

2 Venture capitalists were not willing to disclose the names of all of the companies that had invested in their funds – only a total of forty-five corporate investors were named by respondents.

3 It was noted in Chapter 2 that since the time of interview the number of dedicated funds managed by Advent International has risen to fourteen.

4 These companies were either based in foreign countries or were UK subsidiaries of foreign companies.

5 Data were available for only fifteen of the forty-four funds. However, these fifteen funds had invested in 152 UK-based investee firms which were considered appropriate for indicating spatial patterns of investment.

6 Even though the number of non-financial companies investing in each fund is very small.

6 TECHONOLOGY-BASED FIRMS AND CVC

1 The total amount invested in firms at the 'other early' stage is somewhat misleading given one particularly high investment by a financial institution of £120 million.

2 In one case the introduction was made via a non-financial company that already had a direct CVC stake in the investee firm.

3 The Managing Director of one investee firm had once been responsible for the management of a major venture capitalist's dedicated corporate fund.

4 At least investee firms were not aware of previous relationships. Since two-thirds of indirect investees did not know who indirect investors were, they could not be sure that they had not established business relationships with them. However, any previous links that may have existed with investors were clearly not influential in the investees' choice of venture capital funds in these cases.

5 It must be remembered that the findings from the survey of corporate execu-

tives were not based solely on investments made in TBFs. Investees were also medium or low tech companies.

6 The author recognises that although this quote illustrates the point, it is not 'politically correct'.

7 However, it must be noted that many companies did not consider a board seat to represent power.

7 CONCLUSIONS

1 Although, as has been recognised throughout this book, geographical proximity to *investee firms* is an important factor for the venture capital fund manager.

BIBLIOGRAPHY

Abbott, S. and Hay, M. (1995) *Investing For the Future: New Firm Funding in Germany, Japan, the UK and the USA*, London: FT Pitman.

ACOST (1990) *The Enterprise Challenge: Overcoming Barriers to Growth in Small Firms*, London: HMSO.

Ahern, R. (1993a) 'The role of strategic alliances in the international organisation of industry', *Environment and Planning A* 25: 1229–1246.

—— (1993b) 'Implications of strategic alliances for small R&D-intensive firms', *Environment and Planning A* 25: 1511–1526.

Allen, J. (1992) *Starting a Technology Business*, London: Pitman.

Amin, A. and Thrift, N. (1992) 'Neo-Marshallian nodes in global networks', *International Journal of Urban and Regional Research* 16: 571–587.

—— (1993) 'Globalization, institutional thickness and local prospects', *Revue d'Economie Régionale et Urbaine* 3: 405–427.

Anderson, M.J. (1993) 'Collaborative integration in the Canadian pharmaceutical industry', *Environment and Planning A* 25: 1815–1838.

Anslow, M. (1994) 'Capital commitments to UK venture capital funds in 1993, *UK Venture Capital Journal* March/April: 16–19.

Aoki, A. (1984) *The Co-operative Game Theory of the Firm*, Oxford: Clarendon Press.

Auster, E.R. (1987) 'International corporate linkages: dynamic forms in changing environments', *Columbia Journal of World Business* 22, 2: 3–6.

Aydalot, P. and Keeble, D. (1988) 'High technology industry and innovative environments in Europe: and overview', in P. Aydalot and D. Keeble (eds) *High Technology Industry and Innovative Environments: The European Experience*, London: Routledge: 1–21.

Badaracco, J.L. (1991) *The Knowledge Link: How Firms Compete Through Strategic Alliances*, Boston, MA: Harvard Business School Press.

Bahrami, H. (1992) 'The emerging flexible organisation: perspectives from Silicon Valley', *California Management Review* Summer: 33–52.

Bahrami, H. and Evans, S. (1995) 'Flexible re-cycling and high-technology entrepreneurship', *California Management Review* 37, 3: 62–89.

Bailey, J. (1984) 'Intrapreneurship – source of high growth start-ups or passing fad?', in J.A. Hornaday, F. Tarpley, J.A. Timmons and K.H. Vesper (eds) *Frontiers of Entrepreneurship Research*, Wellesley, MA: Babson College: 358–367.

Bailey, P. (1985) 'Venture capital and the corporation', paper presented to the European Chemical Marketing Research Association, Berlin, Germany, 17 October: 1–15.

Bakker, H., Jones, W. and Nichols, M. (1994) 'Using core competencies to develop new business', *Long Range Planning* 27, 6: 13–27.

Batchelor, C. (1987a) 'Trying to fire the imagination', *Financial Times* 10 February.
—— (1987b) 'Success rate proves patchy', *Financial Times* 29 April: 10.
Baty, G.B. (1990) *Entrepreneurship for the Nineties*, Englewood Cliffs, NJ: Prentice Hall.
Beamish, P.W. and Inkpen, A.C. (1995) 'Keeping international joint ventures stable and profitable', *Long Range Planning* 28, 3: 26–36.
Belotti, C. (1995) 'Technological renewal in small firms: the nature and role of linkages between large and small firms', paper presented at the Babson Entrepreneurship Research Conference, London Business School.
Benassi, M. (1993) 'Organizational perspectives of strategic alliances: external growth in the computer industry', in G. Grabber (ed.) *The Embedded Firm: On the Socio-Economics of Industrial Networks*, London: Routledge: 95–116.
Bennett, N. (1995) 'High-tech British firms flock to American market', *The Times* 7 August: 37.
Bettis, R.A. and Hitt, M.A. (1995) 'The new competitive landscape', *Strategic Management Journal* 16: 7–19.
Bidault, F. and Cummings, T. (1994) 'Innovating through alliances: expectations and limitations', *R&D Management* 24, 1: 33–45.
Bigbie, J-E. (1994) 'Consortia back in business', *Acquisitions Monthly* April: 54–55.
Binks, M. (1993) 'The financing of small and medium sized enterprises in the U.K.: 1993 summary report on the findings of CBI Discussion Group', February.
Birley, S. and Norburn, D. (1985) 'Small vs large companies: the entrepreneurial conundrum', *Journal of Business Strategy* Summer: 81–87.
Bleicher, K. and Paul, H. (1987) 'The external corporate venture capital fund – a valuable vehicle for growth', *Long Range Planning* 20, 6: 64–70.
Blenker, P. and Christensen, P.R. (1994) 'Interactive strategies in supply chains: a double-edged portfolio approach to SME subcontractors positioning', paper presented at the 8th Nordic Conference on Small Business Research, Halmstad University, Sweden, 13–15 June.
Block, Z. (1982) 'Can corporate venturing succeed?', *Journal of Business Strategy* Fall: 21–33.
—— (1983) 'Some major issues in internal corporate venturing', in J.A. Hornaday, J.A. Timmons and K.H. Vesper (eds) *Frontiers of Entrepreneurship Research*, Wellesley, MA: Babson College: 382–389.
Block, Z. and MacMillan, I.C. (1993) *Corporate Venturing: Creating New Businesses Within the Firm*, Boston, MA: Harvard Business School Press.
Boocock, G., Woods, M. and Caley, K. (1993) 'The equity gap in the East Midlands: an initial assessment of the operation of a new venture capital fund', paper presented to the National Small Firms Policy and Research Conference, Nottingham, November.
Borys, B. and Jemison, D.B. (1989) 'Hybrid arrangements as strategic alliances: theoretical issues in organizational combinations', *Academy of Management Review* 14, 2: 234–249.
Botkin, J.W. and Matthews, J.B. (1992) *Winning Combinations: The Coming Wave of Entrepreneurial Partnerships Between Large and Small Companies*, New York: John Wiley.
Bower, J.D. and Whittaker, E. (1993) 'Client communication and innovative efficiency in US and UK biotechnology companies', paper presented at the Conference on New Technology-Based Firms in the 1990s, Manchester Business School, 25–26 June.
Boynton, A.C. and Victor, B. (1991) 'Beyond flexibility: building and managing the dynamically stable organization', *California Management Review* Fall: 53–66.

BIBLIOGRAPHY

British Venture Capital Association (BVCA)(1987) *Report on Investment Activity 1986*, London: British Venture Capital Association.
——(1988) *Report on Investment Activity 1987*, London: British Venture Capital Association.
—— (1989) *Report on Investment Activity 1988*, London: British Venture Capital Association.
—— (1990) *Report on Investment Activity 1989*, London: British Venture Capital Association.
—— (1991) *Report on Investment Activity 1990*, London: British Venture Capital Association.
—— (1992) *The British Venture Capital Association Directory 1992/3*, London: British Venture Capital Association.
—— (1993) *Report on Investment Activity 1992*, London: British Venture Capital Association.
—— (1994) *Report on Investment Activity 1993*, London: British Venture Capital Association.
—— (1995a) *Report on Investment Activity 1994*, London: British Venture Capital Association.
—— (1995b) *Tax Submission 1995*, London: British Venture Capital Association.
Brokaw, L. (1994) 'Working a deal', *INC 500* 24–31.
Brouthers, K.D., Brouthers, L.E. and Wilkinson, T.J. (1995) 'Strategic alliances: choose your partner', *Long Range Planning* 28, 3: 18–25.
Brown, L. and Pattinson, H. (1995) 'Information technology and telecommunications: impacts on strategic alliance formation and management', *Management Decision* 33, 4: 41–51.
Bruno, A.V. and Tyebjee, T.T. (1984) 'The entrepreneur's search for capital', in J.A. Hornaday, F. Tarpley, J.A. Timmons and K.H. Vesper (eds) *Frontiers of Entrepreneurship Research*, Wellesley, MA: Babson College: 18–31.
Brusco, S. (1982) 'The Emilian model: productive decentralisation and social integration', *Cambridge Journal of Economics* 6: 167–184.
Brush, C.G. and Chaganti, R. (1995) 'Cooperative strategies: extent of use and an articulation of content dimensions in non-high tech new ventures', paper presented at the Babson Entrepreneurship Research Conference, London Business School.
Buckley, P.A. and Casson, M. (1988) 'A theory of cooperation in international business', in F.J. Contractor and P. Lorange (eds) *Cooperative Strategies in International Business*, Lexington, MA: Lexington Books: 31–53.
Burdett, J.O. (1991) 'A model for customer–supplier alliances', *Management Decision* 29, 5: 28–34.
Burgelman, R.A. (1983) 'A process model of internal corporate venturing in the diversified major firm', *Administrative Science Quarterly* 28, 2: 223–244.
Burns, P. (1992) 'Financing SMEs in Europe: a five country study', paper presented at the 15th National Small Firms Policy and Research Conference, Southampton.
Burrows, B.C. (1982) 'Venture management – success or failure', *Long Range Planning* 15, 6: 84–99.
Burstein, D. and Hofmeister, S. (1985) 'Our money, your brains', *Venture* 7, 8: 40–42.
Buxton, J. (1995) 'Expansion along Scottish routes', *Financial Times* 18 April: 13.
Bygrave, W.D. and Timmons, J.A. (1992) *Venture Capital at the Crossroads*, Boston, MA: Harvard Business School Press.
Camagni, R. (1991) 'Introduction: from the local "milieu" to innovation through

cooperation networks', in R. Camagni (ed) *Innovation Networks: Spatial Perspectives*, London: Belhaven: 1–9.

Canadian Venture Capital (1990) 'Corporate venture capital: some new ideas and some fading interest', August.

Cary, L. (1993) *The Venture Capital Report: Guide to Venture Capital in the UK and Europe*, London: Management Today, sixth edition.

Case, J. (1995) 'The wonderland economy', *INC, Special Issue: The State of Small Business*: 14–29.

Chemical Week (1992) 'Minority stakes: pros and cons: access to new markets', 7 October: 25.

Chesnais, F. (1988) 'Technical co-operation agreements between firms', *Science Technology Industry Review* 4: 51–119.

Ciborra, C. (1991) 'Alliances as learning experiments: cooperation, competition and change in hightech industries', in L.K. Mytelka (ed.) *Strategic Partnerships: States, Firms and International Competition*, London: Pinter: 51–77.

Clark, G.L. (1993) 'Global interdependence and regional development: business linkages and corporate governance in a world of financial risk', *Transactions of the Institute of British Geographers* 18: 309–325.

Collins, T.M. and Doorley, T.L. (1991) *Teaming Up for the 90s: A Guide to International Joint Ventures and Strategic Alliances*, Homewood, IL: Business One Irwin.

Connell, R. and Phillips, B. (1988) 'Finding funds for small firms', *Management Today* November: 143–164.

Contractor, F.J. and Lorange, P. (1988) 'Why should firms cooperate?: the strategy and economic basis for cooperative ventures', in F.J. Contractor and P. Lorange (eds) *Cooperative Strategies in International Business: Joint Ventures and Techology Partnerships between Firms*, Lexington, MA: Lexington Book: 3–28.

Cooke, P. (1988) 'Flexible integration, scope economies, and strategic alliances: social and spatial mediations', *Environment and Planning D* 6: 281–300.

—— (1992) 'Computing and communications in the UK and France: innovation, regulation and spatial dynamics – an introduction', in P. Cooke, F. Moulaert, E. Swyngedouw, O. Weinstein and P. Wells (eds) *Towards Global Localization*, London: UCL Press: 1–18.

Cooke, P. and Morgan, K. (1993) 'The network paradigm: new departures in corporate and regional development', *Environment and Planning D* 11: 543–564.

Cooke, P. and Wells, P. (1991) 'Uneasy alliances: the spatial development of computing and communication markets', *Regional Studies* 25, 4: 345–354.

—— (1992) 'Globalization and its management in computing and communications', in P. Cooke, F. Moulaert, E. Swyngedouw, O. Weinstein and P. Wells (eds) *Towards Global Localization*, London: UCL Press: 61–78.

Cookson, C. (1994) 'Gloom among U.K.'s high tech entrepreneurs', *Financial Times* 23 September: IV.

Corrigan, F. (1992) 'Venture capital', paper to the London and Southern Gas Association, London.

Cosh, A. and Hughes, A. (1994) 'Size, financial structure and profitability: UK companies in the 1980s', in A. Hughes and D.J. Storey (eds) *Finance and the Small Firm*, London: Routledge: 18–63.

Crackett, D. (1992) 'Large company initiatives for small firms – mutual benefit', paper presented to the 22nd European Small Business Seminar, Amsterdam, September.

Crevoisier, O. and Maillat, D. (1991) 'Milieu, industrial organization and territorial production system: towards a new theory of spatial development', in R. Camagni (ed.) *Innovation Networks: Spatial Perspectives*, London: Belhaven: 13–34.

Culpan, R. (1993) 'Multinational competition and cooperation: theory and practice', in R. Culpan (ed.) *Multinational Strategic Alliances*, Binghampton, NY: Haworth Press: 13–32.

Culpan, R. and Kostelac, E.A. (1993) 'Cross-national corporate partnerships: trends in alliance formation', in R. Culpan (ed.) *Multinational Strategic Alliances*, Binghampton, NY: Haworth Press: 103–122.

Curran, J. and Blackburn, R. (1994) *Small Firms and Local Economic Networks: The Death of the Local Economy?*, London: Paul Chapman.

Dawkins, W. (1985) 'Campaign to encourage entrepreneurial skill', *Financial Times* 18 September.

—— (1986) 'Why windows on technology are difficult to open', *Financial Times* 24 June.

Deger, R. (1994) 'Courting entrepreneurs', *Venture Capital Journal* August/September: 37–38.

DTI/CBI (1993) *Innovation: The Best Practice*, London: Department of Trade and Industry/Confederation of British Industry.

Devlin, G. and Bleackley, M. (1988) 'Strategic alliances – guidelines for success', *Long Range Planning* 21, 5: 18–23.

Dicken, P. and Thrift, N. (1992) 'The organization of production and the production of organization: why business enterprises matter in the study of geographical industrialization', *Transactions of the Institute of British Geographers* 17: 279–291.

Dickson, K., Lawton Smith, H. and Smith, S. (1990) 'The small firm perspective on inter-firm collaboration for innovation', in D. O'Doherty (ed.) *The Cooperation Phenomenon: Prospects for Small Firms and the Small Economies*, London: Graham and Trotman: 51–70.

Dickson, M. (1993) 'Market upswing sparks a revival', *Financial Times* 24 September: VII.

Dodgson, M. (1992) 'Tecnological collaboration: problems and pitfalls', *Technology Analysis and Strategic Management* 4, 1: 83–88.

—— (1993) *Technological Collaboration in Industry: Strategy, Policy and Internationalisation in Innovation*, London: Routledge.

Dollinger, M.J. and Golden, P.A. (1992) 'Interorganizational and collective strategies in small firms: environmental effects and performance', *Journal of Management* 18, 4: 695–715.

Donckels, R. and Lambrecht, J. (1995) 'Joint ventures: no longer a mysterious world for SMEs from developed and developing countries', *International Small Business Journal* 13, 2: 11–26.

Doz, Y.L. (1988) 'Technology partnerships between larger and smaller firms: some critical issues', in F.J. Contractor and P. Lorange (eds) *Cooperative Strategies in International Business: Joint Ventures and Technology Partnerships between Firms*, Lexington, MA: Lexington Books: 317–338.

Doz, Y.L., Angelmar, R. and Prahalad, C.K. (1985) 'Technological innovation and interdependence: a challenge for the large, complex firm', *Technology in Society* 7: 105–125.

Duhamel, M., Franzetti, P. and Heese, C. (1994) *Research into the Financing of New Technology-Based Firms (NTBFs)*, final report of the European Commission, 25 July.

Duijnhouwer, A.L. (1994) 'Competitiveness, autonomy and business relationships', in J.M. Veciana (ed.) *SMEs: Internationalization, Networks and Strategy*, Aldershot: Avebury: 174–200.

Dunn, K. (1992) 'Corporate partners: corporate venturing', in G. Sharp (ed.) *The Insider's Guide to Raising Venture Capital*, London: Kogan Page: 167–174.

Ehrlich, S.B., De Noble, A.F., Moore, T. and Weaver, R.R. (1994) 'After the cash arrives: a comparative study of venture capital and private investor involvement in entrepreneurial firms', *Journal of Business Venturing* 9: 67–82.

Eisenhardt, K.M. and Schoonhoven, C.B. (1994) 'Triggering strategic alliances in entrepreneurial firms: the case of technology-sharing alliances', paper presented at the Babson Entrepreneurship Research Conference, Babson College, Boston, MA.

Elder, T. and Shimanski, J.M. (1987) 'Redirection decisions in successful corporate ventures', in N.C. Churchill, J.A. Hornaday, B.A. Kirchhoff, O.J. Krasner and K.H. Vesper (eds) *Frontiers of Entrepreneurship Research*, Boston, MA: Babson College: 510–526.

Esposito, E., Lo Storto, C. and Raffa, M. (1993) 'The complexity in the relationships between large and small firms: some empirical evidence', paper presented at the Babson Entrepreneurship Research Conference, Houston, Texas.

Ettington, D.R. and Bantel, K.A. (1994) 'Intent to use strategic alliances for commercialization', paper presented at the Babson Entrepreneurship Research Conference, Babson College, Boston, MA.

European Venture Capital Journal (1990a) 'Focus on corporate venturing: corporate venture capital: trends, strategies and programmes in Europe', March/April: 3–12.

—— (1990b) 'Corporate venturing followup', May/June: 9–10.

—— (1991) 'Investor profiles: Advent's corporate venture capital strategies', July/August: 14–19.

—— (1994) 'Advent signs up Dutch postal group', April/May: 7–8.

Farrell, C. and Doutriaux, J. (1994) 'Collaborative strategies or internal development: when are they most appropriate for small Canadian high-tech firms and why?', paper presented at the Babson Entrepreneurship Research Conference, Babson College, Boston, MA.

Fassin, Y. and Lewis, C. (1994) 'IPO markets in Europe and the United States: principle and practice', in W.D. Bygrave, M. Hay and J.B. Peeters (eds) *Realizing Investment Value*, London: FT Pitman: 39–63.

Fast, N.D. (1978) *The Rise and Fall of Corporate New Venture Divisions*, Ann Arbor, MI: UMI Research Press.

—— (1981) 'Pitfalls of corporate venturing', *Research Management* March: 21–24.

Fast, N.D. and Pratt, S.E. (1981) 'Individual entrepreneurship and the large corporation', in K.H. Vesper (ed.) *Frontiers of Entrepreneurship Research*, Wellesley, MA: Babson College: 443–450.

Faulkner, W. (1989) 'The new firm phenomenon in biotechnology', in P. Rosa (ed.) *The Role and Contribution of Small Business Research*, Aldershot: Avebury: 131–144.

Financial Times (1992) 'Venture capital famine forecast', 21 January: 12.

Florida, R.L. and Kenney, M. (1988) 'Venture capital, high technology and regional development', *Regional Studies* 22, 1: 33–48.

Flynn, D.M. (1995) 'A preliminary examination of organizational and other factors affecting performance in new ventures: the view of venture capitalists', *Entrepreneurship and Regional Development* 7: 1–20.

Forrest, J.E. (1990) 'Strategic alliances and the small technology-based firm', *Journal of Small Business Management* July: 37–45.

Forrest, J.E. and Martin, M.J.C. (1992) 'Strategic alliances between large and small research intensive organisations: experiences in the biotechnology industry', *Research and Development Management* 22, 1: 41–53.

Fredriksen, O., Olofsson, C. and Wahlbin, C. (1992) 'Why don't venture capitalists add value? Or do they?', paper to the 12th annual Babson Entrepreneurship Research Conference, INSEAD, Fontainebleau, France.

Freear, J. and Wetzel, W.E. (1990) 'Who bankrolls high-tech entrepreneurs?', *Journal of Business Venturing* 5: 77–89.

—— (1991) 'Who are the real venture capitalists?', in D.V. Gibson (ed.) *Technology Companies and Global Markets: Programs, Policies, and Strategies to Accelerate Innovation and Entrepreneurship*, Savage, MD: Rowman and Littlefield: 189–206.

Fried, V.H. and Hisrich, R.D. (1988) 'Venture capital research: past, present and future', *Entrepreneurship Theory and Practice* 13: 15–28.

Gabizon, A. (1985) 'Venture capital funds for investment in specific industry sectors', in S.E. Pratt and S.E. Lloyd (eds) *Guide to European Venture Capital Sources*, Boston, MA: Venture Economics: 47–49.

Garnsey, E. and Wilkinson, M. (1994) 'Global alliance in high technology: a trap for the unwary', *Long Range Planning* 27, 6: 137–146.

Garud, R. and Kumaraswamy, A. (1995) 'Technological and organisational designs for realizing economies of substitution', *Strategic Management Journal* 16, S1: 93–109.

Gaston, R.J. (1989) *Finding Private Venture Capital For Your Firm: A Complete Guide*, New York: Wiley.

Gatewood, E.J., Trevino, M. and Hoy, F.S. (1995) 'Technology management decisions and strategic choices: the case of 3M and Ferro', paper presented at the Babson Entrepreneurship Research Conference, London Business School.

Gertler, M.S. (1992) 'Flexibility revisited: districts, nation-states, and the forces of production', *Transactions of the Institute of British Geographers* 17: 259–278.

Gibb, A.A. (1992) 'Can academe achieve quality in small firms policy research?', *Entrepreneurship and Regional Development* 4: 127–144.

Gilbert, N. (1991) 'Strategic alliances spur small-business R&D', *Financier: The Journal of Private Sector Policy* 15, 6: 18–21.

Ginsberg, A. and Hay, M. (1993) 'Managing the dilemmas of corporate venturing', paper presented to the Rent VII Research in Entrepreneurship Workshop, Budapest, Hungary, November 25–26.

Glamholtz, E.G. and Randie, Y. (1993) 'How to make entrepreneurship work in established companies', in R.L. Kuhn (ed.) *Generating Creativity and Innovation in Large Bureaucracies*, Westport, CT: Quorum Books: 131–150.

Golden, P.A. and Dollinger, M. (1993) 'Cooperative alliances and competitive strategies in small manufacturing firms', *Entrepreneurship Theory and Practice* Summer: 43–56.

Gompers, P.A. (1994) 'The rise and fall of venture capital', *Business and Economic History* 23, 2: 1–26.

Gordon, R. (1991) 'Innovation, industrial networks and high-technology regions', in R. Camagni (ed.) *Innovation Networks: Spatial Perspectives*, London: Belhaven Press: 174–195.

Gorman, M. and Sahlman, W.A. (1989) 'What do venture capitalists do?', *Journal of Business Venturing* 4: 231–248.

Gourlay, R. (1994a) 'Cult of the big company', *Financial Times* 6 December: 12.

—— (1994b) 'Fresh U.S. capital in fewer, larger funds', *Financial Times* 23 September: v.

—— (1995a) 'Marriages of convenience', *Financial Times* 6 June: 14.

—— (1995b) 'Easdaq gets a step closer', *Financial Times* 14 March: 16.

—— (1995c) 'Early stagers put on hold', *Financial Times* 4 April: 12.

—— (1995d) 'An old beast stirs into life', *Financial Times* 23 May: 12.

Grabher, G. (1993) 'Rediscovering the social in the economics of interfirm relations', in G. Grabher (ed.) *The Embedded Firm: On the Socioeconomics of Industrial Networks*, London: Routledge: 1–31.

Greenthal, R.P. and Larson, J.A. (1983) 'Venturing into venture capital', *McKinsey Quarterly* Spring: 70–79.

Gugler, P. (1992) 'Building transnational alliances to create competitive advantage', *Long Range Planning* 25, 1: 90–99.

Gugler, P. and Dunning, J.H. (1993) 'Technology-based cross-border alliances', in R. Culpan (ed.) *Multinational Strategic Alliances*, Binghampton, NY: Haworth Press: 123–165.

Gupta, A.K. and Sapienza, H.J. (1992) 'Determinants of venture capital firms: preferences regarding the industry diversity and geographic scope of their investments', *Journal of Business Venturing* 7: 347–362.

Haar, N.E., Starr, J. and MacMillan, I.C. (1988) 'Informal risk capital investors: investment patterns on the East Coast of the USA', *Journal of Business Venturing* 3: 11–29.

Hagedoorn, J. (1993a) 'Strategic technology alliances and modes of cooperation in high-technology industries', in G. Grabher (ed.) *The Embedded Firm: On the Socioeconomics of Industrial Networks*, London: Routledge: 116–137.

—— (1993b) 'Understanding the rationale of strategic technology partnering: interorganizational modes of cooperation and sectoral differences', *Strategic Management Journal* 14: 371–385.

—— (1995) 'A note on international market leaders and networks of strategic technology partnering', *Strategic Management Journal* 16: 241–250.

Hagedoorn, J. and Schakenraad, J. (1992) 'Leading companies and networks of strategic alliances in information technologies', *Research Policy* 21: 163–190.

—— (1994) 'The effect of strategic technology alliances on company performance', *Strategic Management Journal* 15: 291–309.

Håkansson, H. and Johanson, J. (1988) 'Formal and informal cooperation strategies in international industrial networks', in F.J. Contractor and P. Lorange (eds) *Cooperative Strategies in International Business*, Lexington, MA: Lexington Books: 369–379.

Hall, G. (1989) 'Lack of finance as a constraint on the expansion of innovatory small firms', in J. Barber, J.S. Metcalfe and M. Porteous (eds) *Barriers to Growth in Small Firms*, London: Routledge: 39–57.

Hamel, G., Doz, Y.L. and Prahalad, C.K. (1989) 'Collaborate with your competitors – and win', *Harvard Business Review* Jan./Feb.: 133–139.

Hamilton, W.F. (1985) 'Corporate strategies for managing emerging technologies', *Technology in Society* 7: 197–212.

Hamilton, W.F. and Singh, H. (1992) 'The evolution of corporate capabilities in emerging technologies', *Interfaces* 22, 4: 13–23.

Hanan, M. (1969) 'Corporate growth through venture management', *Harvard Business Review* Jan./Feb.: 43–61.

—— (1976) 'Venturing corporations – think small to stay strong', *Harvard Business Review* May/June: 139–148.

Hara, G. and Kanai, T. (1994) 'Entrepreneurial networks across oceans to promote international strategic alliances for small businesses', *Journal of Business Venturing* 9: 489–507.

Hardymon, G.F., DeNino, M.J. and Salter, M.S. (1983) 'When corporate venture capital doesn't work', *Harvard Business Review* May/June: 114–120.

Harrigan, K.R. (1988) 'Strategic alliances and partner asymmetries', in F.J. Contractor and P. Lorange (eds) *Cooperative Strategies in International Business*, Lexington, MA: Lexington Books: 205–226.

Harrison, R.T. and Mason, C.M. (1992) 'The roles of investors in entrepreneurial companies: a comparison of informal investors and venture capitalists', in N.C. Churchill, S. Birley, W.D. Bygrave, D.F. Muzyka, C. Wahlbin and W.E. Wetzel (eds) *Frontiers of Entrepreneurship Research 1992*, Wellesley, MA: Babson College: 388–404.

Hart, M.M., Stevenson, H.H. and Dial, J. (1995) 'Entrepreneurship: a definition revisited', paper presented at the Babson Entrepreneurship Research Conference, London Business School.

Harvey, D. (1989) *The Condition of Postmodernity*, Oxford: Basil Blackwell.

Healey, M.J. and Rawlinson, M.B. (1993) 'Interviewing business owners and managers: a review of methods and techniques', *Geoforum* 24, 3: 339–355.

Hegg, G.L. (1990) 'A corporate view of venture capital', in *Managing R&D Technology: Building the Necessary Bridges*, The Conference Board Research Report, No. 938: 28–30.

Henricks, M. (1991) 'The power of partnering', *Small Business Reports* 16, 6: 46–57.

Hergert, M. and Morris, D. (1988) 'Trends in international collaborative agreements', in F.J. Contractor and P. Lorange (eds) *Cooperative Strategies in International Business*, Lexington, MA: Lexington Books: 99–109.

Herod, A. (1993) 'Gender issues in the use of interviewing as a research method', *Professional Geographer* 45, 3: 305–317.

Hirst, P. and Zeitlin, J. (1989) 'Introduction', in P. Hirst and J. Zeitlin (eds) *Reversing Industrial Decline: Industrial Structure in Britain and Her Competitors*, Oxford: Berg: 1–16.

Hisrich, R.D. (1986) 'Entrepreneurship and intrapreneurship: methods for creating new companies that have an impact on the economic renaissance of an area', in R.D. Hisrich (ed.) *Entrepreneurship, Intrapreneurship and Venture Capital*, Lexington, MA and Toronto: Lexington Books: 71–104.

Hitt, M.A., Hoskisson, R.E. and Harrison, J.S. (1991) 'Strategic competitiveness in the 1990s: challenges and opportunities for US executives', *Academy of Management Executive* 5, 2: 7–22.

Hladik, K.J. (1988) 'R&D and international joint ventures', in F.J. Contractor and P. Lorange (eds) *Co-operative Strategies in International Business: Joint Ventures and Technology Partnerships between Firms*, Lexington, MA: Lexington Books: 187–203.

HM Government (1931) *Report of the Committee on Finance and Industry* (MacMillan Report), Cmnd 3897, London: HMSO.

—— (1959) *Report of the Committee on the Working of the Monetary System* (Radcliffe Report), Cmnd 827, London: HMSO.

—— (1971) *Report of the Inquiry on Small Firms* (Bolton Report), Cmnd 4811, London: HMSO.

—— (1979) *Interim Report on the Financing of Small Firms* (Wilson Report), Cmnd 7503, London: HMSO.

Hobson, E.L. and Morrison, R.M. (1983) 'How do corporate start-up ventures fare?', in J.A. Hornaday, J.A. Timmons and K.H. Vesper (eds) *Frontiers of Entrepreneurship Research*, Wellesley, MA: Babson College: 390–410.

Hofstede, G. (1980) *Culture's Consequences: International Differences in Work Related Values*, Beverly Hills, CA: Sage.

Honeyman, K.F. (1992) 'Corporate Venturing as a Development Tool: Benefits, Pitfalls and Strategies for Success', undergraduate dissertation, Middlesex Business School.

Houlder, V. (1995) 'Revolution in outsourcing', *Financial Times* 6 January: 7.

Hull, F. and Slowinski, E. (1990) 'Partnering with technology entrepreneurs', *Research – Technology Management* 33, 6: 16–20.

Hull, F., Slowinski, E., Wharton, R. and Azumi, K. (1988) 'Strategic partnerships between technological entrepreneurs in the United States and large corporations in Japan and the United States', in F.J. Contractor and P. Lorange (eds) *Cooperative Strategies in International Business: Joint Ventures and Technology Partnerships between Firms*, Lexington, MA: Lexington Books: 445–456.

Hurry, D., Miller, A.T. and Bowman, E.H. (1992) 'Calls on high-technology: Japanese exploration of venture capital investments in the United States', *Strategic Management Journal* 13: 85–101.

Hutchinson, R. and McKillop, D. (1992) *The Financial Services Industry in Northern Ireland*, Report No. 91, Northern Ireland Economic Council, Belfast.

Imrie, R. (1994) 'A strategy of the last resort? Reflections on the role of the subcontract in the United Kingdom', *OMEGA* 22, 6: 569–578.

James, H.S. and Weidenbaum, M. (1993) *When Businesses Cross International Borders: Strategic Alliances and their Alternatives*, New York: Praeger.

Jarillo, J.C. (1989) 'Entrepreneurship and growth: the strategic use of external resources', *Journal of Business Venturing* 4: 133–147.

—— (1993) *Strategic Networks: Creating the Borderless Organization*, London: Butterworth-Heinemann.

Jenkins, G. (1989) 'Venture capital is cautious: who will seed start-ups?', *Harvard Business Review* 67, 6: 117.

Journal of Accountancy (1984) 'Survey findings released on collaborative corporate ventures', 158, 5: 24–30.

Journal of Applied Corporate Finance (1992) 'Roundtable on US risk capital and innovation (with a look at Eastern Europe)', 4, 4: 48–78.

Kanter, R.M. (1988) 'The new alliances: how strategic partnerships are reshaping American business', in H.L. Sawyer (ed.) *Business in the Contemporary World*, Lanham, MD: University Press of America: 59–82.

—— (1989) *When Giants Learn to Dance: Mastering the Challenge of Strategy, Management and Careers in the 1990s*, New York: Simon and Schuster.

—— (1994) 'Collaborative advantage: the art of alliances', *Harvard Business Review* July/August: 96–108.

Keeble, D. (1994) 'Regional influences and policy in new technology-based firm creation and growth', in R. Oakey (ed.) *New Technology-Based Firms in the 1990s*, London: Paul Chapman: 204–218.

Keeble, D. and Walker, S. (1994) 'New firms, small firms and dead firms: spatial patterns and determinants in the United Kingdom', *Regional Studies* 28, 4: 411–427.

Kehoe, L. (1993) 'Rebels turned diplomats', *Financial Times* 8 February: 8.

Klein, L.E. (1987) 'How a venture capital initiative can help the corporate "intrepreneur": a case study', *Business Development Review* Winter: 22–27.

Kodama, F. (1992) 'Technology fusion and the new R&D', *Harvard Business Review* July/August: 70–78.

Kogut, B. (1988) 'Joint ventures: theoretical and empirical perspectives', *Strategic Management Journal* 9: 319–332.

Kogut, B. and Singh, H. (1988) 'Entering the United States by joint venture: competitive rivalry and industry structure', in F.J. Contractor and P. Lorange (eds) *Cooperative Strategies in International Business*, Lexington, MA: Lexington, Books: 227–251.

Kotkin, J. (1989) 'Natural partners: a new source of start-up financing', *INC* June: 67–80.

Kuhn, R.L. (1993) 'Strategic alliances for Japanese mid-sized firms', in R.L. Kuhn (ed.) *Generating Creativity and Innovation in Large Bureaucracies*, Westport, CT: Quorum Books: 227–242.

Kukalis, S. and Jungemann, M. (1995) 'Strategic planning for a joint venture', *Long Range Planning* 28, 3: 46–57.

Landström, H. (1990) 'Co-operation between venture capital companies and small firms', *Entrepreneurship and Regional Development* 2: 345–362.

Larson, A.L. (1990) 'Partner networks: leveraging external ties to improve entrepreneurial performance', in N.C. Churchill, W.D. Bygrave, J.A. Hornaday, D.F. Muzyka, K.H. Vesper and W.E. Wetzel (eds) *Frontiers of Entrepreneurship Research 1990*, Wellesley, MA: Babson College: 539–553.

—— (1992) 'Network dyads in entrepreneurial settings: a study of the governance of exchange relationships', *Administrative Science Quarterly* 37: 76–104.

Lash, S. and Urry, J. (1987) *The End of Organised Capitalism*, Cambridge: Polity Press.

—— (1994) *Economies of Signs and Space*, London: Sage.

Lawton Smith, H., Dickson, K. and Smith, S.C. (1991) "There are two sides to every story": innovation and collaboration within networks of large and small firms', *Research Policy* 20: 457–468.

Lerner, J. (1995) 'Xerox technology ventures: March 1995', unpublished paper, Harvard Business School.

Lewis, J.D. (1990) *Partnerships For Profit: Structuring and Managing Strategic Alliances*, New York: Free Press.

Littler, D.A. and Leverick, F. (1995) 'Joint ventures for product development: learning from experience', *Long Range Planning* 28, 3: 58–67.

Littler, D.A. and Sweeting, R.C. (1983) 'New business development in mature firms', *OMEGA* 11, 6: 537–545.

—— (1984) 'Business innovation in the U.K.', *R&D Management* 14, 1: 1–10.

—— (1985) 'Radical innovation in the mature company', *European Journal of Marketing* 19, 4: 33–44.

—— (1987a) 'Corporate development: preferred strategies in UK companies', *Long Range Planning* 20, 2: 125–131.

—— (1987b) 'Innovative business development: selection and management issues', *Futures* 19, 2: 155–167.

Lorange, P. and Roos, J. (1992) *Strategic Alliances: Formation, Implementation and Evolution*, Oxford: Blackwell.

Lorange, P., Roos, J. and Brønn, P.S. (1992) 'Building successful strategic alliances', *Long Range Planning* 25, 6: 10–17.

Lorenz, C. (1993) 'Corporate venturing back in vogue', *Financial Times* 2 July: 13.

McCann, J.E. (1991) 'Patterns of growth, competitive technology, and financial strategies in young ventures', *Journal of Business Venturing* 6: 189–208.

MacDonald, M. (1991) *Creating Threshold Technology Companies in Canada: The Role for Venture Capital*, Science Council of Canada Discussion Paper.

McDowell, L. (1992) 'Valid games? A response to Erica Schoenberger', *Professional Geographer* 44, 2: 212–215.

McFarlan, F.W. and Nolan, R.L. (1995) 'How to manage an IT outsourcing alliance', *Sloan Management Review* Winter: 9–23.

McGee, J.E. (1994) 'Cooperative strategy and new venture performance: the role of managerial experience', unpublished paper, University of Nebraska at Omaha.

McGee, J.E. and Dowling, M.J. (1994) 'Using R&D cooperative arrangements to leverage managerial experience: a study of technology-intensive new ventures', *Journal of Business Venturing* 9: 33–48.

McGrath, R.G., MacMillan, I.C., Yang, E.A-Y. and Tsai, W. (1992) 'Does culture endure, or is it malleable? Issues for entrepreneurial economic development', *Journal of Business Venturing* 7: 441–458.

McKee, B. (1992) 'Ties that bind large and small', *Nation's Business* 80, 2: 24–26.

MacMillan, I.C. (1986) 'Progress in research on corporate venturing', in D. Sexton and R. Smilor (eds) *The Art and Science of Entrepreneurship*, Cambridge, MA: Ballinger: 241–263.

MacMillan, I.C., Block, Z. and Subba Narasimha, P.N. (1984) 'Obstacles and experience in corporate ventures', in J.A. Hornaday, F. Tarpley, J.A. Timmons and K.H. Vesper (eds) *Frontiers of Entrepreneurship Research*, Wellesley, MA: Babson College: 280–293.

—— (1986) 'Corporate venturing: alternatives, obstacles encountered, and experience effects', *Journal of Business Venturing* 1: 177–191.

MacMillan, I.C. and George, R. (1985) 'Corporate venturing: challenges for senior managers', *Journal of Business Strategy* 5, 3: 34–43.

MacMillan, I.C., Kulow, D.M. and Khoylian, R. (1988) 'Venture capitalists' involvement in their investments: extent and performance', *Journal of Business Venturing* 4: 27–47.

Maillat, D. (1995) 'Territorial dynamic, innovative milieus and regional policy', *Entrepreneurship and Regional Development* 7: 157–165.

Malecki, E.J. (1991) *Technology and Economic Development: The Dynamics of Local, Regional and National Change*, Harlow: Longman.

—— (1995) 'Flexibility and industrial districts', *Environment and Planning A* 27: 11–14.

Mamis, R.A. (1995) 'Crash course', *INC* February: 54–63.

Manardo, J. (1991) 'Managing the successful multinational of the 21st century: impact of global competition', *European Management Journal* 9, 2: 121–126.

Manigart, S. and Struyf, C. (1995) 'Financing the high technology startups in Belgium: an explorative study', paper presented at the Babson Entrepreneurship Research Conference, London Business School.

Mariti, P. and Smiley, H. (1983) 'Co-operative agreements and the organization of industry', *Journal of Industrial Economics* 31, 4: 437–451.

Martin, R. (1989) 'The growth and geographical anatomy of venture capitalism in the United Kingdom', *Regional Studies* 23, 5: 389–403.

Mason, C.M. and Harrison, R.T. (1991a) 'The small firm equity gap since Bolton', in J. Stanworth and C. Gray (eds) *Bolton 20 Years On: The Small Firm in the 1990s*, London: Paul Chapman: 112–150.

—— (1991b) 'Venture capital, the equity gap and the north–south divide in the U.K.', in M. Green (ed.) *Venture Capital: International Comparisons*, London: Routledge: 202–247.

—— (1992) 'The supply of equity finance in the UK: a strategy for closing the equity gap', *Entrepreneurship and Regional Development* 4: 357–380.

—— (1994) 'The role of informal and formal sources of venture capital in the financing of technology-based SMEs in the United Kingdom', in R. Oakey (ed.) *New Technology-Based Firms in the 1990s*, London: Paul Chapman: 104–124.

—— (1995) 'Closing the regional equity capital gap: the role of informal venture capital', *Small Business Economics* 7: 153–172.

Mason, C.M. and Lumme, A. (1995) 'The value-added impact of business angels', paper presented to 5th Global Entrepreneurship Research Conference, Salzburg, Austria.

Mast, R. (1991) 'The changing nature of corporate venture capital programs', *European Venture Capital Journal* March/April: 26–33.

Miles, R.E. and Snow, C.C. (1986) 'Organizations: new concepts for new forms', *California Management Review* 27, 3: 62–73.

—— (1992) 'Causes of failure in network organizations', *California Management Review* Summer: 53–72.

Miller, A. and Camp, B. (1985) 'Exploring determinants of success in corporate ventures', *Journal of Business Venturing* 1: 87–105.

Mitton, D.G. (1991) 'Tracking the trends in designer genes: a longitudinal study of the sources and size of financing in the developing biotech industry in San Diego', in N.C. Churchill, W.D. Bygrave, J.G. Covin, D.L. Sexton, D.P. Slevin, K.H. Vesper and W.E. Wetzel (eds) *Frontiers of Entrepreneurship Research*, Wellesley, MA: Babson College: 501–514.

Mohr, J. and Spekman, R. (1994) 'Characteristics of partnership success: partnership attributes, communication behavior, and conflict resolution techniques', *Strategic Management Journal* 15: 135–152.

Moore, B. (1994) 'Financial constraints to the growth and development of small high-technology firms', in A. Hughes and D.J. Storey (eds) *Finance and the Small Firm*, London: Routledge: 112–144.

Moore, B., Moore, R. and Sedaghat, N. (1992) 'Early stage finance for small high-technology companies: a preliminary note', paper to an Anglo-German seed capital workshop, Oxford Science Park.

Morgan, K. (1991) 'Competition and collaboration in electronics: what are the prospects for Britain?', *Environment and Planning A* 23: 1459–1482.

Morrison, A.J. (1993) 'Strategic alliances: theory and practice in the hotel industry', paper presented at the National Small Firms Policy and Research Conference, Nottingham.

Mowery, D.C. (1988) 'Collaborative ventures between US and foreign manufacturing firms: an overview', in D.C. Mowery (ed.) *International Collaborative Ventures in US Manufacturing*, Cambridge, MA: Ballinger: 1–22.

Moye, H.M. (1993) 'Reassessing human resources in large-scale bureaucracies', in R.L. Kuhn (ed.) *Generating Creativity and Innovation in Large Bureaucracies*, Westport, CT: Quorum Books: 151–156.

Murray, G. (1991a) 'The changing nature of competition in the UK venture capital industry', *NatWest Bank Quarterly Review* November: 65–80.

—— (1991b) *Change and Maturity in the UK Venture Capital Industry 1991–95*, report for the BVCA, London.

—— (1992a) '"The second equity gap": exit problems for seed and early stage venture capitalists and their investee companies', paper presented at the European Foundation for Entrepreneurship Research, London, December.

—— (1992b) 'A challenging marketplace for venture capital', *Long Range Planning* 25, 6: 79–86.

—— (1993) 'Third party equity support for New Technology Based Firms in the U.K. and continental Europe', paper presented at the Institute for Management, Innovation and Technology Seminar: Finance for Small Firms, Brussels, 29 November.

—— (1994a) 'The European Union's support for new technology-based firms: an assessment of the first three years of the European Seed Capital Fund Scheme', *European Planning Studies* 2, 4: 435–461.

—— (1994b) 'Third party equity – the role of the U.K. venture capital industry', in T.W. Davis and R. Buckland (eds) *Finance in Growing Firms*, London: Routledge.

—— (1994c) 'Evolution and change: an analysis of the first decade of the U.K. venture capital industry', unpublished paper, Warwick Business School.

—— (1995) 'Managing investors' risk in venture capital financed, new technology based firms', paper presented at the ESRC Risk Conference, London, 16–17 May.

Murray, G. and Lott, J. (1995) 'Have U.K. venture capitalists a bias against investment in new technology-based firms?', *Research Policy* 24: 283–299.

Muzyka, D.F. (1988) 'The management of failure: a key to organisational entrepreneurship', in B.A. Kirchhoff, W.A. Long, W.E. McMullen, K.H. Vesper and W.E. Wetzel (eds) *Frontiers of Entrepreneurship Research*, Wellesley, MA: Babson College: 501–517.

Myrick, T. (1986) 'Conflicting guidance: will accounting rules impair corporate venture capital?', *FE: The Magazine for Financial Executives* 2, 11: 34–36.

Mytelka, L.K. (1991) 'Introduction', in L.K. Mytelka (ed.) *Strategic Partnerships: States, Firms and International Competition*, London: Pinter: 1–6.

NEDO (1986) *Corporate Venturing: A Strategy for Innovation and Growth*, Report GPB 8008, London: HMSO.

Niederkofler, M. (1991) 'The evolution of strategic alliances: opportunities for managerial influence', *Journal of Business Venturing* 6, 4: 237–257.

Oakey, R.P. (1984) 'Innovation and regional growth in small high technology firms: evidence from Britain and the USA', *Regional Studies* 18, 3: 237–251.

—— (1993) 'Predatory networking: the role of small firms in the development of the British biotechnology industry', *International Small Business Journal* 11, 4: 9–22.

Oakley, A. (1981) 'Interviewing women: a contradiction in terms', in H. Roberts (ed.) *Doing Feminist Research*, London: Routledge and Kegan Paul: 30–61.

Oakley, P.G. (1987) 'External corporate venturing: the experience to date', in R. Rothwell and J. Bessant (eds) *Innovation: Adaptation and Growth*, Amsterdam: Elsevier: 287–296.

Oates, D. (1987) 'Corporate venturing: big help for small firms', *Director* 40, 11: 66–67.

O'Doherty, D. (ed.) (1990) *The Cooperation Phenomenon: Prospects for Small Firms and the Small Economies*, London: Graham and Trotman.

Ohmae, K. (1985) *Triad Power: The Coming Shape of Global Competition*, New York: Free Press.

—— (1989) 'The global logic of strategic alliances', *Harvard Business Review* March/April: 143–154.

—— (1990) *The Borderless World: Power and Strategy in the Interlinked Economy*, London: Collins.

Olleros, F-J. and MacDonald, R.J. (1988) 'Strategic alliances: managing complementarity to capitalize on emerging technologies', *Technovation* 7: 155–176.

Onians, R. (1995) 'Making small fortunes; success factors in starting businesses', paper presented to the Royal Society of Arts, 11 January.

Ormerod, J. and Burns, I. (1986) 'Corporate venturing is good business', *Accountancy* 98, 1119: 107–108.

—— (1988) *Raising Venture Capital in the U.K.*, London: Butterworths.

Osland, G.E. and Yaprak, A. (1993) 'A process model on the formation of multinational strategic alliances', in R. Culpan (ed.) *Multinational Strategic Alliances*, Binghampton, NY: Haworth Press: 81–100.

—— (1995) 'Learning through strategic alliances: processes and factors that enhance marketing effectiveness', *European Journal of Marketing* 29, 3: 52–66.

PA Consulting Group (1991) *Chief Executives' Attitudes to Technological Innovation in UK Manufacturing Industry*, London: PA Consulting Group.

Parkhe, A. (1993) 'Strategic alliance structuring: a game theoretic and transaction cost examination of interfirm cooperation', *Academy of Management Journal* 36, 4: 794–829.

Pegg, O., Peterson, R. and Peridis, T. (1992) 'Strategic alliances between small and large firms: an oxymoron?', paper presented at Babson Entrepreneurship Research Conference, INSEAD, France.

Pekar, P. and Allio, R. (1994) 'Making alliances work – guidelines for success', *Long Range Planning* 27, 4: 54–65.

Perlmutter, H.V. and Heenan, D.A. (1986) 'Cooperate to compete globally', *Harvard Business Review* March/April: 136–152.

Perrow, C. (1986) *Complex Organizations*, New York: Random House.

Peters, T. (1990) 'Get innovative or get dead', *California Management Review* 33, 1: 9–26.

—— (1991) 'Get innovative or get dead', *California Management Review* 33, 2: 9–23.

Peterson, R.W. (1967) 'New venture management in a large company', *Harvard Business Review* May/June: 68–76.

Pfeffer, J. and Salancik, G.R. (1978) *The External Control of Organizations: A Resource Dependence Perspective*, New York: Harper and Row.

Philpott, T. (1994) 'Banking and new technology-based small firms: a study of information exchanges in the financing relationship', in R. Oakey (ed.) *New Technology-Based Firms in the 1990s*, London: Paul Chapman: 68–80.

Pinchot, G. (1985) *Intrapreneuring*, New York: Harper and Row.

Piol, E. (1985) 'Corporate venture capital – the Olivetti approach', in S.E. Pratt and S.E. Lloyd (eds) *Guide to European Venture Capital Sources*, Boston, MA: Venture Economics: 53–56.

Piore, M.J. and Sabel, C.F. (1984) *The Second Industrial Divide*, New York: Basic Books.

Pisano, G.P., Russo, M.V. and Teece, D.J. (1988) 'Joint ventures and collaborative arrangements in the telecommunications equipment industry', in D.C. Mowery (ed.) *International Collaborative Ventures in U.S. Manufacturing*, Cambridge, MA: Ballinger: 23–70.

Porter, M. (1980) *Competitive Strategy: Techniques for Analyzing Industries and Competitors*, New York: Free Press.

—— (1985) *Competitive Advantage*, New York: Free Press.

Povey, T. (1986) 'Igniting a small spark', *Financial Times* Venture Capital Special, 8 December: 4.

Powell, W.W. (1987) 'Hybrid organizational arrangements: new form or transitional development', *California Management Review* 30, 1: 67–87.

—— (1990) 'Neither market nor hierarchy: network forms of organization', *Research in Organizational Behavior* 12: 295–336.

Pratt, G. (1990) 'Venture capital in the United Kingdom', *Bank of England Quarterly Bulletin* February: 78–83.

Pratt, S.E. (1994) 'The organized venture capital community', in S.E. Pratt (ed.) *Pratt's Guide to Venture Capital Sources*, Boston, MA: Venture Economics: 82–86.

Pucik, V. (1988) 'Strategic alliances, organizational learning, and competitive advantage: the HRM agenda', *Human Resource Management* 27, 1: 77–93.

Radtke, M.L. and McKinney, G.W. (1991) 'Corporate strategic partnerships', in S.E. Pratt (ed.) *Pratt's Guide to Venture Capital Sources*, Boston, MA: Venture Economics: 80–82.

Rind, K.W. (1981) 'The role of venture capital in corporate development', *Strategic Management Journal* 2: 169–180.

—— (1994) 'Dealing with the corporate strategic investor', in S.E. Pratt (ed.) *Pratt's Guide to Venture Capital Sources*, Boston, MA: Venture Economics: 93–96.

Ring, P.S. and Van de Ven, A.H. (1994) 'Developmental processes of cooperative interorganizational relationships', *Academy of Management Review* 19, 1: 90–118.

Rizzoni, A. (1991) 'Technological innovation and small firms: a taxonomy', *International Small Business Journal* 9, 3: 31–42.

Roberts, E.B. (1980) 'New ventures for corporate growth', *Harvard Business Review* 58, 4: 134–142.

—— (1990) 'Initial capital for the new technological enterprise', *IEEE Transactions on Engineering Management* 37, 2: 81–94.

—— (1991) *Entrepreneurs in High Technology: Lessons from MIT and Beyond*, New York and Oxford: Oxford University Press.

Rosenstein, J., Bruno, A.V., Bygrave, W.D. and Taylor, N.T. (1989) 'Do venture capitalists on boards of portfolio companies add value besides money?', in R.H. Brockhaus, N.C. Churchill, J.A. Katz, B.A. Kirchhoff, K.H. Vesper and W.E. Wetzel (eds) *Frontiers of Entrepreneurship Research*, Wellesley, MA: Babson College: 216–229.

Rothwell, R. (1975) 'From invention to new business via the new venture approach', *Management Decision* 13, 1: 10–21.

—— (1983) 'Innovation and firm size: a case for dynamic complementarity; or, is small really so beautiful?', *Journal of General Management* 8, 3: 5–25.

—— (1984) 'The role of small firms in the emergence of new technologies', *OMEGA* 12, 1: 19–29.

—— (1989) 'SMFs, inter-firm relationships and technological change', *Entrepreneurship and Regional Development* 1: 275–291.

—— (1992) 'Successful industrial innovation: critical factors for the 1990s', *R&D Management* 22, 3: 221–239.

—— (1993) 'The changing nature of the innovation process: implications for SMEs', paper presented at the Conference on New Technology-Based Firms in the 1990s, Manchester Business School, 25–26 June.

Rothwell, R. and Dodgson, M. (1994) 'Innovation and size of firm', in M. Dodgson and R. Rothwell (eds) *The Handbook of Industrial Innovation*, Aldershot: Edward Elgar: 310–324.

Rudman, R.J. (1993) 'Corporate venturing', paper presented to the Financial Forum for SMART Stage II Award Holders, London.

Sabel, C.F. (1989) 'Flexible specialization and the re-emergence of regional economies', in P. Hirst and J. Zeitlin (eds) *Reversing Industrial Decline? Industrial Structure and Policy in Britain and her Competitors*, Oxford: Berg: 17–70.

Sadtler, D.R. (1993) 'How venture capitalists add value', *Journal of General Management* 19, 1: 1–16.

Saget, F. (1992) 'The impact of economic globalization on small business: learning to form alliances', paper presented at the Conference on Small Business in the Global Economy, Workshop 1, Montreal, Canada.

Sandham, A. and Thurston, J. (1993) 'Successfully negotiating a partnership: structuring a deal that maximizes the benefits for both parties', paper presented at the Financing and Investing in Biotechnology conference, London, 22–23 November.

Sapienza, H.J., Manigart, S. and Herron, L. (1992) 'Venture capitalist involvement in portfolio companies: a study of 221 portfolio companies in four countries', paper presented at the Babson Entrepreneurship Research Conference, INSEAD, Fontainebleau, France.

Sargent, M. and Young, J.E. (1991) 'The entrepreneurial search for capital: a behavioural science perspective', *Entrepreneurship and Regional Development* 3: 237–252.

Sayer, A. and Walker, R. (1992) *The New Social Economy: Reworking the Division of Labour*, Cambridge, MA: Blackwell.

247

Schoenberger, E. (1991) 'The corporate interview as a research method in economic geography', *Professional Geographer* 43, 2: 180–189.

—— (1992) 'Self-criticism and self-awareness in research: a reply to Linda McDowell', *Professional Geographer* 44, 2: 215–218.

Schollhammer, H. (1982) 'Internal corporate entrepreneurship', in C. Kent, D.L. Sexton and K.H. Vesper (eds) *Encyclopedia of Entrepreneurship*, Englewood Cliffs, NJ: Prentice-Hall: 209–229.

Schumann, P.A. (1993) 'Creativity and innovation in large organisations', in R.L. Kuhn (ed.) *Generating Creativity and Innovation in Large Bureaucracies*, Westport, CT: Quorum Books: 111–130.

Scottish Enterprise (1993) *Scotland's Business Birth Rate*, Glasgow: Scottish Enterprise/Insider.

Segers, J-P. (1993) 'Strategic partnering between new technology based firms and large established firms in the biotechnology and micro-electronics industries in Belgium', *Small Business Economics* 5: 271–281.

—— (1995) 'Technology based entrepreneurship in Flanders (Belgium): new technology based firm creation as a focal goal of technology based regional policy', unpublished paper, University of Limburg Diepenbeek, Belgium, Research Group ESO.

Sexton, D.L. and Bowman-Upton, N.B. (1990) 'Corporate venturing', in D.L. Sexton and N.B. Bowman-Upton (eds) *Entrepreneurship – Creativity and Growth*, New York: Macmillan: 267–284.

Shamdasani, P.N. and Sheth, J.N. (1995) 'An experimental approach to investigating satisfaction and continuity in marketing alliances', *European Journal of Marketing* 29, 4: 6–23.

Shan, W. (1990) 'An empirical analysis of organizational strategies by entrepreneurial high-technology firms', *Strategic Management Journal* 11: 129–139.

Shaughnessy, H. (1995) 'International joint ventures: managing successful collaborations', *Long Range Planning* 28, 3: 10–17.

Shutt, J. and Whittington, R. (1987) 'Fragmentation strategies and the rise of small units: cases from the North West', *Regional Studies* 21, 1: 13–23.

Siegel, R., Siegel, E. and MacMillan, I.C. (1988) 'Corporate venture capitalists: autonomy, obstacles and performance', *Journal of Business Venturing* 3: 233–247.

Silver, D.A. (1979) 'Venture capital at the corporate planning desk', *Planning Review*, May: 23–29.

—— (1993) Strategic Partnering, New York: McGraw-Hill.

Skapinker, M. (1992) 'Music factory falls foul of recession', *Financial Times* 28 November.

Skjerstad, T. Å. (1994) 'Strategic partnerships and Trojan horses: winners and losers from successful product development', paper presented in Trondheim, 22 April.

Slatter, S. (1992) *Gambling on Growth: How to Manage the Small High-Tech Firm*, Chichester: John Wiley.

Slowinski, G., Farris, G.F. and Jones, D. (1993) 'Strategic partnering: process instead of event', *Research: Technology Management* May/June: 22–25.

SBRC (1992) *The State of British Enterprise: Growth, Innovation and Competitive Advantage in Small and Medium Sized Firms*, University of Cambridge: Small Business Research Centre.

SBRT (1989) *Risk Capital for Small Firms: A Guidebook and Directory*, London: Small Business Research Trust.

Smith, R.D. (1994) 'The role of the UK financial markets in funding early stage technology companies', paper presented to the High Technology Small Firms Conference, Manchester Business School.

Smollen, L.E. (1978) 'Corporate activities in venture formation', in W. Naumes (ed.) *The Entrepreneurial Manager in the Small Business: Text, Readings and Cases*, London: Addison-Wesley: 43–47.

Sommerlatte, T. (1990) 'The third channel for innovation – how established companies and young high technology firms complement each other', in D. O'Doherty (ed.) *The Cooperation Phenomenon: Prospects for Small Firms and the Small Economies*, London: Graham and Trotman: 20–30.

Stafford, E.R. (1994) 'Using co-operative strategies to make alliances work', *Long Range Planning* 27, 3: 64–74.

Standeven, P. (1993) 'Financing the Early Stage Technology Firm in the 1990s: An International Perspective', discussion paper prepared for the Six Countries Programme Conference on 'Financing the Early Stage Technology Company in the 1990s: An International Perspective', Montreal.

Steier, L. and Greenwood, R. (1995) 'Venture capitalist relationships in the deal structuring and post-investment stages of new firm creation', *Journal of Management Studies* 32, 3: 337–357.

Stewart, D.B. (1993) 'Strategic alliances: a small and medium sized firm perspective', paper presented to the Administrative Sciences Association of Canada Conference, Lake Louise, Alberta.

Stiles, J. (1994) 'Strategic alliances: making them work', *Long Range Planning* 27, 4: 133–137.

Storper, M. (1995) 'The resurgence of regional economies, ten years later: the region as a nexus of untraded interdependencies', *European Urban and Regional Studies* 2, 3: 191–221.

Storper, M. and Harrison, B. (1990) 'Flexibility, hierarchy and regional development: the changing structure of industrial production systems and their forms of governance', paper presented at Networks of Innovators – An International and Inter-Disciplinary Workshop, Montreal, May.

Storper, M. and Scott, A.J. (1990) 'Work organization and local labour markets in an era of flexible production', *International Labour Review* 129, 5: 573–591.

Storper, M. and Walker, R. (1989) *The Capitalist Imperative*, Oxford: Basil Blackwell.

Susbauer, J.C. (1978) 'Intracorporate entrepreneurship programs in American industrial enterprise', in W. Naumes (ed.) *The Entrepreneurial Manager in the Small Business: Text, Readings and Cases*, London: Addison-Wesley: 140–145.

Sweeting, R.C. (1991a) 'Early-stage new technology-based businesses: interactions with venture capitalists and the development of accounting techniques and procedures', *British Accounting Review* 23: 3–21.

—— (1991b) 'UK venture capital funds and the funding of new technology-based businesses: process and relationships', *Journal of Management Studies* 28, 6: 601–622.

Sykes, H.B. (1986a) 'Lessons from a new ventures program', *Harvard Business Review* May/June: 69–74.

—— (1986b) 'The anatomy of a corporate venturing program: factors influencing success', *Journal of Business Venturing* 1: 275–293.

—— (1990) 'Corporate venture capital: strategies for success', *Journal of Business Venturing* 5: 37–47.

—— (1993) 'Business research: a new corporate function', *Journal of Business Venturing* 8: 1–8.

Sykes, H.B. and Block, Z. (1989) 'Corporate venturing obstacles: sources and solutions', *Journal of Business Venturing* 4: 159–167.

Taurins, S. (1992) 'Internal corporate venturing: a guide for practitioners', *U.K. Venture Capital Journal* Nov./Dec.: 12–26.

Taylor, L. (1989) 'Raising venture capital', *Journal of Business Strategy* July/August: 61–64.

Taylor, M. (1987) 'Technological change and the business enterprise', in J.F. Brotchic, P. Hall and P.W. Newton (eds) *The Spatial Impact of Technological Change*, London: Croom Helm: 208–227.

—— (1995) 'The business enterprise, power and patterns of geographical industrialization', in S. Conti, E. Malecki and P. Oinas (eds) *The Industrial Enterprise and its Environment: Spatial Perspectives*, Aldershot: Avebury.

Teece, D. (1986) 'Profiting from technological innovation', *Research Policy* 15, 6: 286–305.

—— (1992) 'Arrangements for regimes of rapid technological progress', *Journal of Economic Behaviour and Organization* 18, 1: 1–25.

Thomas, L.G. (1988) 'Multifirm strategies in the US pharmaceutical industry', in D.C. Mowery (ed.) *International Collaborative Ventures in U.S. Manufacturing*, Cambridge, MA: Ballinger: 147–181.

Timmons, J.A. and Gumpert, D.E. (1982) 'Discard many old rules about getting venture capital', *Harvard Business Review* Jan./Feb.: 152–156.

Timmons, J.A. and Sapienza, H.J. (1992) 'Venture capital: the decade ahead', in D.L. Sexton and J.D. Kasarda (eds) *The State of the Art of Entrepreneurship*, Boston, MA: PWS-Kent: 402–437.

Tyler, B.B. and Steensma, H.K. (1995) 'Evaluating technological collaborative opportunities: a cognitive modelling perspective', *Strategic Management Journal* 16: 43–70.

UK Venture Capital Journal (1985) 'Major corporations and venture capital', Special Report, January: 10–14.

—— (1987) 'Current issues facing the UK venture capital industry', Special Report, March: 10–17.

Urry, M. (1995) 'Questions over youth's behaviour', *Financial Times* 23 August: 13.

Vachon, M. (1993) 'Venture capital reborn', *Venture Capital Journal* January: 32–36.

Van Gils, A. and Zwart, P.S. (1994) 'Partnerships between small and medium sized enterprises: a research methodology', paper presented at 8th Nordic Conference on Small Business Research, Halmstad University, Sweden, 13–15 July.

Vatne, E. (1995) 'Local resource mobilisation and internationalisation strategies in small and medium sized enterprises', *Environment and Planning A* 27: 63–80.

Venkatachalam, M. and Weaver, K.M. (1989) 'A conceptual model of the corporate entrepreneuring process', paper presented at the 34th World Conference of the International Council for Small Businesses, Quebec.

Venture Capital Journal (1990) 'Apple and Advent aiming to harvest European technology', August.

—— (1992) 'BP hits secondary market, again', June.

Venture Economics (1993) *National Venture Capital Association 1992 Annual Report*, Arlington, VA: NVCA.

—— (1994) *National Venture Capital Association 1993 Annual Report*, Arlington, VA: NVCA.

—— (1995) *National Venture Capital Association 1994 Annual Report*, Arlington, VA: NVCA.

Vesper, K.H. (1984) 'Three faces of corporate entrepreneurship: a pilot study', in J.A. Hornaday, F. Tarpley, J.A. Timmons and K.H. Vesper (eds) *Frontiers of Entrepreneurship Research*, Wellesley, MA: Babson College: 294–320.

Walker, D.A. (1989) 'Financing the small firm', *Small Business Economics* 1: 285–296.

Walker, J. (1993) 'Specialists in a sea of generalists – the specialised investor in the 1990s', *Venture Capital Report* September.

Warren, R.J. and Kempenich, R.E. (1984) 'Corporate venturing: a complement to acquisition', *Mergers and Acquisitions* 18, 4: 65–70.

Weinstein, O. (1992) 'High technology and flexibility', in P. Cooke, F. Moulaert, E. Swyngedouw, O. Weinstein and P. Wells (eds) *Towards Global Localization*, London: UCL Press: 19–38.

Wells, P. and Cooke, P. (1992) 'The computer hardware industry in the 1980s: technological change, competition and structural change', in P. Cooke, F. Moulaert, E. Swyngedouw, O. Weinstein and P. Wells (eds) *Towards Global Localization*, London: UCL Press: 129–151.

Wetzel, W.E. and Freear, J. (1996) 'Promoting informal venture capital in the United States: reflections on the history of the venture capital network', in R.T. Harrison and C.M. Mason (eds) *Informal Venture Capital: Evaluating the Impact of Business Introduction Services*, Hemel Hempstead: Woodhead-Faulkner.

Weyer, M.V. (1995) 'The venture capital vacuum', *Management Today* July: 60–63.

Williamson, O. (1975) *Markets and Hierarchies: Analysis and Antitrust Implications*, New York: Free Press/Macmillan.

Winters, T.E. and Murfin, D.L. (1988) 'Venture capital investing for corporate development objectives', *Journal of Business Venturing* 3: 207–222.

Wissema, J.G. and Euser, L. (1991) 'Successful innovation through inter-company networks', *Long Range Planning* 24, 6: 33–39.

Yoshino, M.Y. and Rangan, US (1995) *Strategic Alliances: An Entrepreneurial Approach to Globalization*, Boston, MA: Harvard Business School Press.

Young, G. (1985) *Venture Capital in High-Tech Companies*, London: Frances Pinter.

Young, S. (1988) 'Manufacturing under pressure', *Management Today* July: 103–107.

INDEX

INDEX

253